CONTENTS

KU-414-395

HOW TO USE THIS BOOK

This book is divided into two distinct sections.

- The AS section describes and explains the reasons for, and the consequences of, the Norman Conquest of England, covering the period 1042–1100. The text of this explained narrative aims to give the student in-depth information and some basic analysis. The summary questions at the end of each chapter challenge the student to use the information in the chapter to explain, evaluate and analyse important aspects of the topic covered by that chapter. In this way, students will acquire a clear understanding of the key features of each topic.

- The A2 section is more analytical in style. The period covered extends from 1100 to 1228 and concentrates upon major themes, particularly political and social reform and change. Students who use the book as part of their A2 studies should also read through the relevant chapters in the AS section of the book. For example, students who are studying Feudalism at A2 level should read Chapter 6 in addition to Section 5.

At the end of each section there is an Assessment section. The AS Assessment section is based on the requirements of the three Awarding Bodies – AQA, Edexcel and OCR – and gives students detailed guidance on how to answer the questions set.

The bibliography suggests the mainstream books that students may wish to consult. It also gives a selection of documentary readings, together with suggestions as to appropriate contemporary accounts. Students are strongly advised to broaden their understanding of the period by reading as widely as possible.

Medieval England 1042–1228

Toby Purser

Series Editors
Martin Collier
Rosemary Rees

Heinemann is an imprint of Pearson Education Limited,
a company incorporated in England and Wales, having
its registered office at Edinburgh Gate, Harlow, Essex, CM20 2JE.
Registered company number: 872828

Heinemann is a registered trademark of
Pearson Education Limited
© Toby Purser, 2004

First published 2004

ARP Impression 98

British Library Cataloguing in Publication Data is available
from the British Library on request.

ISBN: 978 0 435327 60 6

Typeset by TechType, Abingdon, Oxon

Original illustrations © Harcourt Education Limited, 2004
Illustrated by TechType, Abingdon, Oxon

Cover design by Hicks Design

Printed in Great Britain by Clays Ltd, St Ives plc

Cover photo: © Bridgeman Art Library

Acknowledgements
The author and the publisher would like to thank the following for permission to reproduce photographs:

Pp.64, 71, 155, 181, 208 Bridgeman Art Library; pp.20, 23, 36 AKG-Images; pp.12, 24 Art Archive; pp.33, 208 Mary Evans Picture Library; pp.44, 197 Corbis; p.88 Alamy Images; p.28 ET Archive; pp.45, 96, 151, 162, 164, 198 ©Toby Purser.

Every effort has been made to contact copyright holders of material reproduced in this book. Any omissions will be rectified in subsequent printings if notice is given to the publishers.

Dedication
To David Whitehead, who first taught me medieval history.

AS SECTION: The Norman Conquest of England, 1042–1100

INTRODUCTION

In January 1066, Edward the Confessor died, leaving no direct heir to the throne of England. He had ruled from 1042 and was a descendant of Alfred the Great, of the ancient House of Wessex. Long before Edward died it was clear that there would be a dispute over the succession. In 1066, there were three contenders for the throne: the king's cousin, William, Duke of Normandy; the king's brother-in-law, Harold Godwinsson, the powerful Earl of Wessex; and the king of Norway, Harald Hardrada, who was not related to Edward the Confessor, but based his claim on a long-forgotten promise and descent from a Danish ruler of England. There was also a great-nephew of Edward's, also of the royal House of Wessex, named Edgar, but he was a boy at the time of the king's death. When Edward died, the chances of a double invasion of England were very high indeed.

The succession

The issue of the succession in 1066 was not simply a matter of the contenders fighting it out, but was a result of a complicated series of events, succession struggles and invasions dating back to 1014, when Edward himself was a boy. The evidence historians have to deal with is limited not only by production but by survival and also by point of view. The information we have is overwhelmingly Norman, written after the Conquest to justify the invasion of 1066. History is written by the winners, and very few Anglo-Saxon written sources survive to tell us the story of the losers.

Conquest and colonisation

Due to the circumstances of his succession, William had to launch an invasion of England, fight a decisive battle and subdue his new subjects by force of arms. Not until 1075 was the kingdom of England fully secure. The significance of this conquest and colonisation of England was enormous. To maintain control of the conquered nation, King

William put to the sword thousands of English natives, not only at the battle of Hastings, but also during the years that followed, in order to crush the rebellions that arose throughout England in the years 1067–71. A fundamental weapon of the Norman occupation was the castle. Castles had never been seen before in England on such a scale. William's troops built hundreds – they dominated the landscape.

To encourage and reward his followers, William granted vast estates from the vanquished realm to his cousins and supporters, who in turn rewarded the soldiers who had come over with them in the shallow longboats. These troops garrisoned the castles and were in turn granted small estates of land to support their military status. The troops – mostly of Norman lineage – replaced the Anglo-Saxon landlords who had been killed in battles or rebellions, or who had simply been dispossessed of their estates. This was a major revolution in the history of landholding in England. It was the biggest land-grab since the Vikings had arrived to plunder and settle in the eighth and ninth centuries, and would remain so until the Dissolution of the Monasteries in the sixteenth century. By the end of the Conqueror's reign in 1087, the vast majority of landlords in England were of Norman-French origin. This altered the social and legal fabric of the country and engendered a new hierarchical system of landholding based primarily upon military service. This has become known to historians as the 'feudal system'. In the Church, Norman bishops and clergy replaced the English ones, either by force or when the native incumbents passed away. The Normans destroyed existing structures and built massive new churches and cathedrals in a new architectural style, to seal their dominance over the English Church. This total change to the English polity was reflected in the exhaustive landholding survey conducted in the last years of William's reign: Domesday Book.

Change or continuity?

One of the central themes of this section is the relationship between change and continuity. There was much change, but there was also a great deal of continuity. For although the Normans crushed English rebellions, disinherited landlords and governed by the sword in the years following the Battle of Hastings, much of Anglo-Saxon England survived. The Normans were adept at exploiting the successes of others. William found an ancient and sophisticated nation state when he invaded in 1066. England was a wealthy country, with well-established laws, administrative boundaries and financial customs. The Normans adopted a policy of leaving what worked well alone, and they found that Edward the Confessor's England worked very well indeed. The country had known peace for over forty years, and society was well-ordered and defined. William the Conqueror kept the shires, sheriffs and earldoms and continued to raise taxes as Edward had done, for his own means. He used Anglo-Saxon law codes to govern the natives and even to dispossess them of their own lands to reward his followers.

Towards Anglo-Norman England

The year 1066 resulted, therefore, in great change. It was a year that changed English history forever. But the events of that year were the result of many years of diplomatic and political dramas and in turn created an amalgam of old legal and financial customs with new social and cultural aspects. In short, England was now neither Anglo-Saxon or Norman England, but *Anglo-Norman* England.

KEY QUESTIONS

The AS section of the book will look at the following questions:

1. What was Edward the Confessor's policy towards the succession of the Crown?

2. Why did William the Conqueror win the Battle of Hastings?

3. What problems did William have in securing his kingdom and how did he deal with them?

4. What changed and what remained the same in Anglo-Norman government?

5. How did William reform the Church?

6. To what extent did William II build upon his father's successes?

7. How did the Conquest affect Anglo-Saxon society?

CHAPTER 1

England before the Conquest

INTRODUCTION: THE MEDIEVAL WORLD

The medieval ('middle age') period falls traditionally between the years 1066 and 1485 and is a construct entirely devised by historians. The period follows the so-called 'Dark Ages', which plunged Europe into decline after the fall of the Roman Empire, and precedes the 'Early Modern Age', which was heralded by the Renaissance.

Such dates and boundaries are artificial, placed to help us understand the past in a scientific, modern and rational manner. The thought processes and beliefs of medieval people were anything but scientific and rational. Medieval people believed that everything they did, and everything they could do, was watched over and would be judged, by God. A person was born into a place in life, and would remain there until their earthly life was over and their journey into the afterlife began. Their time on earth was very short; they had to do their utmost to lead a good, Christian life so that they would spend eternity in Heaven. In the words of Bede, an eighth-century monk and historian, life on earth was comparable to the flight of a bird through the lord's great hall, coming in at one end, and flying out of the other. The time spent in the hall was the time a person spent on earth. All that came before and after, was in the hands of the Almighty.

WHAT WAS 'ENGLAND'?

England as a political entity emerged in the tenth century. It was, by 1066, a defined state with borders, administrative units, laws and taxation records. It was a unique blend of a variety of cultures melded together and continually evolving. This was a process that had already been going on since the first century AD.

The Romans invaded **Britain** in AD 43 and stayed until AD 410. When Roman rule collapsed, a century and a half of immigration by Germanic peoples from the European mainland followed. These peoples were Angles, Saxons, Jutes and Frisians, all from north-west Europe. Over this

KEY THEME

Britain The Romans called the British Isles *Britannica*, but after they left the concept of a united island fell apart. When Anglo-Saxon England emerged in the eighth and ninth centuries, rulers often looked back to a Golden Age of 'Britain', but the Scots, Welsh and Irish retained much of their culture and language throughout the Middle Ages, so that there was always a clear distinction between the 'English' and the more general 'British'.

period many of the Celts were pushed westwards into Cornwall and Wales, where Celtic art and language survived.

The new settlers quickly established areas of control, which emerged as kingdoms. These were formed in East Anglia, Mercia, Northumbria and Wessex. What also followed rapidly was these pagan tribes' conversion to Christianity, by the end, if not the middle, of the seventh century. The coming of Christianity formed part of the formal framework of the kingdoms; the tribal leaders realised that the universal appeal of Christianity gave their rule legitimacy and power.

It used to be thought that the invading Germanic tribes wiped out the native Celts. However, it is now understood that there was a great deal of continuity and assimilation from the Romano-British era. The people were neither Germanic or Celtic, but through the fusion of different laws, language, customs and culture, they became English.

The four kingdoms of the English came under a sustained assault from a very different culture from the end of the eighth century to the early eleventh century. The Vikings, raiders from Scandinavia, threatened the very existence of Anglo-Saxon England. The first raids on England were reported at the end of the eighth century but it was not until towards the end of the ninth century, in the 860s, that the great Danish armies came to settle. Northumbria, East Anglia and Mercia were overwhelmed but Wessex, under the leadership of Alfred, fought on, and at the Peace of Wedmore (878) it was agreed that the Danes would settle the east of the country, known as Danelaw. The old Roman road of Watling Street was the boundary. Danelaw areas included East Anglia, the East Midlands, Lincolnshire and East Yorkshire. Danish military bases were established at Derby, Nottingham, Northampton and Huntingdon.

The Peace of Wedmore gave Alfred the opportunity to reorganise and extend his power. After 878 he constructed a series of fortified towns across Wessex, called *burhs*. When the Vikings returned in force in 892, they were defeated by this network of towns and garrisons and dispersed in 896. Alfred's son Edward the Elder and his daughter Aethelflaed reconquered Danish Mercia and East Anglia as far as the Humber, building fortresses all across the Midlands.

England, c. 1060, showing the earldoms and major towns

Devastating raids into Scotland completed the mastery of the West Saxon kings over Britain in 934 and 937.

How was Anglo-Saxon England governed?

The power and authority of the West Saxon kings over Danish England is reflected in the titles they used on **charters** and coins. 'King' derives from the Old English *cyng*; the Latin for 'king' is *rex* and the attribution of national authority ('English', 'Anglo-Saxon') in the tenth century illustrates their growing power. Whereas Alfred was styled *rex Saxonum* (king of the Saxons), a charter of his grandson Athelstan dated to 931 called him *rex Anglorum* (king of the English). In the later 930s Athelstan's charters inflate his authority to imperial status, styling him *rex totius Britanniae* (king of all of Britain), thus asserting power not only over England but all of Britain.

How was Anglo-Saxon England administered?

The kings of England were far more than military warriors. The kingdoms they ruled over and the single kingdom that

KEY TERM

Charter A medieval document which normally included grants of land or promises of trade and good government.

England became in the tenth century developed into a sophisticated and highly organised state. This was partly in response to the Danish invasions, but the legacy of Roman Britain remained strong.

By the early eleventh century the four kingdoms of Northumbria, Mercia, Wessex and East Anglia had become earldoms, ruled by **earl**s. The earldoms were territorial units that covered large areas. The administrative unit of England was the shire (Old English *scir*), which first emerged in Wessex, in Hampshire in the eighth century, probably based in and around Southampton. It spread across Wessex and into the Midlands with the reconquest of Mercia by Edward the Elder and Athelstan. The shire was the administrative and fiscal unit of the emerging English state, and the unit of local government of England, the means by which kings of England throughout the Middle Ages enforced taxation and law. Each shire was divided into 'Hundreds', an area covering a dozen or so villages. The smallest unit of land was the **hide**.

How were Anglo-Saxon England's finances organised?

Any state needs money to pay for defence and for the administration of government. What emerged in England in the tenth and eleventh centuries was an efficient system of taxation based upon a sound currency. The minting of coins expanded considerably under the West Saxon kings so that by the 980s there were approximately 60 mints around the country. Royal control was absolute; every five years all coins in circulation ceased to be legal tender by royal decree and were to be handed in and exchanged. The Anglo-Saxon monetary system of pounds, shillings and pence (12 pence to the shilling, 240 pence to the pound) remained in use from this period to 1971.

The combination of a coinage system with the administrative organisation of shires and hundreds enabled Anglo-Saxon kings to raise very large sums of money. Unfortunately, during the reign of Ethelred (978–1016), much of this went in buying off the Danes during their repeated attacks. £48,000 was raised in 1012 and a massive £82,000 in 1018, perhaps two-thirds of the entire issued coinage. This payment was known as 'Danegeld', a special tax to buy off the invaders. The government raised this tax through the shires; the local courts knew the hidage assessment of each estate so that the appropriate amount of geld could be imposed on each landowner.

Did Anglo-Saxon England survive the next Danish invasions?

Late tenth-century England saw the return of the Vikings and by the turn of century it was clear that Ethelred the Unready was in trouble. In 1013 an army led by King Svein of Denmark invaded the north of England and settled. Ethelred fled with his family to Normandy but returned on the death of Svein in 1014. Unable to capitalise on Svein's death, Ethelred himself died in 1016, leaving his son by his first marriage, Edmund 'Ironside', to deal with Svein's young son, Canute. However, Edmund only survived his father by seven months and in November, Canute received the submission of Wessex, having already gained control over Mercia and the Danelaw. Edward, Ethelred's son by his second marriage, aged around thirteen, went to Normandy and spent twenty-five years there in exile.

But the reign of Canute did not see the elimination of Anglo-Saxon society. Canute kept the Anglo-Saxon bishops and earls in place and used the existing system of shires and hides to raise taxes. When Canute died in 1035, England had enjoyed nineteen years of peace, but he left two sons by different mothers and, due to the uncertainty of succession procedure in both English and Danish custom, the succession to the throne was not clear. The man on the spot, Harold 'Harefoot' became king but died in 1040. His half-brother, Harthacanute, who had been away in Scandinavia in 1035, then arrived to take the crown. His triumph was short-lived; he died at a wedding feast and the way was open for the last man standing, who also happened to be on the spot: Edward, Prince of the Royal House of Wessex.

How was Anglo-Saxon society organised?

By the eleventh century, the contemporary idea of society was that of three levels: those who fought, those who prayed, and those who worked. This was a God-given, unchangeable structure. The aristocratic class of landowners did not dirty their hands; they served the king in battle and in administration. The churchmen had their hierarchy stretching from the Pope in Rome, to the bishops, abbots, monks and the village priest. The peasants, who comprised the vast majority of the population, worked the land all day, virtually every day.

However, late Anglo-Saxon society was subtle and sophisticated. There were merchants, craftsmen and sailors who did not fit into the three-level system. There was a rich cultural mix of Saxon, Danish and Celt, given the migrations and settlements outlined above. The peasant class was itself subdivided into recognised levels. A remarkable source dating from the time of Edward the Confessor (1042–66), a treatise on estate management called 'The Rights and Ranks of People' (*Rectitudines Singularum Personarum*) provides a useful insight into village society.

The *Rectitudines* illustrates peasant life on the eve of the Conquest. Society was ordered as follows:

- At the highest level of village society was the thegn, who held the estate by right of charter ('book-right') and had to do armed service, repairing fortresses and bridges in order to keep his land.
- Below the thegn was the geneat, a riding-servant or bailiff, serving the thegn in various capacities.
- Next was the cottar, who worked for the lord on Mondays and three days a week during harvest; he had five acres (two hectares) of his own land to farm the rest of the time.
- Below the cottar was the gebur or boor, equating to the later villein of medieval England. The boor was the main worker on the land, doing two days' work a week for the lord, sometimes three. He had to plough the lord's acreage, provide hunting dogs and carrying services and pay taxes, and at his death his belongings returned to the lord.
- The *Rectitudines* also describes the many other characters of village life, including bee-keepers, swineherds, sowers, shepherds, cheesemakers and slaves.

Evidence from the *Rectitudines* and other pre-Conquest surveys suggests that village life in Anglo-Saxon England had well-established customs and social hierarchies. The impact of the Norman Conquest was limited. Domesday Book records the continuity from the reign of Edward the

Confessor to the end of the reign of William the
Conqueror.

CAN WE TRUST THE EVIDENCE?

The first thing the student of medieval history has to
understand is that evidence dating from the period
1042–1228 is far more limited than those from any more
recent period of history. Not only is there less evidence, but
what has survived the passage of almost a thousand years
presents all the usual problems for the historian, that is:
authorship, point of view and reliability. The key point
about evidence for the Norman Conquest is that much of
the evidence is Norman, written after the Conquest.
History is written by the winners, not the losers. The
Normans won the Battle of Hastings and conquered
England; they then wrote the histories to justify that
invasion. The main sources for the invasion are *The Deeds of
Duke William* written by the duke's chaplain, William of
Poitiers, in the 1070s, and the astonishing pictorial record,
the Bayeux Tapestry (technically an embroidery), made in
the 1070s. It is still uncertain who commissioned the
Tapestry and where it was made. It has been suggested that
it was made at Winchester by English nuns for Queen
Matilda, or in Bayeux, on Bishop Odo's orders, or in
England on the orders of Count Eustace of Boulogne. Both
The Deeds of Duke William and the Tapestry were created to
justify the invasion but are immensely useful and
insightful.

The main Anglo-Saxon source for the years before and
during the Conquest is collectively known as the *Anglo-
Saxon Chronicle*. Up until 1065 there exist three versions: C,
D and E, derived from a common source but with some
differences. From 1065 to 1079 two versions survive and
thereafter only one version. The 'C' version was written at
Abingdon, 'D' possibly at Worcester and York and 'E' at
Canterbury, later copied by monks at Peterborough. These
chronicles supply a uniquely English account of political
events before 1066 and allow us to make comparisons with
the rather obvious Norman propaganda of William of
Poitiers.

The major economic and social source is Domesday Book
(see below, pages 62–6). This was a survey of land, property
and lordship with details of tax owed to the king. It was

compiled in 1086, twenty years after the Conquest and with deliberate reference to pre-1066 England. The record is unique and a triumph of Anglo-Norman government and administration.

Other evidence relating to land ownership is to be found in charters (legal documents drawn up to confirm land transactions). These are very rare outside the royal court, reflecting the lack of the written word. Law codes are few and letters even fewer. As a result of this scarcity of evidence, medieval historians often have to phrase their conclusions with 'possibly' and 'probably'.

The twelfth century saw an explosion of written sources. Charters, law codes, letters and taxation records appear far more. Royal government expanded its Chancery and the Exchequer developed to account for the vast income and expenditure of the Anglo-Norman kings. The expansion of monasticism encouraged the strong tradition of monastic histories and accordingly the twelfth century is better equipped with sources than the eleventh.

CONCLUSION: THE MAKINGS OF A NATION STATE

The evidence for historians for the eleventh century is scarce, but there is enough to define the ranks of society and to determine the chief national events. Much evidence relating to events after 1066 is written by Norman historians and has to be evaluated in the light of justification, but that is not to say that their evidence is not useful.

England before the Conquest was a sophisticated Anglo-Saxon state. So much so, that when the Danes returned in 1018 and conquered the whole of England, very little changed; the English state was run by a few foreigners from 1018 to 1042 until the royal line of Wessex was restored in the person of Edward the Confessor. It was his failure to produce an heir that sparked the Norman Conquest of England and changed the course of English history.

SUMMARY QUESTIONS

1. To what extent was pre-Conquest England a civilised and sophisticated state?

2. What problems does the historian encounter with the sources from this period?

CHAPTER 2

Who would succeed Edward the Confessor?

Bayeux Tapestry: Edward the Confessor on the throne

INTRODUCTION

When **Edward the Confessor** died childless in January 1066, three men believed that they could succeed him: Harold Godwinsson, William Duke of Normandy and Harald Hardrada. There was a fourth contender, too, a boy named Edgar the Atheling. To understand why there were so many contenders for Edward's throne, it is necessary to examine the events at the start of the eleventh century that were to have repercussions fifty years later.

WHAT PROBLEMS DID EDWARD THE CONFESSOR FACE WHEN HE BECAME KING?

Edward the Confessor was crowned by the archbishops of Canterbury and York on Easter Day, 1043, in a ceremony that had existed since the late tenth century. After the king had approached the altar, the bishops asked the clergy and the people present if they would accept Edward as their king; Edward was then anointed with holy oil, an act that transformed him from a mere mortal to a priest-like leader of his people. He was then invested with the regalia: the ring, sword, crown, sceptre and rod. This was at once a religious and secular ceremony, heavy with symbolism. The **coronation** ceremony was an established ritual by 1043, and would be used again in 1066 at the coronations of both Harold and William. However, the procedure of

KEY PERSON

Edward the Confessor
Edward was a son of Ethelred, King of England 978–1016, a direct descendant of Alfred the Great, King of Wessex. From there he could trace his ancestry to Cerdic, founder of the kingdom of the West Saxons in the early sixth century. The Royal House of Wessex was thus of ancient and venerated descent.

KEY THEME

Coronation The religious ceremony that created a king. By the mid-eleventh century it followed an established procedure. The new king was anointed (his forehead was brushed with holy oil) by the archbishop, which gave the king special powers to rule his people. The archbishop then placed the crown on the king's head.

KEY TERM

Succession crisis, 1066
The crisis that followed the death of Edward the Confessor without a son and heir. It was resolved by the Norman invasion led by William, Duke of Normandy.

KEY PERSON

Queen Emma (c. 985–1052) In an age when women had little real power, Emma stands out. The daughter of Richard, Duke of Normandy, she first married Ethelred, with whom she had several children, including Edward. She next married Canute, with whom she also had children. Whether she chose to marry Canute or whether the marriage simply provided her with a powerful protector is not known. Certainly after the death of Ethelred and the exile of Edward, she supported her Danish family over Edward. She was disgraced and stripped of her wealth and power when Edward discovered her plotting with Magnus of Norway. What power Emma wielded behind the scenes can never be known – surely she had some influence – but her career as queen to two kings of England and mother of two kings (Harthacanute and Edward) was remarkable.

recognising a new king in Anglo-Saxon England was not firmly established, and it is this that lies at the heart of the **succession crisis** of 1066.

Why did Edward become king?

Edward's succession to the throne was not guaranteed; Scandinavian princes, such as Svein Estrithsson, king of Denmark and Canute's nephew, and Magnus of Norway certainly voiced an interest. Rumours of a possible invasion of England by Magnus lasted until the latter's death in 1047. Edward's mother, the redoubtable **Emma**, conspired with him, championing the Scandinavian cause after her long marriage to Canute.

After Canute's defeat of Ethelred and the death of Edmund, Ethelred's son Canute became king of England in 1018. Edward, a boy, fled to Normandy, where he remained until 1040, returning when Harthacanute, Canute's son, became king. When Harthacanute died, Edward was hailed as his successor, and the ancient line of Wessex was restored to the throne. Edward's succession was remarkable in that both Canute's sons had died young and childless; Edward was one of Ethelred's many sons, all of whom had predeceased him. There was no guarantee that the House of Wessex would return to England after a period of Danish dominance. This Danish dominance haunted Edward for the whole of his twenty-four-year reign. It dictated his domestic and foreign policies and would lead to the succession crisis of 1066. The crisis was, in part, driven by the Godwin family.

Who was Godwin?

Godwin was the son of a Saxon thegn who was without doubt a master politician of his time. His marriage to Gytha, a Danish aristocrat and sister-in-law to Canute, enabled him to gain centre stage during Canute's reign, during which he was made earl of Wessex, the richest and most ancient earldom of the kingdom.

When Harthacanute died childless in 1042, Earl Godwin backed Edward's claim, along with the Londoners and southerners. Indeed Edward was in the right place at the right time and, probably due to Godwin's support, was elected and crowned king of England in 1043. Godwin was

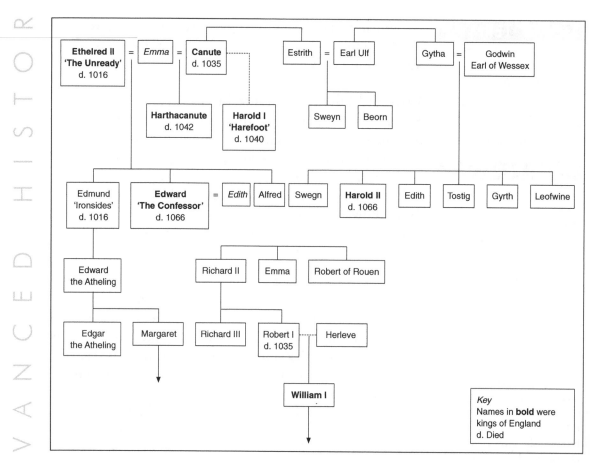

```
Ethelred II          Emma      Canute          Estrith  =  Earl Ulf        Gytha  =  Godwin
'The Unready'    =          =  d. 1035                                               Earl of Wessex
d. 1016

                    Harthacanute      Harold I              Sweyn    Beorn
                    d. 1042           'Harefoot'
                                      d. 1040

Edmund          Edward              Alfred   Swegn   Harold II   Edith   Tostig   Gyrth   Leofwine
'Ironsides'  =  'The Confessor' = Edith              d. 1066
d. 1016         d. 1066

Edward                Richard II   Emma   Robert of Rouen
the Atheling

Edgar        Margaret    Richard III   Robert I    Herleve
the Atheling                           d. 1035

                                    William I
```

Key
Names in **bold** were
kings of England
d. Died

The English succession, 1016–66

rewarded for his support in 1043 when his eldest son, Swegn, was made an earl and his second son, Harold, was also promoted. Most important for Godwin was the marriage of his daughter Edith to Edward early in 1045, setting the seal on his rise from obscure thegn to **dynast**.

Why was Edward's marriage childless?

Marriage to Edith, beautiful daughter of the most powerful man in the kingdom, made good sense to Edward. Urged in his coronation oaths to provide an heir to the kingdom, he was forty at the time of his marriage to Edith, who was probably around twenty. Both were healthy. Later sources, written thirty or more years on, encouraged the story that Edward was **chaste** and remained a virgin all his married life. But this lacks authority, written with hindsight after the disputes between Godwin and Edward and the Norman succession, which was, in Norman eyes, God-granted. Certainly in Edward's old age he became increasingly devoted to the Church, investing all his

KEY WORD

Dynast The term used for a founder of a great family, usually a royal family.

KEY THEME

Chaste People who are chaste have no sexual relations. Monks and nuns swore a vow (promise) of chastity.

energies in the rebuilding of Westminster Abbey. But in 1045 there is nothing to suggest that he and Edith did not lead a normal married life. Unfortunately, she was unable to conceive – and that changed the course of English history.

WHY DID THE GODWINS FALL FROM POWER IN 1051?

In September 1051, Godwin and his family fell from power and fled out of England and into exile. Their fall from grace was swift and remarkable. The consequences were significant for the succession to Edward's throne.

- The immediate cause was the death of Eadsige, Archbishop of Canterbury, in October 1050. The monks of Canterbury wished to elect one of their own number, Elric, a kinsman of Godwin, who supported him, but Edward chose his own favourite, Robert of Jumièges, who had been bishop of London since 1044 and who possibly accompanied Edward when he came to England in 1041.
- Robert of Jumièges and Godwin antagonised each other periodically through the 1040s, and Edward used his royal patronage to build up his own factions (groups of supporters) within the court.
- These, however, were not necessarily purely Norman factions, though Edward's Norman nephew, Ralf of Mantes, appeared in the late 1040s and was granted lands in Herefordshire, where several other Normans were granted estates.
- In addition to this, Godwin's prestige at court had been damaged by the behaviour of his eldest son, Swegn. This included the murder of Beorn who was both Godwin's and Canute's nephew, brother to the king of Denmark and an earl in King Edward's court since 1046. Swegn's crime was enormous; the king and his army declared Swegn *nithing* – in utter disgrace.

The fracas at Dover

The spark that lit the fuse leading to the explosive row between the king and his chief earl, Godwin, was ignited by a street-fight in Dover in 1051. Eustace, Count of Boulogne, had visited the king and on his return journey through Dover found that accommodation and supplies were denied to his party (possibly on the orders of Godwin). Eustace's men attempted to intimidate the local people and the result was an ugly brawl that left seven of Eustace's men and a number of Dover men, women and children dead. When the king heard, he blamed the people of Dover and ordered Godwin to punish the town.

- Godwin, already sidelined in the royal court by the Norman-French followers of the king, and by the damaging actions of his son Swegn, refused to punish Dover, whereupon the king summoned his council and an army to Gloucester.
- Godwin arrived with his own army and it was agreed that the Godwins would be tried in a council in London. However, on the way to London many of Godwin's men deserted to the royal army.
- Godwin did not receive the support of the earl of Northumbria, Siward, or of the earl of Mercia, Leofric. This highlighted how limited his power was.
- Godwin suspected treachery and by the time he and his sons reached London, the king had decisive military supremacy. There was nothing for it but to flee the country.

DID WILLIAM OF NORMANDY VISIT ENGLAND?

It was during this period of open struggle between Edward and Godwin that the first significant event regarding Edward's succession occurred. *The Anglo-Saxon Chronicle* records that, during the winter of 1051/2, 'Earl William' visited with a large force of Frenchmen and was received by the king. Given Godwin's absence and the supremacy of Edward's Norman faction at court, this was a good time for **Duke William** to visit his cousin, the king of England. Did Edward offer William the throne of England?

- Circumstances meant that the timing could not have been better: Edward was supreme in England, and William was by now master of Normandy.
- It was clear that Edith was not going to give the king a son (she had been sent to a nunnery after her father's downfall).
- But the *Chronicle* does not state that Edward offered William the throne.
- Furthermore, the Norman sources have it another way: that Edward sent Robert of Jumièges, Archbishop of

KEY PERSON

William, Duke of Normandy Born around 1027, son of Duke Robert and Herlève, his mistress. When Duke Robert died in 1035, he left his seven-year-old illegitimate boy as heir to the duchy. William spent over ten years establishing himself as duke of Normandy, surviving at least one assassination attempt and winning campaigns against the king of France and count of Anjou. By the 1050s he was secure in the duchy; by 1066 he was the most powerful man in north-western Europe. William's rise was remarkable because he was illegitimate. In a highly spiritual age, where marriage and inheritance depended upon children born within wedlock, William's survival was rare.

KEY EVIDENCE

William of Jumièges, *Gesta Normannorum Ducum* (written 1070s) 'Edward, king of the English, being, according to the dispensation of God, without an heir, sent Robert, Archbishop of Canterbury, to the duke with a message appointing the duke as heir to the kingdom which God had entrusted him.'

KEY EVIDENCE

***The Anglo-Saxon Chronicle* (Worcester version) for 1051** 'Then came Duke William from beyond the sea with a great retinue of Frenchmen, and the king received him and as many of his companions as it pleased him and let him go again.'

Canterbury, to Normandy to offer William the throne. This avoided portraying the duke as a **petitioner** for the crown; instead, he was the heir-designate.

It will never be known whether William visited England or was visited on Edward's orders, but it should be understood that he was not the only possible contender for the throne. Eustace of Boulogne, the king's brother-in-law, had visited in the summer, perhaps making overtures towards the succession; Ralf of Mantes, now earl of Hereford, was still in the frame, as he was Edward's nephew. William was, therefore, one of several contenders, but in the eyes of the Norman chroniclers writing after the Conquest, he was Edward's rightful heir and his appointment as such dates from this point.

HOW POWERFUL WAS HAROLD GODWINSSON?

The return of Earl Godwin

Whatever Norman-French plans Edward may have had with regard to his succession, they were destroyed by the successful return of the earl of Wessex and his family in the late summer of 1052. Godwin and his sons took a large fleet up the Thames, gathering support either by force or by his popularity, and arrived at Southwark in mid-September. The people of London granted him safe passage, and he faced the king's army and navy on the north bank of the Thames and demanded the restoration of his estates. The king's army would not fight and Siward and the northern thegns remained aloof. Edward realised this and was forced to make his peace with Godwin. His Norman followers fled at this point and Godwin was restored to the earldom of Wessex, Harold to East Anglia and Queen Edith brought back to the court. Swegn, the family disaster, was not present; he had died on his way back from a pilgrimage to Jerusalem. It was exactly a year after Godwin's fall. On both occasions the country had avoided civil war, due less to the diplomacy of the great men and the king, than to the reluctance of Englishmen to kill one another. Godwin did not have it all his way:

- Archbishop Robert, whose influence on the king had been too great, died in exile in Jumièges.
- Ralf of Mantes was allowed to remain in Herefordshire.

- Stigand, Bishop of Winchester, was the new archbishop of Canterbury, acceptable to all parties (though he never gained the approval of the Pope).
- The king was not by any means the prisoner of Godwin; he probably accepted Godwin's return with resignation. The northern earls, Leofric and Siward, would not allow Godwin too much power.

The death of Godwin and the rise of Harold

Godwin did not live long to enjoy his success. He suffered a stroke in April 1053 and died a few days later. Harold, aged only twenty-seven, was promoted to the earldom of Wessex by Edward. The later years of the 1050s saw a greater dominance of the Godwin siblings than Godwin could ever have dared to hope:

- Tostig was given the earldom of Northumbria in 1055, on the death of Siward.
- Gyrth was granted an earldom in East Anglia.
- Leofwine was granted an earldom in the south-east.
- Harold, Earl of Wessex, absorbed Ralf of Mantes's Herefordshire lands on his death in 1057.

England in the period 1053–65 saw relative stability. The Godwin brothers, with their sister as queen fully restored to her position at court, dominated the political life of England. Harold, head of the family and the king's right-hand man, was the most powerful person in the realm. He was even called *subregulus* ('deputy-king') by one chronicler. The greatest family triumph came with a decisive defeat of the Welsh in 1063. There was at this time no hint that there would be an invasion of England or that Harold would become the criminal of Norman historiography. This period of time was seen as a time of Godwin success and political unity. The chronicle *Vita Aedwardi* (Life of Edward) saw the unity of the Godwin brothers as key to English survival. When the brothers fell out in 1065, the country was open to foreign invasion.

The Hungarian connection

The underlying issue, however, remained the question of Edward's heir. If the king was not going to produce a son and the return of Godwin dashed the possibility of a Norman succession then another solution had to be sought. As in 1041, the establishment looked for a member of the

KEY EVENT

The war against the Welsh In a pincer movement, Harold attacked from the south and Tostig from the north, isolating the rebellious king, Gruffydd, who was murdered by his own men. Harold sent his head to King Edward. This was a remarkable victory, and paved the way for the Norman conquest of Wales after 1066.

royal House of Wessex to bring out of exile. The nearest living relative to Edward was the son of his half-brother Edmund Ironside, also Edward. On the death of Ironside in 1016, Canute had sent Edmund's children to the king of Sweden to have them murdered, but instead, they had been conveyed to the safety of the king of Hungary. In July of 1054, Ealdred, Bishop of Worcester, set off for Germany to seek out the Saxon Prince Edward. Ealdred remained in Cologne for a year, and returned home empty-handed. But the prince did eventually come to England, with his young son, **Edgar**, and arrived in London in 1057.

KEY PERSON

Edgar the Atheling The title 'atheling' meant 'man of noble/royal descent' and Edgar was considered a possible successor. He survived into adulthood and remained at large for another forty years, sometimes a dangerous opponent of the Norman kings, but never became king of England.

Unfortunately, he died soon after arriving in England, probably never meeting his half-uncle. His son, Edgar 'the Atheling', was probably only five years old, with his chances of surviving to adulthood still uncertain. Edward took the boy and his three sisters into his care and brought them up as his own. It is possible that he regarded his great-nephew as his heir and hoped that if he lived another decade or so, the boy would be old enough to succeed him.

WHAT DID HAROLD PROMISE TO WILLIAM?

Nothing more is heard from English sources regarding the succession problem until the eve of the king's death. But the Norman sources describe in detail a visit made by Harold to Normandy in the summer of either 1064 or 1065. Put simply, the Norman version is that Harold was sent by Edward to William to swear fealty to the duke and confirm the offer of William's succession in 1052 by an oath. He was captured *en route* by the count of Ponthieu and rescued by the duke. At a council Harold then swore an oath in front of the great barons of Normandy, promising to secure the kingdom for William on the death of Edward and swearing to become his **vassal**. Before returning home to England, Harold was honoured by William by going with him on a campaign to Brittany.

KEY TERM

Vassal A vassal swore an oath of loyalty, or homage, to his lord, who swore a return oath to defend his vassal. This contract, enhanced by the personal bond of homage, tied feudal relationships together.

Problems with the evidence

The Norman evidence is too unreliable to establish the absolute truth about Harold's visit to Normandy.

- The chief Norman writer, William of Poitiers, writing in the 1070s, places the oath at Bonneville, near Lisieux, even though he was not present.
- The Bayeux Tapestry, again made during the 1070s, puts the oath at Bayeux.

- Where William of Poitiers is very detailed in his justification of the duke's rise to power and ultimate rightful succession to the English throne, the Tapestry tells us very little. The commentary in the border does not say exactly what it was that Harold swore, though it clearly shows him making an oath of some description.
- The Tapestry does not tell us why Harold was in Normandy in the first place.
- William of Poitiers alludes to the deal struck between William and Edward in 1052, but does not hold a consistent view on that event.
- If Harold had sworn a solemn oath at Edward's behest, why were hostages not given to guarantee the treaty, which was the usual practice? Edgar the Atheling would have been the obvious hostage for Harold to take.
- Why did William not come to England to be crowned in Edward's lifetime? This was not normal English custom, but no evidence suggests favour towards William. Edward could have granted him lands and received him at court before his death.

Bayeux Tapestry: Harold's oath to Duke William

If Harold did visit Normandy and swear an oath to William on the command of the king, Edward may have returned to an earlier policy of a Norman succession. But if Harold did not visit Normandy on such a mission, other scenarios should be considered:

- Harold may well have made a visit on other business that resulted in an oath being extorted from him.
- Harold might, in gratitude, have made an oath of fealty promising to maintain William's interests in England in return for William rescuing him from Ponthieu.

- Harold may have been touring the continent on his own business and attempted to enlist William's support but found himself making promises he could not keep.
- Harold's visit may have been entirely unconnected to the succession and he may simply have sworn an oath of friendship between England and Normandy, acting as Edward's chief counsellor and most powerful earl.

Whatever the real reasons for Harold's visit to Normandy, if it did indeed occur, the fact is that Norman writers used it relentlessly to portray Harold as a **perjurer** and usurper; Duke William used it when he asked for papal support of his invasion of England in order to justify it and turn it into a holy campaign. In the Bayeux Tapestry, King Edward seems angry on Harold's return, which may suggest that Harold may not have been on an official mission for the king, or that he gave too much away.

DID EDWARD OFFER THE THRONE TO HAROLD?

In November 1065, Edward suffered the first of a series of strokes. His mental state was affected and by December it was clear that he was not going to survive. Now, at last, the jockeying for positions of power at the royal court began in earnest. At the centre of this struggle was Harold, Earl of Wessex, the most powerful man in the realm. His influence had increased after the exile of his brother, Tostig, Earl of Northumbria, from England.

How significant was Tostig's fall from power?

Tostig's fall from power after ten years as earl of Northumbria was shocking; it was the beginning of the end for the Godwin family. Tostig stood accused by Northumbrian rebels of murder and harsh rule. In October the rebels had marched on York and killed all Tostig's household troops and servants; they then outlawed Tostig and requested that Morcar, son of Leofric, sometime earl of Mercia, be installed in his place.

Harold was sent to negotiate. The rebels refused to take Tostig back. The king called out his entire army to crush them by force but nobody turned up. The English did not want a civil war. The rebellion was against Tostig, not the king. Harold was in a difficult situation. He tried to make peace, but failed; the rebels stood firm and the king lacked force of arms. Tostig and his family went into exile in Flanders, where his wife's family lived. Tostig would only return to England in 1066 to make war on his brother. The rejection of Tostig, a southerner, demonstrated both the continuing independence of the north and Edward's weakness in not being able to deal with them effectively.

Could Harold become king?

The king probably had his first stroke when he heard of the rebels' victory. The unity of the Godwins was destroyed. Edith, a supporter of Tostig, was bitter towards Harold. Was it at this point that Harold thought that he could, or might have to, take the throne for himself?

- The earls of Northumbria and Mercia, the brothers Morcar and Edwin, were very young.
- Harold had put the peace of the realm before his own brother. He had allowed Morcar to remain earl of Northumbria over and above Tostig; he then married the sister of Edwin and Morcar, Eadgyth. The brothers were in Harold's debt; did they dare oppose his bid for the throne in favour of Edgar the Atheling, who was fourteen in 1066, or Duke William, the king's cousin?
- In any case, the problem seems to have been solved by the king himself. When it became apparent that he lay dying, many nobles and clergy from all across England assembled at Westminster that Christmas, 1065, to witness the consecration of the king's new abbey and probably to see the king die. Those assembled were representative of the kingdom, and not just of the Godwin party. William, Duke of Normandy was absent.

Edward's offer of the throne to Harold – did he or didn't he?

The king had another stroke on Christmas Eve, a Saturday. On 28 December Westminster abbey was consecrated in his absence and the king sank into a coma. At the end he was roused and the queen, Harold and the Archbishop of Canterbury gathered by his bedside, as depicted in the Bayeux Tapestry and recorded in English sources, all, unfortunately, written after the conquest of England.

- The Bayeux Tapestry has the dying king touching hands with a person: was that Harold? It does not say.

KEY EVENT

William's absence Why, we should ask, was the duke of Normandy absent, if he had been declared heir to the king by Harold's supposed oath in 1064/5? His absence is significant and damaging to the Norman version of the rightful Norman succession.

- The *Life of King Edward*, written for Queen Edith, is neutral: Edward 'commended the kingdom to Harold's protection'.
- The equally ambiguous northern and Abingdon versions of *The Anglo-Saxon Chronicle* say, 'the wise ruler entrusted the realm to a man of high rank, to Harold himself'.
- The Canterbury version is less equivocal: 'And Earl Harold succeeded to the realm of England, just as the king had granted it to him, and as he had been chosen to the position'.

These are English sources and could have been written to justify a *coup d'état* by Harold and his followers. But most significantly is the admission by William of Poitiers, the greatest advocate of Norman propaganda, that Edward bequeathed the throne to Harold on his deathbed. William of Poitiers accepts the English version, but from the Norman point of view, this makes Harold's treachery even greater.

It has been shown that Edward was forced by circumstance to change his plans regarding the succession. His Norman cousin, Duke William, was one of several petitioners, including Ralf of Mantes and Eustace of Boulogne, the king's Norman-French nephews, Edgar the Atheling, his English great-nephew and Earl Harold, his brother-in-law. Furthermore, the words of a dying man in the Middle Ages were the most solemn words that could be uttered. By modern standards, Edward was delirious, but by the standards of the time, he spoke directly from God. Quite possibly pressure was put upon the dying man to say the right words from God, and it was thus put about that Harold was now the true heir. This would supersede any oath Harold may or may not have sworn on his accidental or planned visit to Normandy in 1064/5.

Bayeux Tapestry: the dying king is touching hands with someone – was that Harold?

Who would succeed Edward the Confessor?　23

HAROLD IS CROWNED

Whatever the dying king indicated to Harold and his followers, Harold was crowned king of England on 6 January, the very day that Edward was buried; both events occurred at Westminster Abbey. Even if Edward had not indicated that Harold was to be his successor, it is clear that the assembled nobility and clergy, there to see the king die and his new abbey consecrated, acquiesced, and probably acclaimed, Harold the new king. Harold had popular support and the assent of his predecessor. Bearing in mind that in Anglo-Saxon custom there was no established means of inheriting the throne, the will of the outgoing monarch and the assent of the ruling classes were more than enough for Harold. What did an obscure oath sworn (possibly under duress) two years before matter?

Bayeux Tapestry: Harold on the throne

DID EDWARD THE CONFESSOR HAVE A POLICY TOWARDS HIS SUCCESSION?

Given the lack of sources and the contradictory nature of what survives, it can never be fully established what, if anything, Edward wished to do with his crown.

- If his marriage to Edith was a healthy relationship, then the couple were merely unable to conceive, though he certainly grew increasingly pious and chaste.
- If Edward, after nine years of childless marriage to Edith, turned back to Normandy in Godwin's absence and offered, or raised the prospect of, an inheritance to William, then this was dashed by Godwin's return.
- The possibility of the great-nephew was an option, but was hampered by Edgar's youth after his father's death on arriving in England from Hungary.
- Edward may well have sent Harold to William to renew

a treaty of friendship in 1064/5; or Harold may have been tricked, or forced, into an oath he had no intention of keeping and which did not have Edward's consent.

- On his deathbed, the king may have changed his mind when he signalled to Harold; but the words of a dying man were as good as the law itself.

CONCLUSION: WHO HAD THE BETTER CLAIM?

The Norman version is straightforward. Edward offered the throne to William in 1052; Harold, his right-hand man, visited the duchy to confirm this offer and then proceeded to seize the throne illegally. Even if Edward had granted the kingdom to Harold, as Norman sources admit, Harold should instead have guarded the throne for William. However, the Norman story is too simplistic to believe.

- At any one time in the period 1042–66 there were several likely contenders to the throne; English, Norman and Scandinavian. It is possible that Edward had plans, but was forced to adapt them.
- The nobility were fully aware of the power of the duke of Normandy and the Scandinavian threats from across the North Sea, and may have believed that England was going to be invaded whoever became king.
- Acclaiming Harold gave them the best man to defend the kingdom. Harold had proven military skill and sound governmental judgement, and had put the peace of the realm before his own brother.

In the context of the Danish invasion of 1014, Edward the Confessor's strong connection with Normandy, the power of the Godwin family and Edward's own childlessness, another invasion of England after Edward's death was highly likely. The Anglo-Saxon nobility knew that Harold was the best man to withstand the fortunes of war to which the kingdom was now open.

SUMMARY QUESTIONS

1. 'Weak, indecisive and dominated by the Godwins.' To what extent is this a fair and accurate assessment of the reign of Edward the Confessor?

2. How certain can the historian be when considering the succession to the throne in 1066? Discuss the sources in your answer.

CHAPTER 3

Why did William the Conqueror win the Battle of Hastings?

INTRODUCTION: 1066: THE YEAR OF THREE BATTLES

Since it was apparent that England was going to be invaded by either a Norman or a Scandinavian force, the whole of Harold's nine-month reign was overshadowed by preparations for the invasions and the invasions themselves. Most of the year was, in effect, a 'phoney war'. Enraged by what he saw as a usurpation of his crown, William of Normandy orchestrated a careful propaganda campaign to assert his legal right to the throne before turning to the military logistics. He had his fleet ready by the summer but the wind was not right for sailing. Harold, his fleet at the ready and his troops along the south coast, waited in vain. Harold's northern army waited for the Scandinavians. Nothing happened. Not until September did the invasions begin. Then, in the space of six weeks, three great battles were fought that determined the course of English history. No single factor determined the final outcome. Instead, a wide range of events and circumstances coalesced to produce the dramatic end piece.

HOW SECURE WAS KING HAROLD?

Harold, brother-in-law to the previous king, proven warrior and administrator, was in a good position. He reinforced his support from the earls Edwin and Morcar by marrying Eadgyth, their sister. He had been acclaimed king by the *witenagemot*, the gathering of nobility and clergy, of whom there were many at the Christmas court; he was crowned in the coronation ceremony in Westminster Abbey and was depicted in the Bayeux Tapestry in full regalia, where he is referred to as *rex* (king). Furthermore, he was not, as Norman sources insist, crowned by Archbishop Stigand, who was seen by many as corrupt, but by the saintly and revered Archbishop of York, Ealdred. The new king issued coins inscribed with *pax* (peace) and an image of himself wearing the crown and clutching his rod of justice.

Norman sources admit to Harold's coronation and to Edward's deathbed offer to Harold, but within the sources there is a concerted effort to airbrush Harold out of history. Whilst the Tapestry refers to him as *rex,* as do very early government documents in William's reign, by the time Domesday Book was drawn up, in 1086, Harold is merely *comes* (earl). The Norman portrait of a usurper and perjurer with no legal rights was complete twenty years after his death.

HOW DID WILLIAM PREPARE FOR HIS INVASION?

William's war of words

The vilification of Harold began right from the start. When William heard of Edward's death and Harold's coronation he was furious. A letter to Harold cut no ice; his barons in Normandy refused to contemplate invading England. But sending his trusted friend Lanfranc to Rome to portray Anglo-Saxon England as a sink of corruption and decline gained the support of the Pope and transformed a power struggle in north-west Europe into a Holy War, a just war. William went into battle at Hastings with the papal banner at his head; thousands flocked to join him now that he had a cause.

People also flocked to William's banner because he was already famous as a winner of battles. His conquest of Maine, the neighbouring county to Normandy, in 1063, earned him the title 'the Conqueror'. The deaths of his rivals Henry, King of France and Fulk of Anjou made him the most powerful man in north-west Europe.

William's military preparations

Now that men were flocking in from Brittany, southern France, and even Italy, William set about building a fleet. His brilliance as a commander cannot be underestimated. William's attempt was dangerous and risky. He might lose his life and the duchy he had spent twenty years acquiring. Therefore the planning was meticulous. Men were fed, horses provisioned, ships built, arms and armour manufactured. The ordinary people of Normandy did not suffer and the harvest was gathered as the summer came and went. In September, William moved his fleet to the mouth of the Somme to exploit the shorter crossing. All he needed now was a favourable wind.

KEY THEME

Medieval warfare Battles during the eleventh century were rare. Kings and princes usually preferred to negotiate and strike a deal, sealing it perhaps by an alliance and a marriage. Fighting a battle was a great risk; armies were often raised to make threats. In Europe, warfare revolved around sieges and counter-sieges of castles, skirmishes and lightning raids. In England, warfare was infrequent after the great Danish invasions of 1016; conflict was avoided in 1051 and again in 1065; Harold's campaign against the Welsh in 1063 was in effect a raid. The Scottish borders saw similar incursions from time to time.

Bayeux Tapestry: William's men gathering arms and armour

HOW DID HAROLD PREPARE THE DEFENCE OF HIS REALM?

Most crucially, Harold had to disband his fleet and southern army on 8 September. He could no longer provision the troops and the harvest was long overdue. Harold had to send the soldiers home after their two months' service was finished. A large part of the army was made up of farmers who had to work the fields to gather the harvest. This, historians argue, was the essential difference between the archaic Anglo-Saxon *fyrd* and the slick, professional war-machine that William could call upon. However, the length of time spent waiting was unprecedented for both sides. William promised his followers (many of whom were mercenaries) land and booty in order to keep them with him.

Duke William did not get to England first, though. On his return to London, Harold heard the news that Harald Hardrada, King of Norway, had landed in Northumbria and burnt Scarborough, Cleveland and Holderness to the ground.

WHY DID THE VIKING INVASION FAIL?

Harald 'Hardrada' (the Hard One) was a legend in his own time, a feared warrior who had campaigned in Scandinavia, Russia and Byzantium (modern Turkey). His claim to the throne of England was based on a promise apparently made by Harthacanute to Magnus, King of Norway, to leave him his possessions if he died first, a promise the Anglo-Saxons had ignored. Magnus had threatened to invade England throughout the 1040s, a threat which only receded at his death; Hardrada resurrected that claim, but also knew that

KEY WORD

Fyrd The Anglo-Saxon army, formed from the thegns who held their land by military service and the peasants who were paid for two months' service (probably on a rotating basis, though this general mobilisation would have called them all out over the summer). Thegns were well armed, with helmets, chain-mail coats (the byrnie), sword or axe and horse; peasants were lightly armed. The Anglo-Saxon army normally fought on foot. The fleet was drawn from men from the coastal ports as part of the *scip-fyrd*. The entire *fyrd* system worked well enough throughout Edward's reign and for Harold; the defeat at Hastings was due to other causes than problems with the *fyrd*.

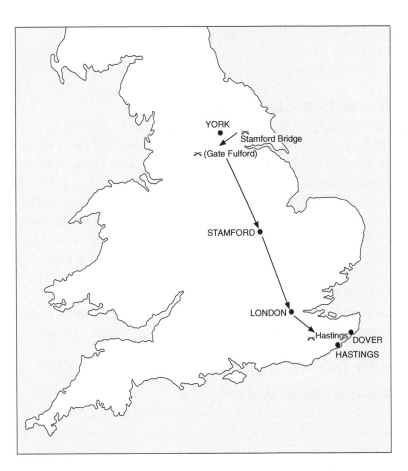

Harold's march from York and Stamford Bridge to meet William at Hastings

he could call upon the support of many Scandinavian people living in the Orkneys, Scotland and the north of England. His aim was to re-establish Canute's empire. He also had on his side the renegade former earl of Northumbria and the new king's brother, Tostig.

If Hardrada's claim was rather flimsy, then his invasion was anything but. The legendary king and most feared warrior in Christendom sailed up the Humber with no less than 300 ships (according to *The Anglo-Saxon Chronicle*), landed at Ricall on the Ouse and marched on York.

The Battle of Gate Fulford

1066 was a year of three battles: Stamford Bridge and Hastings are the most famous, but the first was significant. Hardrada found his way to York barred by the young earls of Mercia and Northumbria, Edwin and Morcar, brothers-in-law of Harold Godwinsson. The battle raged all day and ended in the total defeat of the northern Anglo-Saxon army. The brothers had certainly shown their loyalty to the

Why did William the Conqueror win the Battle of Hastings?   29 king, as had their army, but defeat inevitably ended in slaughter. The king had still to defeat two rival claimants to his throne and had already lost thousands of troops.

The Battle of Stamford Bridge

Harold was probably on his way north, accompanied by those troops of the southern army whom he had been able to recall, when he heard of the defeat at Gate Fulford. He stormed north in a brilliant forced march, covering 190 miles in four days and completely surprising Hardrada who was camped at Stamford Bridge on the river Derwent, on 20 September. In another long and bloody battle, Harold Godwinsson won a total victory over Hardrada's Viking force. The most feared warrior in Christendom was killed, along with Tostig and most of his army. The sources indicate that the remainder of the Viking army needed only twenty-four of their original 300 ships in which to leave.

WHY DID THE NORMAN INVASION SUCCEED?

William's army lands

Harold may have thought that William was either unable or unwilling to come to England that year. Summer was over; the days were getting shorter and the sea crossing less safe. But while Harold was resting his exhausted and depleted army in the north, the wind changed direction and William crossed the Channel and landed unopposed at the Roman shore fort at Pevensey on 28 September.

William was lucky. Norman sources show him praying and pleading for the wind to change. The army of loyal followers, mercenaries and opportunists he had bribed, cajoled and persuaded to join him would not stay in one place indefinitely. Next year was another year and circumstances might be very different. It was now or never. So when the wind changed, he led his men across the Channel with great haste. He knew the Saxon coast lay undefended and his spies had told him of Hardrada's invasion. It was a great risk, but a calculated one.

From Pevensey, William moved to Hastings, where he knew the port afforded shelter for a possible rearguard action. Then he laid waste to the surrounding countryside, partly to preserve his own supplies, partly to draw Harold into battle. A set-piece battle was the only way William

Edwin and Morcar These young brothers were the earls of Mercia and Northumbria and were important to Harold's power. After the expulsion of Tostig in late 1065, Morcar became earl of Northumbria. Harold supported him over his brother and married the brothers' sister, Eadgyth. In return for this, the brothers backed Harold when he took the throne and fought for him at Gate Fulford. It is not clear whether they were at Stamford Bridge, and Harold's march south to Hastings was so rapid that they were not at Hastings. The brothers were involved in the rebellions against King William in 1068–71 and lost their earldoms.

could conclude the campaign. It was in Harold's interest to delay, to starve William out and allow doubt and fear to sink into the minds of the few thousand Norman troops in a foreign land.

But Harold moved quickly, perhaps hoping to emulate the blinding success of his Stamford Bridge campaign, perhaps stung by the attack on his own people in Wessex. He may also have planned on confining William to the coast, preventing him from breaking out with his mounted troops and rampaging far and wide across Sussex. He reached London on 6 October and remained only until 11 October. Many of his foot-soldiers and archers were still moving south from York; his stay in London was not long enough to gather the many thousands he had at his disposal. He did not wait to remobilise the 30,000 or 40,000 *fyrd* troops from the shires of all England. Forcing the pace again, he arrived on the South Downs on the night of 13 October; his men were exhausted.

THE BATTLE OF HASTINGS

William's scouts had warned him of Harold's approach, and he was ready. He left Hastings before dawn on Saturday 14 October, and began the attack on Harold's army, which was encamped on a hill barring the route to London. If Harold had hoped to surprise William and scatter his men before they could retreat to their ships, he was wrong. In the words of *The Anglo-Saxon Chronicle*, the only English account, William came upon Harold 'by surprise' and 'before his army was drawn up in battle array'. Even if Harold had not planned on fighting a defensive battle – or even a battle at all, if William's troops were surprised – he was able to adapt to the situation. The English army was already on a hill; if William wanted to finish off Harold decisively and march on London to the take the crown he believed was rightfully his, then he would have to get Harold off that hill. And with each hour lost, more men would come flooding into the area to support Harold.

Tactics and troops

Harold's army probably numbered around 7000, including the élite **housecarls**, the king's well-armed bodyguards; the thegns, Saxon landlords, mercenaries and the mass of less well-armed peasant-farmers drawn from the Kent,

---

KEY WORD

Housecarl The king and his earls often kept soldiers in their households who provided them with a bodyguard and formed the heart of their armies in time of war when they were expected to fight to the last man. They were rewarded with the spoils of war and land. Most of the housecarls died in the great battles of 1066.

Sussex and London *fyrd*. The Bayeux Tapestry shows that they all fought on foot, as was the Anglo-Saxon custom of warfare. The housecarls wore a chain-mail coat and conical helmet, and had as their prize weapon a two-handed axe that could cut a man in half with one blow; the peasants were armed with anything they could find: scythes, hooks, daggers, spears and stones. The well-armed housecarls and thegns were spread all along the ridge, their three-foot-high shields locked tightly together to form the famous shield-wall, or 'war-hedge'.

William had brought horses with him. The Bayeux Tapestry shows the specially built flat-bottomed boats with horses crossing the Channel. This was the essential difference between the two armies, and represented not only a new type of warfare, but a new type of society. This was a society based around the education and provisioning of the **knight**, whose function in life was to follow his lord and pay for his lands by undertaking war-service. William had several thousand men on horseback, each fighting in special units, the *conroi,* and following the *gonfanon*, or banner, of their leader. In this way, the mass of cavalry was broken into household and familial units of highly trained men able to follow specific orders without confusion. This degree of discipline was to enable the Norman cavalry to pretend retreat and to draw the less disciplined Saxon army off the hill to their deaths in the marshy valley below.

The course of the battle

At nine o'clock William began his attack, sending in the infantry to soften up the English defence. This did not have much impact. Archers fired up into the shield-wall, but the line held firm. Then William sent in the feared cavalry. These were the knights on their warhorses with couched lances. The horses were trained to kick and bite humans, the knights had sat in the saddle from the age of five and knew how to cut a man down. But still the shield-wall held firm. The advantage of the steep incline began to pay off; the Norman knights wheeled about, seeking gaps in the line, hit by stones and missiles hurled at them by the jeering Saxons.

This continued for several hours before reaching a crisis point. After one of the cavalry charges, the Normans pulled

KEY EVIDENCE

**William of Poitiers,
Gesta Willelmi (1070s)**

'Realising that they could not without severe loss overcome an army massed so strongly in close formation, the Normans and their allies feigned flight and simulated a retreat ...The barbarians [English] thinking victory within their grasp shouted with triumph ... gave rapid pursuit to those who they thought to be in flight; but the Normans suddenly wheeling their horses surrounded them and cut down their pursuers so that not one was left alive. Twice was this ruse employed with the utmost success ...'

KEY EVIDENCE

**The Anglo-Saxon
Chronicle (D version) for
1066** 'King Harold assembled a large army and came against him at the hoary apple tree and William came against him by surprise before his army was drawn up in battle array. But the king nevertheless fought hard against him, with the men who were willing to support him, and there were heavy casualties on both sides. There King Harold was killed and Earl Leofwine his brother, and Earl Gyrth his brother, and many good men, and the French remained masters of the field, even as God granted it to them because of the sins of the people.'

Bayeux Tapestry: Norman cavalry charge against the Saxon shield-wall

back and a cry went up that the duke had been killed. Panic set in, and retreat verged on rout, but William was very much alive. Taking off his helmet, he bellowed at the men nearest him that he was alive. Certainly three horses were killed under him that day and this was probably one of those occasions.

It was at this point that some of the English front line, now composed not so much of housecarls as of peasants who had borne the brunt of the Norman assaults, also believed that the battle was won, and left the hilltop. Harold, unable or unwilling to commit his army to a general advance – which might at that moment have swept William back into the sea – watched and despaired as hundreds streamed down the hill towards the retreating cavalry and were cut down as the Normans, seeing that William was alive, recovered and reformed.

The **feigned retreat** was used at least twice that afternoon and the shield-wall was gradually worn down. At last, towards dusk, the Norman knights got in amongst the remaining English on the top of the hill, where their superiority in the saddle counted for everything. English peasants began to desert. William ordered his archers to fire high and it was at the last moment, as the sun set, that Harold, with his brother Gyrth and a small group of loyal housecarls, were ridden down by the cavalry and killed. Harold was hit in the eye by an arrow before being hacked to pieces by the broadswords of the knights. The longest and most decisive battle in English history was over.

WHY DID WILLIAM WIN THE BATTLE OF HASTINGS?

The Battle of Hastings is one of the best-known events in English history. Much ink has been spilt, however, on the precise reasons why William won. There are no single outstanding factors, rather a combination of events, including skill, luck and – in medieval eyes – the hand of God.

- **Logistics and circumstances** Facing a double invasion put an enormous strain on Harold's reserves. This alone, it has been suggested, marks Old English society out as out of date, but such a situation was unprecedented. Harold had to keep his armies and fleet mobilised from May through to September, itself a notable feat. He managed to remobilise and defeat Hardrada in a lightning strike, a brilliant campaign. His army was equal in size to William's at Hastings.
- **Harold's mistakes** Harold played into William's hands. His men, severely weakened in number and spirit by the two battles in the north, did not have a chance to rest before meeting William. Edwin and Morcar, Harold's loyal brothers-in-law, were still marching south when Harold was at Hastings. Harold could have drawn upon thousands more troops. It was in his interest to delay, to starve William out, but he did not, hoping to surprise William's men out foraging and to exact revenge for the damage done to his lands in Wessex. It was a personal matter between the two leaders.
- **Generalship** Harold was, in the last analysis, out-generalled. His rapid return south and forced march from London to Hastings (58 miles in three days) exhausted his men further. He perhaps planned on trapping William on the coast, but William had already moved inland. Harold, not William, was taken by surprise. The casualties amongst the housecarls at Gate Fulford and Stamford told when the peasants broke the shield-wall and ran down onto the Norman cavalry. The archers left behind could not counter William's bowmen. Harold was not courageous enough or imaginative enough to adapt to the feigned retreats; he

---

KEY TERM

Feigned retreat This was a pretend retreat by Norman cavalry to lure the enemy after them so that they could wheel their horses around and surprise the scattered foot-soldiers, using pennants (*gonfalons*) to signal to one another. William's horsemen at Hastings enacted this highly controversial cavalry manoeuvre. This tactic required great skill, discipline and courage. Given the Norman skill in horseback fighting and precedents for this tactic in southern Italy in 1060, it is likely that it was achieved at Hastings and turned the course of the battle.

could neither seize the moment for a general charge nor command his troops to remain on the hill until nightfall when they could slip away and raise another army for another battle.

- **William was lucky,** the wind had changed at the right moment for him. He faced an English army complacent with success but depleted by two battles. But William worked hard for his luck. He had prepared an army which was supremely fit and well equipped. He shipped over horses and archers by the thousands in specially designed boats. He drove his men on and organised it all down to the last arrow-head. On landing at Pevensey he built a wooden castle using ready-made timber within the walls of the Roman fort, and another at Hastings so that his retreat was covered. His spies informed him of Harold's approach. His tactics of wasting Harold's private lands had paid off; he had his chance for the one big battle to decide the kingdom against his old adversary.

- **The Holy War** Finally, William believed he had God on his side. The psychological advantage of the papal banner must, in an age of deep-seated spiritualism, have been great. In medieval battle, God granted the victory. Whereas William was merely unhorsed three times, Harold was struck in the eye. An eye for an eye, a kingdom for a kingdom. The perjurer and usurper was no more.

Key debate: was Harold hit in the eye by an arrow?

The Bayeux Tapestry shows the death of Harold in two scenes. First a figure in mail armour is standing, clutching his eye which has an arrow in it; next a mounted Norman soldier hacks a figure down. On close inspection, the Tapestry reveals that originally, an arrow was also embroidered into that person's eye but later removed. Above the two figures is the line *Harold Rex interfectus est* (King Harold is killed).

CONCLUSION: THE END OF THE BEGINNING?

Harold and his two brothers, Gyrth and Leofwine, all died at Hastings. Tostig, the other brother, had died at Stamford Bridge. The Godwinsson regime had ended brutally and bloodily. William camped his army, itself severely depleted by the fierce fighting, among the English and Norman dead on the hilltop. To give thanks to God for his victory, he founded an abbey on the site of Harold's defensive line. But when William woke up on the morning of Sunday 15 October, he awoke to find himself in a foreign land, his 5000 or so men surrounded by a population of two million Anglo-Saxons. He had won the battle, but his conquest of England had barely begun.

Bayeux Tapestry: the death of Harold

SUMMARY QUESTIONS

1. To what extent was the Anglo-Saxon army incapable of dealing with a double invasion?

2. 'The battle of Hastings was lost by Harold rather than won by William.' How far do you agree with this statement?

CHAPTER 4

How did the Normans secure the kingdom?

INTRODUCTION

William had won a decisive victory at Hastings, but he had yet to win the kingdom. Archbishop Stigand immediately put Edgar Atheling, Edward the Confessor's great-nephew, forward as the new king. However, William's brutal march through Kent, Berkshire and Winchester in October and November isolated London and the remaining figures of Harold's regime: Edwin, Morcar, Edgar Atheling and his sister, Edith, all surrendered to William, who was duly crowned on Christmas Day 1066 with all the full coronation rites of an Anglo-Saxon king.

William felt confident enough to return in triumph to Normandy early in 1067 with the leading Anglo-Saxons in his train, and booty plundered from the churches and halls of England. But from 1067 to 1071 a series of revolts across England posed a great threat to his fragile government. He put them down with great brutality; any pretence he had to being the legitimate heir of Edward the Confessor was ended during this period. To underpin his occupation he built hundreds of castles across the kingdom, garrisoned by armed, mounted troops. Only after 1075, after a rebellion by his own earls, was the first phase of the conquest complete, and by this time England was under virtual military law.

William's son, King William II, who reigned from 1087 to 1100, continued his father's work, establishing and consolidating the borders with Wales and Scotland. William II also faced rebellion from Norman earls, twice, in 1088 and 1095, each time successfully defeating the rebels and, as a result, increasing the power of the crown.

HOW DID WILLIAM DEAL WITH THE REBELLIONS?

William left England under the care of two of his most trusted lords: his cousin William fitzOsbern and his half-brother, Odo, Bishop of Bayeux. The period of peace was short-lived. Rebellions broke out all across England; William subdued them with brutal, forceful and decisive action.

The Welsh border (1067)

Later in the year Edric 'the Wild' raised a revolt in Herefordshire, along the Welsh border, encouraging Welsh princes to join him. They failed to take control of the border, and retired to Wales with much booty.

The south-west (1068)

William returned to England late in 1067 to face more serious threats in the south-west. In 1068, the city of Exeter refused to accept William's rule but eventually did so after an eighteen-day siege. William installed his other half-brother, Robert of Mortain, as earl of Cornwall, and submitted Bristol and Gloucester to his rule on the way back. During the summer of 1068 the sons of Harold Godwinsson landed on the Somerset coast but were repelled by the English troops. William celebrated Easter at Winchester, and soon afterwards his wife Matilda was crowned queen at Westminster, where the king held a great court. William ended the year 1068 with a series of lightning rides through Warwick, Nottingham, York, Lincoln, Huntingdon and Cambridge to show his presence as the new king.

The north (1069–70)

Despite these brilliant efforts, the remaining Anglo-Saxon leaders, earls Edwin and Morcar, and Edgar Atheling defected from William's court and fled north during 1068. The north was still semi-independent of the south. Northern earls had not intervened to save Godwin in 1051 or help Edward in 1052, and had thrown out Tostig in 1065. Their political and ethnic separatism was potentially very dangerous to William's fragile hold on power at this stage.

In January 1069 rebels burned to death the Norman Earl Robert of Commines in the bishop's house in Durham. The insurrection spread to York, where the Norman garrison came under attack. William stormed north and relieved the garrison. However, in the summer there occurred the last Viking invasion of England that was to imperil William's fledgling kingship.

KEY EVIDENCE

The Anglo-Saxon Chronicle (D version) for 1069 'And there came to meet them Prince Edgar and Earl Waltheof and Maerleswegen and Gospatric with the Northumbrians and all the people riding and marching with an immense army rejoicing exceedingly and so they all went resolutely to York and stormed and razed the castle and captured an incalculable treasure in it and killed many hundreds of Frenchmen and took many with them to the ships …When the king found out about this he went northwards with all his army that he could collect, and utterly ravaged and laid waste that shire.'

KEY EVIDENCE

William the Conqueror's deathbed confession, from Orderic Vitalis, 'The Ecclesiastical History', written 1123–41 'I fell on the English of the northern shires like a ravening lion. I commanded their houses and corn, with all their implements and chattels, to be burnt without distinction, and large herds of cattle and beasts of burden to be butchered wherever they were found … and by so doing – alas! – became the barbarous murderer of many thousands, both young and old, of that fine race of people.'

A Viking army in a fleet of 240 ships, led by the sons of Swegn Estrithsson, landed at the Humber and marched on York. Swegn was the nephew of Canute and Earl Godwin, and had been king of Denmark since 1047. After their landing, Swegn's sons found much support amongst the native Anglo-Scandinavians in the east of England, as well as the English, including Edgar Atheling. They seized York and their success encouraged revolts in Dorset, Somerset, Staffordshire and Cheshire. Furthermore, the king of Scotland, Malcolm Canmore, allied himself to Edgar Atheling by marrying his sister, Margaret. William now faced the possibility of a Scandinavian kingdom in northern England or a separate kingdom created for Edgar, the last prince of the royal House of Wessex.

The 'Harrying of the North'

William reacted with characteristic vigour, skill and utter brutality. He marched north with seasoned troops from Nottingham to York, devastating the countryside as he went and slaughtering all the adult males. He burned York and, after Christmas, set about a systematic destruction of Yorkshire. What his troops inflicted on the people was so terrible that chroniclers remembered it over fifty years later. Corpses rotted on the roads, refugees fled in terror, disease and famine inevitably ensued. Domesday Book, the unique record of taxation and landownership made in 1086, simply records 'waste' (that is, uncultivated and depopulated lands and villages) for much of the land that William had devastated. Over 80 per cent of the wasteland recorded in Domesday Book was in Yorkshire. Swathes of land were depopulated, villages left deserted, farms empty, and this was fifteen years later. Yorkshire must have been a desert in 1070.

From Yorkshire, William pushed his troops across the Tees in the teeth of the winter and south-west across the Pennines, into Cheshire. He took Chester, subdued Stafford and was back in Winchester before Easter 1070. The Vikings, seeing their English allies defeated, accepted a bribe and left the Humber.

East Anglia (1070–71)

If William had broken English resistance, he had not quite dealt with the Vikings. In the summer, King Swegn of Denmark himself appeared and entered East Anglia, occupying the Isle of Ely. He was joined by a Lincolnshire thegn named Hereward (the 'Wake'), and the earls Edwin and Morcar. Together, they looted and burned Peterborough Abbey. William reacted with political skill, buying off the Danes, who departed the coast with much booty, leaving the English rebels to fend for themselves. When William advanced on Ely, Morcar surrendered, Edwin fled north and was murdered by his own followers, and Hereward disappeared.

Scotland (1072)

William's devastation of the north had created a vacuum of political authority into which Malcolm of Scotland rode, devastating Durham and Cleveland. William spent the summer of 1072 carefully preparing another army. In the autumn he took them through Durham all the way to Perth, into the heart of Malcolm's kingdom. His fleet sailed into the Tay estuary and met the army. This was a hazardous expedition and left the Norman troops fearfully exposed, but it worked. Malcolm met William at Abernethy and recognised him as king of England. To show good faith, Malcolm expelled Edgar Atheling from his court.

The revolt of the Norman earls (1075)

Edgar Atheling's part in Anglo-Norman history was not yet over. Having gone to Flanders after leaving Scotland, he returned to the Scottish court with honour in 1074. In order to discomfort William further, King Philip I of France offered Edgar a strategically threatening castle at Montreuil-sur-Mer, where Edgar could establish a base to oppose William. William took this seriously enough to offer the Atheling a place back at court in England. Edgar from this point faded as a threat to William; he befriended William's eldest son, Robert, later duke of Normandy, and appeared in southern Italy in the 1080s and on the First Crusade to the Holy Land in the 1090s.

A potentially far greater threat to William emerged in 1075 from his own Norman lords, including the son of his most trusted earl. This rebellion was led by Ralph de Gael, a Breton whose father had held a position at the court of Edward the Confessor and had gone on to assist William in his conquest of England. Ralph recruited Roger de Breteuil, Earl of Hereford, son of William fitzOsbern, the Earl of Hereford, who had been killed in battle in 1071.

The plot seems to have been hatched at the feast that was held for Ralph's wedding to Roger's sister in Norfolk. Ralph, as a Breton, was encouraged by Bretons and Philip of France, always eager to bring down his arch-rival the king of England and duke of Normandy. For good measure, Ralph appealed to Denmark for help.

The revolt was stifled from the outset. Lanfranc, now Archbishop of Canterbury, was acting as William's **regent** during his absence in Normandy and urged the king to remain in the duchy. Earl Roger was bottled up in Herefordshire by loyal Norman troops under the command of the Abbot of Evesham, and Odo of Bayeux and others forced Ralph to retreat to Norwich, where he left his wife in command whilst he fled to Brittany. Another great Danish fleet arrived, led by Canute, son of Swegn Estrithsson, but it was too late. In time-honoured fashion, the Vikings sailed up the east coast, looting and pillaging before departing for home. William returned to England at Christmas 1075. The Breton rebels were blinded and murdered and Roger de Breteuil, perhaps on account of his father's loyalty (see Case Study 1, on page 46), was banished from Herefordshire and imprisoned.

DID THE REBELLIONS CHANGE WILLIAM'S POLICY TOWARDS THE EARLS?

The widespread rebellions against William and the brutality with which he dealt with them had a great impact on the nature of his kingship and conquest of England. Although the nature of William's invasion meant that he was never going to be a mere figurehead amongst an Anglo-Saxon ruling class, he clearly made efforts to be **conciliatory** in the very early years of his reign. Edwin and Morcar kept their earldoms until they fled William's court in 1068; after the murder of the Norman Earl Robert in Durham in 1069, William made Gospatric, a Saxon, earl of Northumbria, but Gospatric joined the general uprising in the summer of that year. As a further concession to the north after the terrible devastation of the winter of 1070, William created Waltheof earl of Northumbria. Waltheof was the son of the previous earl of Northumbria, Siward, who had been succeeded by Tostig Godwinsson in 1057, as Waltheof had been too young at the time. Waltheof repaid William's trust in him by joining, or at least having knowledge of, the 1075 revolt by Ralph de Gael and Roger

How did the Normans secure the kingdom?   41

de Breteuil. After a period of imprisonment Waltheof, the
last Anglo-Saxon earl, was beheaded in 1076.

HOW DIFFERENT WERE THE ANGLO-NORMAN EARLDOMS?

The old Anglo-Saxon earldoms of Wessex, Mercia, East
Anglia and Northumbria were either divided up very soon
after William's coronation, or allowed to lapse, during, or
as a result of, the rebellions. Harold, King of England and
Earl of Wessex, was not replaced; instead, Odo, Bishop of
Bayeux and William's half-brother, was made earl of Kent.
William fitzOsbern, a cousin and lifelong companion to the
Conqueror, was made earl of Hereford and lord of the Isle
of Wight, two crucial defensive points of the new
kingdom, both carved out of Harold's territories. (For
fitzOsbern, see Case Study 1, page 46.) These posts were
granted very soon after the Battle of Hastings, for it was
Odo and William fitzOsbern who were governors of
England on the king's triumphant return to Normandy
early in 1067.

Although William made some concessionary moves, it was
clear from the severity of the rebellions that he would have
to react drastically. The rebellions forced William to
impose not only new personnel but new boundaries on the
old Anglo-Saxon earldoms.

The earldom of Mercia lapsed after the murder of Edwin in
the wake of the 1071 rebellion. After William's
concessionary policy of appointing first Gospatric and then
Waltheof to Northumbria, that earldom also lapsed;
following Ralph de Gael's treachery in 1075, the earldom
of East Anglia was not filled in the Conqueror's reign. Thus
the great Anglo-Saxon earldoms passed out of existence
well within a decade of the new Norman government. The
rebellions also led to the creation of the smaller earldoms of
Cheshire and Shropshire some time before 1077, again as
defensive measures.

WHY WERE CASTLES SO IMPORTANT?

In addition to having to reorganise the Anglo-Saxon
earldoms before, and as a result of, the rebellions, William
consolidated his hold on his newly conquered kingdom by
building castles. These were erected at the very beginning
of his campaign, even before the battle of Hastings, and

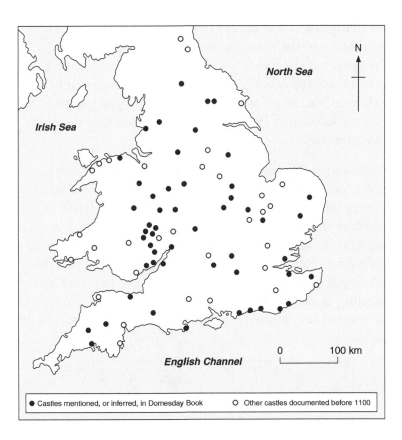

The early castles of the Norman kings

● Castles mentioned, or inferred, in Domesday Book   ○ Other castles documented before 1100

were virtually unheard of in England. England had only ever seen the large, public fortresses built by the Romans and the walled towns (burhs) under Alfred the Great. Castles were small, and private, fortifications. The only castles seen in England before 1066 were the motte-and-baileys built in Herefordshire by Edward the Confessor's Norman nephew, Ralf of Mantes, in the 1050s. William built hundreds of castles all across England. Castles were an integral part of his conquest of England, and also formed part of the fabric of Anglo-Norman society. Castles were a new phenomenon that altered the **geopolitical** landscape of Britain forever.

Motte-and-bailey castles

These early castles were not the great stone castles of the later medieval era, complete with gatehouses, towers and damsels in distress; instead, they looked rather like small wooden stockades. A timber tower was placed on top of a large earth mound – the motte – and adjacent to the motte was the bailey, or outer compound, again with a timber fence. The bailey accommodated stables, a chapel, a forge and living space; the small garrison of mounted soldiers could retire to the tower on the motte in times of danger. The genius of the motte-and-bailey fortress was that they could be erected quickly and simply; William brought with him 'kit castles' which his carpenters put together after the landing at Pevensey, within the walls of the old Roman fortress.

Motte-and-bailey castles were a common sight in north-west Europe. William had spent his life engaged in warfare to consolidate his power in Normandy, but the Battle of Hastings was only the second battle he had fought (he fought three in total). Set-piece battles were rare; medieval warfare was conducted through skirmishes, raids, ambushes and sieges. Control over territory meant the building and manning of castles. William's rise to power in Normandy is the story of his domination of the countryside by the use of castles.

Bayeux Tapestry: scene of motte-and-bailey castle at Dinant

Securing the realm

William began a comprehensive programme of castle-building in England before the rebellions began, and built more following the rebellions.

- His right-hand man, William fitzOsbern, Earl of Hereford and Lord of the Isle of Wight, built a stone keep at Chepstow, dominating the River Wye and the Severn estuary. This was one of the very few stone castles in England.
- William himself began the mighty stone keep at the Tower of London (the White Tower).

Chepstow Castle in Monmouthshire, Wales: an example of a Norman keep

The Anglo-Saxon Chronicle (D version) for **1066** 'And Bishop Odo and Earl William stayed behind and built castles here far and wide throughout this country, and distressed the wretched folk, and always after that it grew much worse.'

Letter from Archbishop Lanfranc to Roger de Breteuil, 1075 'Our lord the king of the English greets you and all of his faithful subjects in whom he places great trust, commanding us to do all in our power to prevent his castles from being handed over to his enemies: may God avert such a disaster.'

- After William's brutal submission of the West Country and the North during the rebellions of 1067–71 he built castles in Exeter, Warwick, Nottingham, York, Lincoln, Huntingdon and Cambridge.
- These castles were deliberately sited in English towns; hundreds of homes were demolished to make way for them in the town centres.
- Castles were, at this stage, a device of war, a means of containing the surrounding area and deploying troops quickly. They were also a visible and psychological symbol of conquest.
- Outside the towns, castles were situated to control the surrounding countryside, either at river crossings, or on hills. On the Welsh borders, very much bandit country, a chain of castles was built to watch over the mountain passes.

In an alien land, with so few Normans, castles were fundamental to the survival of William's kingship. They underlined with a sense of permanence the terror inflicted on the north by his troops during the winter of 1069. Even though the motte-and-bailey forts could be erected quickly and simply, some of them were very substantial and incorporated not only a military garrison but also the seat of local government. Royal control over the castles was essential, and the men appointed to manage the castles were of the highest calibre. During the 1075 revolt, the king's regent and archbishop of Canterbury, Lanfranc, wrote to Earl Roger de Breteuil, urging him not to let the castles of Herefordshire fall into the wrong hands. In the end, it was the lack of support and the maintenance of the castles in royal hands that led to the failure of the rebellion.

CASE STUDY 1

WILLIAM FITZOSBERN, EARL OF HEREFORD

An examination of the life and career of one of the most powerful men in the early years of Anglo-Norman England throws considerable light on how William actually effected his conquest. This was essentially through a network of kinship and loyalty, backed up with courage and audacity.

A childhood friendship

William fitzOsbern was the son of Osbern Herfastsson – the 'fitz' being a corruption of *fils* (son) – who had been William the Conquerer's **steward**. As a boy, William had witnessed the brutal murder of his father in his own bedchamber, and had grown up in the ducal household; the boy duke, the writer William of Poitiers tells us, 'loved him above the other members of his household'. They were also related, as fitzOsbern's father was the grandson of Duke Richard of Normandy's half-brother, Rodulf. Another friend of Duke William's youth was Roger of Montgomery, who later became earl of Shrewsbury. FitzOsbern participated in much of the duke's struggle to gain control over his duchy during the wars of the 1040s and 1050s.

Schooled in the art of warfare from an early age and witness to William's brutal triumph over his enemies in Normandy, fitzOsbern was the duke's steward at the time of the Conquest. It was fitzOsbern, apparently, who persuaded the sceptical Norman barons to invade England; it was fitzOsbern who, when the duke fell on his face on disembarking at Pevensey, shouted to the shocked troops (who saw it as a bad omen): 'Do not take this as unlucky – he has claimed England, taking possession of it with both hands'. And it was fitzOsbern who was with the duke on a patrol after the landing as they laughed and joked along a coastal path.

Earl of Herefordshire and Lord of the Isle of Wight

After Hastings, where fitzOsbern fought in the thick of the battle with the duke, he was richly rewarded, as befitted a

KEY WORD

Steward Duke William had a household, which was a large group of followers, servants and soldiers, and in the household were servants with specific tasks. The steward's role was very important; he ran the household and was the duke's deputy. Most dukes, kings and princes had similar households by this period.

cousin, lifelong friend and ally. FitzOsbern was granted the earldom of Herefordshire, extensive lands in Gloucestershire, Worcestershire, Oxfordshire, Dorset, Berkshire, Hampshire, Somerset and the Isle of Wight. These lands were much the same lands that Swegn Godwinsson had held twenty years earlier, followed by Ralf of Mantes (King Edward's nephew), then Harold, and now fitzOsbern. Keeping these estates together under different owners reflected the new king's initial policy of conciliation towards the Anglo-Saxon ruling class. Although fitzOsbern was a Norman, the lands he held were the same territories held by his Anglo-Saxon predecessors.

If fitzOsbern's lands were based on past titles, then the power he wielded was unique. Vice-regent with the king's half-brother, Odo, fitzOsbern immediately set about the invasion of Wales from his base in Herefordshire. Within a couple of years, the Normans had advanced deep into South Wales, possibly as far as Swansea. FitzOsbern was also **castellan** of York Castle, and was with the king on the notorious 'Harrying of the North' during the winter of 1069–70.

The end of an era?

William fitzOsbern was killed in a small battle in Flanders in 1071. His death left the king bereft of a childhood friend and the most loyal and powerful man in his new-found kingdom. His death marks a turning point in the Conqueror's policy. It came soon after the great rebellions of 1067–71 and it left a power vacuum. FitzOsbern's son never had the power his father had enjoyed, and his participation in the rebellion in 1075 was partly due to his resentment. The second generation could never emulate the achievements of their fathers. After Roger de Breteuil's rebellion, the earldom of Herefordshire was not replaced until the 1120s. The new earldoms of Shrewsbury and Cheshire were much smaller. The unique bond of trust between the king and his closest noblemen began to dissolve. Most of the leading Norman landowners were related to the king, but as time passed, that family loyalty began to be replaced by a more venal, political motivation. Had fitzOsbern not been killed in battle, there might never have been a rebellion in 1075 and the earldoms of

KEY TERM

Castellan The official appointed by the king to manage a castle – an important job. The castellan was usually a man of high rank and had to be loyal to the Crown.

Herefordshire, East Anglia and Northumbria might have continued as before.

William fitzOsbern was also a **benefactor**. Before the Conquest he had founded two abbeys, at Lyre and Cormeilles in Normandy, and arranged for money and lands from his English territories to be donated to them after 1066. There was no contradiction in this great warlord, witness to many atrocities and battles and, in the words of one chronicler, 'terror of the English' turning to pious devotion. Medieval people were all too aware of their own mortality. William fitzOsbern, soldier, patron and governor, typifies the spirit and energy of the Norman Conquest of England. Cousin and advisor to the duke, deputy to the king, his life and career are a window on the Anglo-Norman world.

TO WHAT EXTENT DID THE NORMANS CREATE AN 'EMPIRE'?

The conquest of England from 1066 to 1075 brought England into the sphere of north-west France, away from the Scandinavian axis that had shaped English government and politics since the Danish invasions of 1014. Both William I and William II saw Normandy as their most important territory. It was the **patrimony**. They also appreciated that not only was there an Anglo-Norman axis of power, but that in conquering England they had inherited from Edward the Confessor and Harold Godwinsson all England's political relations with Wales and Scotland. Rapid inroads were made into Wales after 1066, thanks largely to Harold's brilliant campaign of 1063, but Scottish affairs met with far greater resistance. Both William I and William II used the borders with England and Normandy to consolidate and entrench their government. In order to do so, they required armies and money and to obtain these, changes in government were effected and resources already at their disposal were ruthlessly exploited. However, the idea of an Anglo-Norman kingdom including England and Normandy was short-lived; the two states were divided between two rulers on William I's death and William II was not duke of Normandy in his brother's absence on the First Crusade.

> **KEY WORD**
>
> **Benefactor** The medieval world was a spiritual world, where people believed that good deeds on earth would help to secure a place in heaven. Those with wealth and power spent their money on founding churches. William the Conqueror and his wife Matilda founded two abbeys in Caen, Normandy.

> **KEY WORD**
>
> **Patrimony** The family homeland, inherited by the eldest son in Norman custom. The younger son inherited lands acquired by conquest or by marriage. Although England was a kingdom and Normandy a duchy, William I ordered that Normandy, the patrimony, should be inherited by his eldest son, Robert, and that the acquisition, England, should be inherited by his younger son, William, when he died in 1087.

England and Normandy, 1087–1100

In 1087, William I's eldest son, Robert, became duke of Normandy, and his second son, William, became king of England; England and Normandy were again divided. William II faced rebellion from Norman barons in 1088 and again in 1095. The problem was that many barons believed that Robert, as the eldest son of the Conqueror, should have inherited both England and Normandy. However, William II was a chip off the old block; he moved fast before Robert could invade, cutting off support from within England and isolating Robert's supporters, who included Odo of Bayeux, who thought he would gain more by supporting Robert.

After 1088, William II was secure on the English throne and it was Robert who faced invasion from England in 1090. The two brothers came to an agreement that whoever died first without heirs would leave his lands to the other. This treaty expressly cut out the Conqueror's youngest son, Henry. In 1093 Robert denounced this treaty and he and William were once again at war. The situation was transformed in 1095 when Pope Urban II preached a crusade against the Muslim world in the Middle East, which was increasingly threatening Christendom. He aimed his appeal for help directly at the restless warlords of northern France and Duke Robert was first in the queue. The two brothers struck another deal: in return for 10,000 marks, Robert pledged the duchy to William. William extorted the cash from England and Robert led a contingent on the crusade, which ended in the famous capture of Jerusalem in 1099. Disloyal to his father and unable to govern his duchy, Robert seems to have made his mark as a crusader.

William II, now secure in England, was the recognised ruler of Normandy from 1096 to 1100 (Robert remained duke, even on the crusade). William utilised the resources of the duchy to secure the frontiers with the neighbouring regions of Maine, Anjou and the Vexin. Within two years he had consolidated and extended these frontiers, with all the energy and vigour his father had displayed. The onus would be on Robert, now on his return journey from Jerusalem, to buy back his duchy.

England and Scotland

Malcolm, king of the Scots, did not recognise William II as

the Conqueror's heir, but instead did homage to Robert.
Malcolm had invaded Northumbria for the fourth time in
1091 and William II raised an army and faced Malcolm on
the Tweed. An agreement was reached (nobody wanted to
fight) whereby Malcolm did homage to William and was
granted a pension and confirmation of his English lands.
Edgar the Atheling, who had returned to the Scottish court
after 1072, was once again removed, and went south with
William II. This was a return to the *status quo* of the reign
of William I. However, in 1092 William returned north,
built a castle at Carlisle, settled it with people from the
south and placed the town within the diocese of Durham,
thus moving the frontier north.

In 1093 Malcolm claimed that William had broken the
treaty between them, but he was killed in an ambush near
Alnwick along with his son and heir, Edward. It was not
until 1097 that Malcolm's son Edgar was put on the throne,
with the help of Edgar the Atheling, Anglo-Norman
soldiers and King William II of England. Edgar reigned
successfully and was followed by both his brothers,
Alexander and David, well into the twelfth century. The
rulers of Scotland were very much reliant upon support
from, and good relations with, the Norman kings of
England.

England and Wales

No such diplomacy existed between Anglo-Norman
England and Wales. The conquest of Wales was a repeat of
the conquest of England, except that it was achieved more
slowly and with more force. After Harold had broken the
power of Llewelyn ap Gruffydd in 1063, the various Welsh
princes contended for the kingdoms of Gwynedd in the
north, Powys in the centre and Deheubarth in the south.
Welsh unity was rare and Norman strategic castle-building
and military precision allowed for rapid advances into the
far south very soon after 1066. The advance into the centre
was halted by the rebellion of 1075, but in 1093 a battle at
Brecon was exploited by Roger of Montgomery, Earl of
Shrewsbury, who went on to occupy Cardiganshire and
Dyfed, and built a castle at Pembroke.

In the north, the earl of Chester, Hugh d'Avranches, and his
cousin, Robert of Rhuddlan, made good progress, reaching
Conwy by 1093, and building castles at Bangor, Caernarfon

The Anglo-Norman 'empire' and its borders

and Anglesey in 1094. But after 1094 the Norman advance suffered major reversals. The Welsh princes of Powys and Gwynedd – Cadwgan ap Bleddyn and Gruffydd ap Cynan – led a revolt that swept the Normans back to Glamorgan and Brecon. William II invaded Wales twice – in 1095 and 1097 – but did not fully recover Powys and Gwynedd.

CONCLUSION: FROM CONCILIATION TO COLONISATION?

After the slaughter of Hastings and the submission of London, William of Normandy was crowned king of England. It does seem as if, for a brief time, he hoped to pursue a conciliatory policy towards the leading Anglo-Saxon lords, but the rebellions and defections led him to react brutally. Castle-building, already underway, was increased greatly; the shocking treatment of Yorkshire ensured that the north never rebelled or encouraged a

How did the Normans secure the kingdom?   51

serious Viking invasion again. William's kingship had become, as a result of the military activity of these years, an occupation.

- After the earls' revolt of 1075 and the execution of the last Anglo-Saxon earl, Waltheof, in 1076, William I faced no further opposition to his rule in England.
- The rebellions of 1069–71, though potentially very great, lacked co-ordination and focus; the rebellion of 1075 lacked support.
- On William's death in 1087, England was at peace, Scotland was subdued and the Welsh borders were in his power.
- Under his son, William II (1087–1100), further rebellions in England were crushed, the kings of the Scots were assured their power only with English support, and parts of Wales, particularly the south, lay under either direct or indirect Norman rule.
- William II, despite opposition from his brother and Norman barons on both sides of the English Channel, had more than consolidated his father's conquest of England. He had also built on his father's provisional efforts on the Anglo-Norman borders of Wales, Scotland, Maine and Anjou by the time of his death in 1100.

SUMMARY QUESTIONS

1. How did the rebellions of 1067–72 change William's attitude towards his new kingdom?

2. How important were castles in securing Norman rule?

3. To what extent was the Norman conquest of England complete by 1100?

CHAPTER 5

The governance of Anglo-Norman England

INTRODUCTION: CHANGE AND CONTINUITY

The fundamental contradiction of William's government of England was that he had conquered the country by force of arms and yet always maintained that he governed through legal and rightful inheritance from Edward the Confessor. Kings after 1066 ruled 'by the grace of God' (Normans believed God had helped them win at Hastings), and with an amalgam of ancient Anglo-Saxon customs and new Norman methods. Although castles dotted the landscape and mounted troops cantered through the streets, William I replied upon Anglo-Saxon tools of government and traditions of kingship.

HOW DID ANGLO-NORMAN KINGSHIP FUNCTION?

The theoretical powers of the king of England were well established by 1066. The king was the chief lawmaker in the realm, the supreme military commander and the maker of foreign and domestic policy. The king after his coronation was no mere mortal; he occupied a priest-like status as the spiritual leader of his people. William I made no great changes to this function of kingship; it was in his interest, as the legal heir to Edward the Confessor (so he claimed) to continue as before.

Charisma and personality

The power of kingship was very much vested in the personality of the king. He had to be physically strong, spending a lifetime in the saddle, on the move from one area to the next and, after 1066, from England to Normandy. Kingship was **itinerant**. The king had to be mentally strong to dominate by sheer force of personality and intellect, the powerful churchmen and barons each with their own vested interests and ambitions, who surrounded him. Edward the Confessor was in conflict with Godwin for many years before reaching some sort of compromise with Harold; Harold, apart from his brother Tostig's rebellion, had the support of the Saxon nobility and William, having promised great rewards to his followers, only faced the one rebellion from the nobility, in 1075, which was quickly dealt with. A measure of William's security and the strength of his kingship was in his frequent and prolonged absences in Normandy. During those times, he appointed deputies, or regents, to govern England, including Odo of Bayeux, William fitzOsbern and Lanfranc, Archbishop of Canterbury. When he was in England, his wife Matilda and Roger de Montgomery, another lifelong friend and ally, ran the duchy while his eldest son Robert was a youth.

The success of the kingship of William I and his son William II depended very much on their ability to exploit and adapt English customs and traditions to their advantage. At times they had to act rapidly and with brutality; other occasions demanded subtle cunning and intelligence in matters of man-management and diplomacy.

The coronation service

The anointing and the coronation were the means by which the new king legitimised his rule. This was especially important to William, who had seized power by victory in battle. The coronation of Harold, William I and his son William II used the same religious service, witnessed by many hundreds of people who would acclaim, or shout their approval of the king. Afterwards there followed great feasting.

For William I, the aspect of continuity in the coronation service was vital, for it was part of Norman policy that he was the true heir to Edward the Confessor, designated by him and crowned only after a brief period of usurpation by Harold Godwinsson. William, in the eyes of his followers at least, was king not only *de facto* (in fact) but *de jure* (in law). This policy was supported by the insistence that William ruled by **hereditary** right, in that he was the cousin of Edward the Confessor. The phrase 'by hereditary right' appears in royal documents very early in William's reign. Furthermore, after the coronation, William ruled with powers from God. The idea that God had helped him win the battle of Hastings over the perjurer and usurper Harold, was developed by William of Poitiers but finds its way into royal documents very soon after 1066, when

KEY TERM

Hereditary Term used to describe something passed on from father to son, or to a member of the same family. This might be a title, an estate or an entire kingdom.

William is described as 'king of the English by the grant of God'. The idea that William I was king by the grace of God and by hereditary right was a new departure after 1066. By using the ancient traditions of Anglo-Saxon kingship ceremonies alongside the unique circumstances that brought him the crown, William and his successors were able to appeal both to English customs and to the Norman sense of righteous conquest.

From the reign of William II (1087–1100) onwards, many of the kings of England issued a Coronation charter, a list of promises of good government. For the first time, William II declared on his seals that he was king 'by the grace of God'. William II also had the added incentive of the threat from his elder brother Robert, Duke of Normandy, whom many saw as the rightful king of England. The dying William I handed his second son a letter to take to Lanfranc, Archbishop of Canterbury, authorising him to crown him; William II promised to regard Lanfranc as his chief adviser and took one of his father's chaplains, Robert Bloet, to authenticate the testament of the old king. William the Conqueror's crown had been passed on by a will approved and administered by the Church, thereby making the coronation service all the more vital.

Visual symbols
The visual symbols of kingship were important in an age when written information was scarce and communications were slow. The Norman kings showed off their power in a number of ways:

- The coronation was a public event; if this was an ancient tradition which William continued, then crown-wearings were rather new. William deliberately wore his crown at sessions where the public could view him, at Winchester (Easter), Gloucester (Christmas) and Westminster (Whitsun).
- William II continued this tradition, which was designed to reinforce the king's majesty. The greatest event was in 1099, when William II held his **court** for the first time at the newly completed great hall at Westminster. Edgar, king of the Scots, carried the sword before William II, symbolising his subordination to William,

and the royal court feasted in the hall with great ceremony and lavish hospitality. Such an event was designed to show off the king's power, wealth and generosity.

- Other visual symbols of kingship were the royal seals and coins. The royal seal was attached to documents to authenticate government commands and decrees. It shows the king on the throne with the royal regalia, as do the seals and coins of Edward the Confessor. There was change here, however: before the Conquest the English royal seal showed the king enthroned in majesty on both sides. After the Conquest, one side showed the king armed and mounted as a knight. This emphasised the military nature of the Conquest. The **iconography** of kingship, as well as the **ideology** of kingship, remained unchanged by the Norman Conquest.

The royal household

The king's household lay at the heart of Anglo-Norman kingship. It was the inner core of the court, which included a wider circle of society invited to attend special events, such as crown-wearings. The household was an integral part of the day-to-day business of kingship. It was both a private and a public body of people, composed of the king's family, domestic servants, priests, secretaries and clerks and men of military experience who formed the king's bodyguard. It was also composed of a wider, more official body of men, the royal administrators, earls and bishops who sat on the royal council and deliberated matters of state. As the king and his household moved around the country, they were joined by the local lords of the area, so that the household was constantly changing, according to where the king was and to who was dispatched on official business to some far corner of the realm.

In summary, the royal household had a triple function:

- a judical, legal body (the *curia*)
- a military nerve-centre of the crown (the *familia*)
- a private, domestic function (the *domus*).

Changing personnel

The royal household after 1066 was not fundamentally changed from that before 1066. What was very different was that the members of the household after 1066 were increasingly Norman. At first, William kept some Anglo-Saxons in his household, including Regenbald the Chancellor, Bundi and Ednoth. But by the time he died, in 1087, the household was overwhelmingly Norman. Men such as William fitzOsbern and Roger Bigod were Stewards, Hugh of Ivry was Butler, Hugh of Montfort-sur-Risle was Constable and Ralph of Tancarville was Chamberlain. All of these men had been trusted followers of William before the Conquest and held offices in Normandy. Under William II, the men at the heart of the household were of similar standing: William, Bishop of Durham, Walkelin, Bishop of Winchester, Roger Bigod again, and Urse d'Abitot, Sheriff of Worcester.

HOW FAR WERE ANGLO-SAXON GOVERNMENT AND ADMINISTRATION ALTERED?

The chancery and the chancellor

If the royal household in the Anglo-Saxon and Norman worlds was roughly similar in design and composition and changed only in its personnel in Anglo-Norman England, then the existence of a chancery and chancellor were quite new to the Normans. It is known that under Edward the Confessor a body of royal clerks had developed traditions of administrative practice and formed a highly organised *scriptorium* (writing office, or chancery). These were the men who wrote up the documents and appended the great royal seal. It is probable that one such clerk took responsibility for the seal and overall control of the office, and this man may have been Regenbald, who worked for both Edward and William I, though he was never actually styled 'chancellor'. No such office or clerks existed in Normandy before 1066, though there was a chancery in France during this time, during the reign of Philip I, king of France after 1060. The first named Anglo-Norman chancellor was Herfast, in 1069, followed by Osmund, Maurice and Gerard, chancellor in 1087, the end of William I's reign. The first three all went on to become bishops but until they did so, they remained officials of the royal household.

Why was Ranulf Flambard so powerful?

One royal clerk who stands out in the reign of William II was Ranulf Flambard, a Norman priest. Flambard served first in Odo of Bayeux's household and then in the

Conqueror's, where he was keeper of the great seal by 1078. In 1087 he served William II and quickly gained his complete trust. Flambard was at the heart of the regency council during the king's absences in Normandy, the north of England or Wales, and in 1098 became president of the council. Flambard's job was to adminster vacant bishoprics and abbeys, supervise the collection of geld, and to visit the shires with the royal barons to ensure royal justice. In doing all this, he incurred the wrath of the propertied classes, who hated his taxes, and he enriched himself and his family, buying the bishopric of Durham from the king as a reward. Such was the hatred for the king's deputy that on his accession in 1100, Henry I had him arrested and put in the Tower of London 'by the advice of those who were around him'. Flambard's adventures had only just begun, however; in 1101 he escaped from the Tower to Normandy and eventually returned to England to govern his bishopric.

The significance of Flambard was that, although he had no greater title than royal chaplain, great powers of government could be invested in one man during the king's absence. The life and career of Ranulf Flambard foreshadow the twelfth-century chief justiciars under Henry I, Henry II, Richard, John and Henry III, and he reflects the growing power of bureaucracy within royal government.

How useful were the writs?

These royal clerks were the men who wrote the **writs** of Edward the Confessor, which were issued with great frequency. A writ was a short, sealed document with a standard greeting, which communicated commands and grants from the king's household to the provinces of England. It was essentially a letter, a terse statement intended for public notification of royal grants and privileges. Nothing like it existed in Normandy. The existence of the writ presupposed the fact that such a command could be issued by a sophisticated government and that it would actually be obeyed by a peaceful, law-abiding society. Both these factors were largely missing in Norman government and society before 1066. Naturally enough, William I seized upon such a powerful tool of state and continued to use them with greater frequency. The very early writs issued by William I were in Anglo-Saxon,

KEY EVIDENCE

A writ, in Anglo-Saxon, from King William I and Earl William fitzOsbern, dated March–December, 1067, while the king was in Normandy 'William the king and William the earl to Giso the bishop and Eadnoth the staller and Tofi the sheriff and all my thegns in Somerset, greeting. I make it known that I have granted to Abbot Wulfwold and the church of St Peter at Bath the land at Charlcombe as fully as it ever was. And I forbid anyone to take away anything of what I have given him.'

becoming Latin after 1070. The use of the writ represents continuity with the pre-1066 government and the Norman skill in adapting pre-existing functions of state.

Shires, sheriffs and local government

A central government with a writing office issuing royal commands and grants was nothing if the royal will could not be transmitted to an officer in the locality. The Normans found England already divided into shires and saw no reason to change this; indeed, the smaller Norman earldoms that grew out of the great Anglo-Saxon earldoms were based increasingly around the shire-town, beginning with Chester and Shrewsbury. The royal official responsible for the king's will in the shire remained the sheriff; again, the Normans saw no need to change this. The functions of the sheriff after 1066 were threefold: to manage the royal estates in the shire, to collect the royal taxes and to supervise royal justice in the shire. These functions remained unchanged since Anglo-Saxon government.

Did the powers of the sheriff increase?

At the start of his reign, William I continued to employ existing Anglo-Saxon sheriffs such as Edric of Wiltshire or Tofi of Somerset. But after 1070 there was a consistent policy of replacing the existing sheriffs with men from the duchy of Normandy. And as the power of the great Anglo-Saxon earldoms diminished, replaced by smaller earldoms, the power of the sheriff grew in the period 1066–1100 and challenged that of the earls, particularly as Norman sheriffs were often castellans. It was the appointment of royal sheriffs in Herefordshire that sparked Roger de Breteuil's rebellion in 1075. Those sheriffs with no background could become unscrupulously greedy or fall under the influence of the local lord; those with connections could form their own faction and foment rebellion. The choice of sheriff was therefore of vital importance, and the Crown was constantly seeking to balance the power of sheriffs by appointing loyal household officials, dispatching royal judges and by permitting the bishops to hold law courts. Many of the first-generation Norman sheriffs were Norman aristocrats whose children and grandchildren were to become earls. The first-generation sheriffs may have inherited an Anglo-Saxon position and tradition, but the power they wielded was far greater than the Anglo-Saxon sheriffs, given the

HEINEMANN ADVANCED HISTORY

power vacuum created by the collapse of the old earldoms. This was a deliberate policy of William I's.

The shire courts

The shire courts were the focal points of royal justice in the provinces under the Normans just as they had been under the Anglo-Saxon kings. No such institution had existed in Normandy before 1066; the Norman kings of England found a useful tool of government and continued to use it.

The shire court usually met twice a year, at Easter (March/April) and Michaelmas (October). The meetings were public events, attended by earls and bishops, the sheriff and freemen of the shire. Legal cases were heard regarding land and family disputes, crime and outlawry; taxation, royal dues and military affairs were discussed. It was in the interest of all the great landowners of the shire to be present.

The hundred courts

The meetings of the shire courts were special occasions. Much of the routine business in the shires was conducted through the hundred court. The division of Anglo-Saxon shires into hundreds remained unchanged after 1066. This court, technically under the jurisdiction of the sheriff but in reality presided over by his deputies, met more frequently than the shire court, and was the lowest public court in the land. It dealt chiefly with local land disputes touching on local law and order.

Laws and customs

The Normans in the first generations after the Conquest initiated no new law codes. Instead, the law was the usual blend of Norman and Anglo-Saxon traditions. William I was keen to ensure that, as he was the legal heir to Edward the Confessor, traditional English laws and customs were preserved. The method of trial by ordeal had long been used on both sides of the English Channel, as had inquiries by means of witnesses or by the production of charters as evidence. Ordeal by fire and water was common in Anglo-Saxon England but judicial combat became the usual method of proof in both criminal and land cases. In addition to this traditional method of

KEY EVIDENCE

From the 'Laws of William the Conqueror', a compilation of legal enactments made at various times by William I (1066–87) 'This I also command and will, that all shall have and hold the law of King Edward in respect of their lands and all their possessions, and with the addition I have ordained for the welfare of the English people.'

KEY EVIDENCE

The report of the trial at Pinnenden Heath, near Maidstone 1075–6, which granted the archbishop the rights of Canterbury that had been plundered by Odo of Bayeux
'The king thereupon gave orders that the whole shire court should meet without delay, and that there should be brought together not only all the Frenchmen in the county, but also and more especially those English who were well acquainted with the traditional laws and customs of the land.

'When the king heard the judgement given in this plea, and had been made aware of those who ratified it, and when he had learnt the many reasons which could be adduced in support of it, he gave thanks, and joyfully confirmed the judgement with the assent of all his magnates.'

ordeal, the use of the jury to give a collective verdict upon oath became increasingly frequent under William I.

One measure taken by William I reflects the nature of his conquest of England. This was the protection of the Norman-French settlers in England. A fine was imposed upon any hundred where a Norman was found murdered and his assassin escaped. This later became the *murdrum* fine collected for unsolved murders of all free men.

The royal household (the *curia regis*) was where the most important legal cases were heard, and where royal grants were made and confirmed, but the shire courts were the main means by which the Norman kings maintained law and order in the provinces. The sheriff was the royal representative of justice, but there is evidence to show that William I and William II used commissioners from the royal households to preside over the shire courts from time to time. It was in these trials that juries were used consistently and in this sense, the shire courts were altered into local sessions of the king's court.

Wealth and taxation

William I acquired a kingdom that had a rich heritage of legal and administrative customs and traditions, but that was also rich itself. The Anglo-Saxon monarchy had created a system of tax collection known as the geld, most particularly the Danegeld, a general tax to pay or fight off the Danish invaders in the late ninth century. The king and his advisers decided on the size of the geld and apportioned it among the various shires; within the shires it was divided among the hundreds. The king had his treasury at Winchester and made decisions relating to financial policy in consultation with the whole court. The rate at which the geld was levied was normally two shillings for every hide of land.

William I and his half-brothers directly owned nearly half the land in England. In addition to this landed income, he drew substantial profits from justice (for example, fines) through the sheriffs, and from trade. England was a kingdom rich in trade with countries such as Sweden, the Low Countries, the Rhineland, Flanders and now Normandy. The royal income under William I has been estimated at around £20,000 or more, a phenomenal sum of money. Coinage could only be minted at a royal mint, and William quickly took control of these. By 1066 a well-established system involved some 60 mints across southern and central England producing silver pennies of standard weight. William added a few more mints, at Durham, Rhuddlan and Cardiff, reflecting the growth of Norman control in those areas. Under William II the new mint at Carmarthen followed expansion further into Wales.

The mints were the places where the coins were produced, by stamping the metal. They were Anglo-Saxon, the wealth was Anglo-Saxon and so too were the moneyers – the people in charge of the mints – many of whom worked for Harold, William I and William II. The Norman kings could not afford to destroy or make too drastic alterations to such a lucrative system.

WHAT DOES DOMESDAY BOOK TELL US ABOUT ANGLO-NORMAN GOVERNMENT?

The sophistication of Anglo-Saxon administrative, legal and financial systems coupled with the skill of William I adapting and continuing these systems in his new Anglo-Norman government, is nowhere better illustrated than in the remarkable survey of England drawn up in 1086. This was Domesday Book, so-called because its verdicts were just as unanswerable as the Book of the Day of Judgement. It was written in Latin, in Carolingian minuscule handwriting on parchment and includes 13,400 place names on 888 pages. Astonishingly, it was written up by one man, probably a native Englishman, or at least someone familiar with the place-names. No other country in the world produced such a detailed historical record at such an early date. Domesday Book is a record of a conquered kingdom, but it is a testament to the survival of that kingdom in many aspects.

Why was Domesday Book created?

Remarkably, Domesday Book was completed within a year of its conception. At his Christmas court held at Gloucester in 1085, *The Anglo-Saxon Chronicle* tells us that the king had 'deep speech' with his council about the country. It was decided to send men all over the country; they would visit every shire to find out what land or cattle the king had and what taxes he was owed; these commissioners also discovered what lands the archbishops, bishops and earls had and what taxes they owed the king. Essentially then, the king wished to find out who had what and who owed what, twenty years after his seizure of the kingdom.

Historians are still debating the exact purpose of Domesday Book. Generally, however, its purpose was threefold: legal, military and financial. The reasons for its production illustrate well the way William governed his kingdom during his final years.

- **Law and Property** A primary purpose of Domesday Book was legal. In the twenty years following the battle of Hastings, almost all of the Anglo-Saxon ruling class had been dispossessed. William needed to find out just who held the lands in his new kingdom and this needed to be confirmed and written down. Many areas had seen long-drawn-out disputes and legal hearings still unresolved in 1086. William, considering himself the legal heir to Edward the Confessor, wished to see these disputes settled and the violent upheaval resulting from his invasion and conquest legalised. Domesday Book was, in this way, a great judicial inquiry.
- **Military** A second purpose of the survey was military. The timing of the survey is significant, for it was commissioned at a period of crisis in William's government of England. For the first time since 1072, he faced possible invasion from Scandinavia. In the winter of 1085 he raised a massive army to deal with the threat, and billeted the army on the people of England. He needed to pay for this army and he needed to find out who his army commanders and soldiers actually were when he required them. Domesday Book, though arranged by Anglo-Saxon shires, focused upon the chief landholders in those shires. These were the tenants-in-chief – the new Anglo-Norman bishops, earls and barons who had totally replaced the Anglo-Saxon ruling class in the twenty years since 1066. To reinforce this

information, William summoned all the landholders to Salisbury in August 1086, during the making of Domesday, and had them swear a special oath of allegiance to him. This was the Oath of Salisbury, which bound his men to him by personal loyalty.

- **Financial** A third purpose of Domesday Book was financial. It provided an exact record of the local contribution to the king's geld, the Danegeld, which was the great general taxation levied on the entire population. *The Anglo-Saxon Chronicle* comments upon very heavy taxes levied on the English people in the year 1086, following a general tax levied early in 1084 which brought the king 21,000 lbs of silver. England was a rich and prosperous kingdom, and it is clear that the Norman kings would milk the country dry if they needed to.

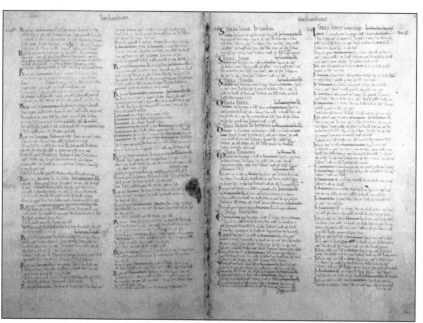

Pages from Domesday Book (Public Record Office)

How was Domesday Book produced?

The means by which Domesday Book was produced reflects the sophistication of Anglo-Norman government at every level. There are in fact two Domesday Books; 'Great' Domesday, covering every shire south of the river Tees except for Norfolk, Suffolk and Essex, which are accounted for in much more detail in 'Little' Domesday. The commissioners sent out to gather the information worked in seven circuits (for example, Circuit V was the West

Midlands) and each circuit used the shire and hundred courts to obtain the details. It is important to note that Domesday Book was arranged by shires (counties) and not by the great estates of the new Norman landlords. This reflects the strength and usefulness of the Anglo-Saxon administration. In each county, the first landholder named is the king, followed by other major landholders. The precise questions asked by the commissioners have survived in a document at Ely Abbey, known as the Ely Inquiry. From this, we know that the sheriff and local barons, with the priest, **reeve** and six villagers, swore on oath testifying who held the lands during the reign of Edward the Confessor, who holds it now, how many hides, how many ploughs, villagers, mills, fishponds, meadows and so on. The names of some of the jurors in each hundred are even listed in the Ely Inquiry. See below (pages 82–4) for a study of a Domesday village and its environs.

The significance of this is that there already existed a sophisticated administrative system available to William's commissioners in 1086. The system of summoning a jury has its origins in early tenth-century England. Law codes and documents from the reign of Ethelred (978–1016), father of Edward the Confessor, reveal that the reeve and twelve senior thegns of a hundred had to present information on oath relating to criminals. Much material relating to the great royal and ecclesiastical estates of Anglo-Saxon England was collected by the commissioners and written up in such a way to be given testimonial sanction at the local courts for the making of Domesday Book. The Domesday commissioners could use these documents for the 1086 survey and in addition pull the levers of the machinery of local administration to obtain further information.

The Norman administration used Anglo-Saxon customs and procedures. Domesday Book could not have been made without such established practices of local government. William was well aware that his commissioners could use the many financial and legal documents housed in the great abbeys and churches of his kingdom and the geld lists drawn up by his own government in recent years. What the Anglo-Norman government brought was a sense of control, urgency and purpose. The use of established

KEY WORD

Reeve The lord's official in charge of overseeing the crops and the animals in the village.

procedure combined with political and military necessity resulted in the speedy production of Domesday Book and it is likely that the first drafts of this remarkable survey were presented to the king before he departed to Normandy later in 1086, never to return to the kingdom he had conquered.

CONCLUSION: DID THE NORMAN GOVERNMENT OPPRESS ENGLAND?

The events of 1086 draw a line under the governance and kingship of William the Conqueror. Domesday Book and the Salisbury Oath legalised and finalised his rule. The last Scandinavian invasion never materialised. William died in 1087, after his horse threw him against the pommel of the saddle and ruptured his spleen. Characteristically, he was at war with his neighbour, the region of Maine adjacent to Normandy, and had burnt the town of Le Mans to the ground. It took him six weeks to die, in an abbey outside Rouen. His loyal and remarkable wife, Matilda, had died in 1083; his eldest son, Robert, hated him and his half-brother, Odo, was in prison at his command. A monk from Caen described the dead king and duke as wise, temperate and pious, but the obituary in *The Anglo-Saxon Chronicle* presents a different picture of how he treated his conquered people in England.

The Conqueror's body lay deserted after his death, stripped and bloated. Those in the land of the living raced to secure their own, worldly futures under one or both of the Conqueror's sons. At the funeral in Caen, the corpse of the Conqueror split open and all those present ran from the church, gagging at the stench, leaving one terrified clerk to mumble the ceremony as quickly as possible.

The view of William II was no more favourable. Few laws and financial records of his reign survive, but it was known that he was not devout, and that he plundered the wealth of the Church. He never married and was probably homosexual. These factors incurred the wrath of the chroniclers so that we have no balanced view of the man. He was a great soldier and taxed the English heavily to finance his wars, for which he was also hated. His death, whilst hunting in the New Forest, a forest created by his

KEY EVIDENCE

The Anglo-Saxon Chronicle for 1087
'He had castles built
And poor men hard oppressed.
The king was very stark
And deprived his underlings of many a mark
Of gold and more hundred pounds of silver,
That he took by weight and with great injustice
From his people with little need for such a deed.'

KEY EVIDENCE

The Anglo-Saxon Chronicle for 1100 'He [William II] was very strong and fierce to his country and his men and to all his neighbours, and very terrible. And because of the counsels of wicked men, which were always agreeable to him, and because of his avarice, he was always harassing this nation with military service and excessive taxes, so that in his days all justice was in abeyance, and all injustice arose both in ecclesiastical and secular matters.'

father for that purpose and at the expense of many English houses and liberties, was seen by some as providential. For William II had red hair, and red was the witch colour (hence his nickname 'Rufus'). A stray arrow hit him in the chest in the depths of the forest the day after Lammas Day (2 August) and his younger brother, the penniless, landless Henry, galloped to nearby Winchester to secure the treasury and the realm while his brother's corpse lay bleeding on a cart.

Whatever was thought of the Conqueror and his son as men, what can be truly established beyond all doubt is the totality of the Norman Conquest of England by 1100. The entire Anglo-Saxon ruling class – earls, bishops and thegns – had been replaced. A new set of values had been introduced into England; these were based upon loyalty and military service. The government of the new king was based upon the traditional procedures and customs of Edward the Confessor but was enforced with a savage energy inspired by unique circumstances.

It was inevitable that the new, Anglo-Norman, government would impact upon the people it ruled and in turn, create a new, Anglo-Norman, society, which we now turn to.

SUMMARY QUESTIONS

1. 'A brutal and merciless ruler from start to finish.' To what extent is this a fair and accurate assessment of William I's rule over England?

2. How far does the making of Domesday Book signify the triumph of Anglo-Saxon sophistication over Norman simplicity?

CHAPTER 6

How did society change after the Conquest?

INTRODUCTION

William I always maintained that he was the rightful heir to Edward the Confessor, but the reality of his kingship was based upon military conquest. He and his son were careful to preserve Anglo-Saxon laws and to utilise the wealth of England (to raise armies to extend their power over England) and to exploit the sophistication of Anglo-Saxon government in order to govern the conquered people more effectively. Whilst this pragmatic government ensured the security of the realm and whilst William I initially kept English earls and leading churchmen in power, by the time Domesday Book was completed, virtually all the ruling class of pre-Conquest England had been replaced by Normans.

THE RULING CLASS AND 'FEUDALISM'

This was no mere cosmetic change. The Normans may have brought very few ideas of law and government with them, but they did bring a fundamentally different set of social values which altered the composition of English society. Networks of kinship and allegiance reached out from the king at the centre to the most insignificant soldier on the Welsh border. This social structure was held together by the taking of oaths and at its heart lay military service. Historians know this structure as 'feudalism' (from the Latin *feudo* or fief, the plot of land granted to a man for services). The surviving evidence suggests that new customs were introduced over a period of several generations, and they were not without precedent in some parts of Anglo-Saxon England.

Who owned England?

After the Conquest William I quickly established the principle that 'all land belongs to the king'. He had, after all, conquered the country, and he directly owned a fifth of all the land surveyed in Domesday Book in 1086. The notion of freeholdings disappeared; all land was 'held' (not owned) either directly from the king by a tenant-in-chief or from a tenant-in-chief by a tenant (from the Latin *tenere*, 'to hold'). Each landholder formed a link in the chain that led ultimately to the king.

Who were the tenants-in-chief?

About a quarter of England was held by the Church and nearly half by the close followers of the king. These individuals, the tenants-in-chief, were very few in number (about 180) and most of them came from the Norman nobility which had emerged earlier in the eleventh century. The tenants-in-chief were generally the earls, archbishops, bishops, abbots and **barons** of Anglo-Norman England. They formed the aristocratic élite of the new society: the nobility.

The inner circle of the tenants-in-chief numbered only eleven; they were granted nearly a quarter of England. Most of these had played a part in the history of Normandy in the period 1040–66. The destruction of the Godwinsson brothers at the Battle of Hastings meant that the earldoms of Wessex (Harold), East Anglia (Gyrth) and Middlesex (Leofwine) were available for redistribution.

These eleven of the inner circle included the king's two half-brothers, Odo of Bayeux and Robert of Mortain, and his cousin, William fitzOsbern. They were granted vast swathes of land from Kent to Chester: Robert of Mortain received Cornwall, fitzOsbern the Isle of Wight, Roger of Montgomery, William de Warenne and William of Briouze received parts of Sussex and when the great Marcher earldoms of Hereford, Shrewsbury and Chester emerged, the titles went to fitzOsbern, Montgomery and Hugh d'Avranches. These were precisely the men who had supported William most in his duchy before the Conquest, and now they received their reward.

Why did William I need the service of knights?

William I had to ensure that the power of the Crown was enhanced, and not diminished. The tenants-in-chief did not hold their lands in absolute ownership as spoils of conquest, but on condition that they provided soldiers for the king. Each tenant-in-chief had to provide a certain number of fighting men, or knights as they are called

---

KEY WORD

Baron (Latin *baro*) This was an old word in north-west France by the year 1000. It meant simply a mature and experienced man, a man of status and quality. The *barones regis* were the king's barons, the great earls and bishops who gathered near the king to assist him in running the country. The estates of a baron were called baronies. The term 'baron' was not a formal title at this time, but it is used to denote the more powerful Norman lords who were not quite of the status of the half-dozen earls.

today. This was a quota, known as the *servitium debitum*, and could in theory produce between four and five thousand troops. William had conquered England by force of military arms, and the events of 1067–71 showed that he held it by force. The ruling class of Anglo-Norman England was an aristocracy organised for war, and it was this military feature which made post-Conquest feudalism a unique and unprecedented feature in English society. Furthermore, it is clear that William expected the archbishops, bishops and abbots to pay for their land in providing armed troops.

When was knight-service introduced?

A lively debate has raged amongst historians for over a century about exactly how and when William introduced the quotas for knights. The imposition of quotas was normally allocated in multiples of ten and may originally have been a rough-and-ready practical response to the hazards of conquest. It may be that some quotas were made with reference to pre-Conquest obligations of service, as Anglo-Saxon England certainly had in place a form of military service which Harold called upon to defend his kingdom in 1066. The earliest post-Conquest piece of evidence is a writ of 1072, which summons the Abbot of Evesham to bring the king the five knights he owes him. This writ may be earlier than 1072 and may even draw upon a pre-conquest obligation of the abbot's.

The reality was that this perfect, feudal army was rarely, if ever, summoned. The problems of logistics, supply and organisation were too great; the rebellions of 1088 and 1095 under William II suggest that the barons were never going to turn up with their allocated soldiers. In fact, very soon after the first generation of Conquest settlement, feudal service was often commuted to a money-payment (*scutage*), so that in effect the quotas became a form of taxation. Both William I and William II preferred to use mercenaries, which saved time and guaranteed fighting troops.

WHO WERE THE KNIGHTS?

Whilst the upper band of aristocracy, the tenants-in-chief, are easily defined by their holdings in Domesday Book, their connections with the king and their titles, the

KEY EVIDENCE

A writ, issued before 1077 and probably in 1072, ordering the Abbot of Evesham to supervise the levy of knights in his area and to bring the knights he himself owes the king 'William, king of the English, to Ethelwig, abbot of Evesham, greeting. I order you to summon all those who are subject to your administration and jurisdiction that they bring before me at Clarendon on the Octovae of Pentecost all the knights they owe me duly equipped. You, also, on that day, shall come to me, and bring with you fully equipped those 5 knights which you owe me in respect of your abbacy. Witness Eudo the steward. At Winchester.'

thousands of knights who formed the lower levels of the Norman aristocracy and who replaced the Anglo-Saxon thegns in the villages of England are less easily identified. These men, sometimes known simply in Latin as *milites* (singular *miles*) are the Roberts, Ralphs and Williams who fill the pages of Domesday Book, having ousted the Ethelberts, Edrics and Wulfnoths of pre-Conquest England. (The English word 'knight' derives from the Old English *cniht*, who was often a mounted retainer.) They were not a homogenous class in 1087, rather a miscellany. When William of Poitiers described William's plan to invade England, he distinguished between the 'noble knights' and the 'common knights'.

Arms and the man: a social code?

It could be said that the post-Conquest *milites* of the Domesday Book fulfilled a similar function to the pre-Conquest thegns and *cnihts*, as landholders and members of the ruling classes. However, the set of values the Norman *milites* brought with them was rather different from the values of pre-Conquest England. Increasingly, Norman knights were dependent upon their lords and masters; a bond of loyalty was established between them. The very word *miles* did not just mean 'soldier' but represented the servant-function of the man to his lord; the word was increasingly linked in the documents to the words *fidelis* (loyal) and *homo* (man). Another contemporary word was

Bayeux Tapestry: William giving armour to Harold

'vassal', a man who owed allegiance to his lord. This social relationship was often reinforced by symbolic acts, such as oath-taking, the granting of arms and armour and 'dubbing' a man to make him a knight (a short blow on the back of the neck). That is why Harold Godwinsson's alleged oath at Bayeux, promising to secure the

How did society change after the Conquest?   71

kingdom for William, was so important to the Normans and their claim that Harold had somehow become William's 'man'. The Bayeux Tapestry also shows the duke giving Harold arms and armour, an act heavy with ritual and symbolism, which was very important to Norman society, so that Harold's seizure of the throne was seen as a direct insult.

What did the knights do?

The actual service these knights did, varied from simple escort duty to garrison duty (guarding a castle) and from going on campaign into Wales or Scotland to putting down rebellion in England. They had to provide for themselves or had provided by their lord, a warhorse, arms and armour – an expensive business. It was a business that also depended on a lifelong education in riding and the use of arms, and this in turn implies a social class with expectations of those activities and with the economic wherewithal to sustain them. These men, trained and educated in service and warfare, were the men who fought at Hastings under their respective lords and masters.

How were the knights supported?

There were two means of support for a knight in this period: landed income and a household position. The land-holding knights named in Domesday Book did not have much status above that of a well-off peasant. Other knights, however, were trained, professional soldiers who served in the baron's household and rode into battle. In the latter group, the term *miles* was functional: they were armed and mounted men with a job to do and were not necessarily recorded in Domesday Book. The two groups of knights were not mutually exclusive; if there was not enough land to go around, a placement in a baronial household was a starting point; good fortune might later grant a fief or an heiress. And if a fief itself did not supply much support, then service in a household could supplement that meagre income.

The landed knights

The knights listed in Domesday were not well off compared to the barons. On average, they held land of less than one-and-a-half hides and an income of around £2 a year (compared with Roger Lacy, a Herefordshire baron of

KEY EVIDENCE

***The Anglo-Saxon Chronicle* for 1086** 'The king wore his crown and held his court at Winchester for Easter, and travelled so as to be at Westminster for Whitsuntide and there dubbed his son, Henry, a knight.'

middle rank, who had an income of £325). This was enough to sustain them but not for them to pursue any great social advancement. They rarely held whole manors, rather, parcels of land or units appurtenant to their lord's manor (see below, pages 79–80, for the manor). The land they had came from the lord's **demesne.** This allowed them to live off the rents from that land without having to work on it themselves. These knights were enfeoffed with their fief, or fee (*feodum* in Latin, from where the modern word 'feudalism' derives). The ceremony of enfeoffment may have involved oath-taking to bind the agreement, as very little was written down at this time. These landed knights may have had parcels of land from one or more lords, and they may have done knight-service to one or more lords. Such was the desire to seize land following the Conquest that tenants-in-chief often enfeoffed more knights than they needed to provide for the king, so some landed knights may not have done military service at all for some lords.

(see below, pages 79–80, for the manor)

Household knights

The royal household was the nucleus of the Anglo-Norman army and a permanent feature of Anglo-Norman government and society. Just as clerks in the chancery hoped to find advancement, young (Norman) men joined the royal household in the hope of social promotion, mixing with the great nobles of the day. The majority were professional soldiers.

The development of baronial households was a distinct feature of Anglo-Norman society. Whereas in pre-Conquest England the king retained household troops (the housecarls), in post-Conquest England the great Norman lords – including abbots and bishops – maintained their own household soldiers. This was partly because they had to feed and house the knights they were expected to provide for the king as part of their *servitium debitum*, and partly because they were foreigners occupying the country and needed troops to protect their own estates from native insurrection. In the first generation after the Conquest, most of these knights were landless and depended on their lord for equipment and food, but there existed a code of social conduct and social advancement. The households of the Norman lords were permanent features. William

---

KEY TERM

Demesne Land belonging to the lord. The royal demesne were the estates kept in the hands of the king. Barons and bishops kept back large parts of their estates in demesne for their own private profit, whilst granting out land to the knights with the rest in return for the knight-service they had to provide for the king.

KEY EVIDENCE

Orderic Vitalis, *The Ecclesiastical History* (written 1123–41). Orderic, a half-English, half-Norman monk, is describing the great household of Hugh d'Avranches, Earl of Chester under William I
'An enormous household, which resounded with the noise of a crowd of youths, both noble and common, was always in attendance upon him. Some good men, clerks as well as knights, also lived with him, and he gladly gave them a share in both his labours and his wealth.'

---

fitzOsbern, close friend and advisor to the king, kept a household so large that it irritated the king; the Bayeux Tapestry shows Duke William's household men well-dressed, armed and mounted.

How different were the Norman knights from the Saxon thegns?

Similarities

- Both did military service.
- Both formed the landholding class in England.

Differences

- The knights held their land in a chain that linked them to the king, through the tenant-in-chief, which the thegns had not done.
- The estates of the knights eventually became hereditary, some before 1087.
- Landless knights had positions in baronial or royal households which did not exist before 1066.
- The system of oaths, when a knight paid homage or fealty to the lord as his vassal, was new to England.
- Knight-service was more specifically military and centred around the castle (garrison duty) and the baronial or royal households.
- The service of a thegn was not always military and was not often specified in the surviving sources.
- Thegns usually held their land for their lifetime, or for three lifetimes, held by 'book-land', as it was specified in a charter, or 'book'. Land was not permanently hereditary.

CASE STUDY 2

WILLIAM BAYNARD, PETER THE KNIGHT AND ROGER LACY

Written evidence outside the royal sphere of influence for knight-service and the conditions of that service is very scarce. This is not only due to poor survival of the documents over a period of 900 years, but also to the fact that little was actually written down. Verbal agreements, confirmed with an oath and witnessed by friends, family and vassals, may have sufficed. Although Domesday Book informs us of the thousands of new Norman landlords, it tells us nothing about the manner in which they held their land.

KEY EVIDENCE

Lease of land by Aldred, Bishop of Worcester, to Wulfgeat, a thegn (1051–52). Land is granted for three generations and the service is not specified

'Here it is declared in this document that Bishop Aldred has granted to Wulfgeat a certain piece of land, namely $1\frac{1}{2}$ hides in the manor called Ditchford, to be held and enjoyed for three lives ... And they shall always be submissive and obedient and acknowledge the lordship of whoever is bishop at that time ...'

KEY WORD

Hereditary In this context, land or possessions that are passed from father to son.

Three documents, however, have survived, and inform us of the intimate details of **enfeoffment** and service. These grants of land were private, non-royal agreements made in 1083, 1085 and in the period 1066–87. They may have been written down in the first place because each deals with the Church. But what is striking is that each agreement differs according to the particular circumstances; taken together, they do not form a composite picture of a 'feudal system' imposed upon England in the first generation following the Conquest. Rather, they show a diverse and complex society at the point of transition between pre- and post-Conquest England, in three different areas: London, Suffolk and Herefordshire.

1 **William Baynard and the Abbot of Westminster (1083)**

The agreement made in 1083 was between Gilbert, Abbot of Westminster, and William Baynard. Baynard was granted a farm in the town of Westminster to have for his lifetime only, 'to house him'. He was granted the land because of the 'love and service' he had shown to the Church, which might suggest that he had served his time as a household knight for the abbey and was being rewarded with enough land to give him an income. William was not the first man to hold this land from the Abbot. He was following in the footsteps of a certain Wulfric Bordewayte, a thegn. This is evidence for continuity from pre-Conquest to post-Conquest landholding. Furthermore, William was not, by the terms of the agreement, allowed to sell, mortgage or give away any of these lands. They were to return to the Abbot at his death.

2 **Peter the knight and the Abbot of Bury St Edmunds (1066–87)**

The language of the second grant, from the Abbot of Bury St Edmunds to a certain Peter, was quite different. Peter is specifically called a knight of 'King William' and he will become the 'feudal man' of the Abbot by doing the ceremony of 'homage'. He will serve on behalf of the Abbot with three or four knights for the king's army. There is no mention of the land he receives for this, or any details about how long he will hold it, or what powers he has over that land. The other problem of this agreement is that the text that survives is a fourteenth-century copy, which is so damaged in parts that the date of the document can only be attributed to the reign of William I (1066–87).

3 Roger Lacy and the Bishop of Hereford (1085)

By far the most detailed and authentic of the three grants is the agreement between Roger Lacy, a Herefordshire baron, and the Bishop of Herefordshire, Robert of Lorraine, dated 1085. Unlike Peter the knight, Roger does not become the 'feudal man' of the bishop. Instead, he actually asked the bishop if he could pay a money rent for the land at Holme Lacy but the bishop refused, requesting two knights' service. As with the Westminster grant, Roger only has the land for his lifetime, though we are told that his father, Walter Lacy, had the estate before him. Roger is not allowed to sell, give away or mortgage the property, and even during his possession of the estate, the bishop's men are permitted to take wood for fuel and to graze their pigs on the land.

Included with the Holme Lacy agreement is another agreement between the bishop and the baron, concerning land at Onibury, in Shropshire. For this estate Roger does indeed pay rent, at 20 shillings a year.

Summary

Several important conclusions can be drawn from comparing these early grants:

- They differ in their conditions of service and the 'feudal' language they use.
- William Baynard is taking over land from a Saxon thegn, which indicates continuity from Saxon to Norman.
- Roger Lacy is taking over land that his father held, which indicates continuity from father to son and the first step to hereditary rights.
- Roger Lacy initially wanted to pay cash for Holme Lacy and does so for Onibury, which indicates that other agreements that were not written down or that have not survived for other estates, may have been paid for in cash, rather than knight-service.

The above conclusions cannot be said to point towards a uniform system of feudalism imposed by William the

> ### KEY EVIDENCE
>
> **From the Holme Lacy charter of 1085** 'But the bishop, by the counsel of his vassals, gave him this same land in return for a promise that he would serve the bishop with 2 knights as his father did whenever the need arose.'

Conqueror on England after the Conquest. Instead, these documents show that different customs and different conditions were employed, depending on circumstances, in order to grant out the land. Was it automatic that Roger Lacy would possess Holme Lacy as his father had done? Did William Baynard have to wait until Wulfric the Thegn had died until he was given Wulfric's farm, or had Wulfric been dispossessed after Hastings (if not killed at Hastings)? The differences between these surviving sources pose enough questions for us to doubt the idea of a single system introduced in one go; rather, it would appear to be a piecemeal, slow process that was beginning during the Conqueror's reign.

The documents do afford us a unique insight into how the first and second generation of Norman settlers were establishing themselves in their newly acquired kingdom. The baronial households listed illustrate well how these new landholders went about conducting business and cast a beam of light onto the aristocratic world of William the Conqueror.

THE FEUDAL DEBATE: CONTINUITY OR CHANGE?

The extent and the timing of the introduction of knight-service and hereditary fiefs have been much debated. Towards the end of the nineteenth century, historians believed that the military arrangements that William I made were adapted from past, pre-Conquest customs. Accepting that William I defined the amount of service owed to him, the Victorian legal historian F.W. Maitland argued that 'it seems questionable whether he introduced any new principle'. But historians at the beginning of the twentieth century, notably J.H. Round, followed by F.M. Stenton and D.C. Douglas (writing later) saw the introduction of a contractual arrangement between the king and his barons, the barons and his men as a new social phase. R.A. Brown took this up in the 1970s and argued that the three fundamentals of feudalism were the knight, vassalic commendation and the fief.

Historians are now revising this, and suggesting that the evidence points not to a coherent system imposed quickly, but rather a variety of customs and traditions utilising

Anglo-Saxon methods and evolving into a new social code over a period of one or two generations. The three agreements discussed above do not point towards a uniform system imposed after the Conquest. Instead, landholders felt their way gradually according to circumstance and time, building upon pre-Conquest patterns of settlement and Norman traditions.

A military state

What must also be emphasised is that the system of knight-service was created out of the necessity to occupy England and reinforce the Norman Conquest. The need for efficient troops led to a quota system; those troops garrisoned the new castles and put down the rebellions. England before 1066 was a peace-loving state; when Godwin fell out with Edward the Confessor in 1051 no side went to war, and in 1065, when Tostig was expelled from Northumbria, Harold avoided war, choosing instead to expel his own brother. English society before 1066 was not a society used to warfare. Normandy before 1066, by contrast, had witnessed intermittent warfare from the moment the boy-duke William succeeded to the duchy in 1035. The rise to power of the duke was the story of his triumph in battles, skirmishes, sieges and counter-sieges over a twenty-year period against rebels within the duchy and his enemies the count of Anjou and the king of France. Norman society developed military services and the oath-taking vassalic relationships that bound that society together. After 1066, they exported these conventions to England and imposed them in order to make their Conquest successful.

The quotas of knight-service may well have been new after 1066 and resulted, eventually, in a new social class, but the feudal army William I could summon was never enough for his needs. He still had to resort to the old Anglo-Saxon *fyrd*. He did this in 1068, to deal with the rebellion at Exeter; in 1073 he took a large force of Englishmen to Maine (France) and in 1075 the earls' revolt was repulsed by the local English levies. The old system that Harold had used in 1066 largely survived, but the new Norman knights were the elite fighting troops and the new landholding class.

HOW DID THE CONQUEST AFFECT THE ORDINARY PEOPLE?

Over 90 per cent of the population of some two million were Anglo-Saxon and Anglo-Danish; 90 per cent of them lived in the countryside. It might be said that after 1066 one ruling class was replaced by another, but the language and culture of the new rulers were quite different. They were only there by force of arms. Changes to society as a whole could be profound, as we have seen in Yorkshire after 1070 and in the towns where great castles appeared. Domesday Book charts the many demographic and economic changes in England in the period 1066–87 and it is not enough to conclude that ordinary life in England continued as before. The Norman Conquest thus impacted upon all levels of society at various times and at various paces.

That said, the Norman Conquest did not bring about the same kind of change in the organisation and conditions of English peasant life as it did in the higher ranks of society. The ranks of society outlined in the *Rectitudines Singularum Personarum* (above, page 9) remained the same after the Conquest. There was no widespread transformation in the agricultural structure in the twenty years following the battle of Hastings; the Normans were unwilling, or unable, to modify the varieties of agricultural structure that existed in pre-Conquest England.

Village life

The village was the primary institution of peasant life throughout the eleventh century. Domesday Book is of course the major evidence for the social and economic condition of the 13,400 English villages recorded in 1066 and in 1086. From this remarkable source we can compile a detailed picture of Anglo-Norman society.

The typical village in Anglo-Norman England consisted of cottages clustered near a church, surrounded by hedgeless fields where the peasantry worked on scattered strips of land, grazing their animals on the common land.

Was there a manorial 'system'?

At the centre of the village was a large house, occupied by the lord or his bailiff. A village under lordship was a manor. The term 'manor' was a definition for legal and fiscal purposes. In the north and west it was common for a manor to include several villages. Danelaw customs survived in the north and east of England. Indeed, so many pre-Conquest provincial traditions persisted until well after the Conquest that there cannot be said to have been a uniform 'manorial system' imposed on England after the Conquest.

Ranks of society: free tenants, cottars and villeins

At the top end of the village social scale were the free tenants, who paid a money-rent for their property and who were free to go where they wished. Towards the bottom end were the cottars, men with smallholdings of around five acres (two hectares) who worked on the lord's land one day a week and provided hired labour. Village craftsmen were usually found in this rank of society.

In between the free tenants and the cottars were the villeins, who formed the largest section of village society. The villein had a holding in the open field, which maintained him and his family and passed to his eldest son. The villeins were not free. On certain days in the week the villein had to work for the lord on his land; this was called 'week-work'. At certain times of the year, such as during the harvest, he had to perform extra duties, known as 'boon-work'. The villein could not leave his land or that of his lord; he paid a fine when his daughter married (the merchet) and another when he took over his father's land (the heriot). The villein could be taxed by his lord at will, providing that his land was not taken from him.

Forest law

William I introduced to England a forest law of Frankish (French) origin to protect his hunting. This law was applicable across large parts of England: by 1100, the whole of Essex was 'forest'. In Hampshire, William widened the private chase of Edward the Confessor's forest to create the 'New Forest' and in doing so destroyed whole villages. The forest law protected the red deer, fallow deer, the roe and wild boar, and the vert (vegetation which nourished the animals). Punishments for poaching became increasingly severe, ranging from mutilation to death. As vast swathes of England were heavily forested, these laws had a significant effect on the people.

KEY EVIDENCE

The *Anglo-Saxon Chronicle* for 1087: William I's obituary

'He made great protection for the game
And imposed laws for the same.
That who so slew hart or hind
Should be made blind.
He preserved the hares and boars
And loved the stags as much
As if he were their father.'

Towns

English towns suffered in the first decades of Norman rule. Some, like York and Exeter, were involved in the rebellions; many towns were partly cleared for the building of castles, for example Gloucester, Oxford, Lincoln and Cambridge, where dozens of houses were demolished. Trade was disrupted as links with Scandinavia were broken. But England and Normandy were thriving centres of commerce and weathered the storms of warfare. William I was keen to ensure English prosperity so that he could raise higher taxes; he confirmed to London its old laws and the customs of many towns were carefully recorded in Domesday Book. William recognised the importance of London before his coronation, beginning the building of the Tower of London. He also built Baynard and Mountfichet castles. His son, William II, completed the Tower and added to London's importance by building the vast and splendid great hall at Westminster, alongside the abbey that had been completed just before the death of Edward the Confessor in 1066.

Winchester, the ancient capital of Wessex, underwent change. Although by the early twelfth century it was no longer the centre of government, William I wore his crown there at Easter and enlarged the royal palace. The Norman Bishop Walkelin demolished the old Saxon cathedral and built a new one that even today has the longest nave in western Europe. William enlarged the castle and the royal treasure had been moved there by the end of the eleventh century.

York, the great regional capital of the north, suffered terribly during the rebellions. The population was reduced by half to between 4000 and 5000. The city declined in stature as the one-time capital of a Viking kingdom and seat of the northern archbishopric; it also declined in prosperity. In 1070 the new archbishop, Thomas of Bayeux, restored the cathedral and revived trade to a certain extent. However, recovery was slow; York remained on a par with the flourishing regional centres of Lincoln, Bristol, Norwich and Exeter.

OUNDLE, NORTHAMPTONSHIRE: A DOMESDAY VILLAGE

In the far east of Northamptonshire, twelve miles from Peterborough, lies what is now a small town, Oundle. The lord of the village in 1086 was the Abbot of Peterborough, a tenant-in-chief and sixth on the list of the sixty tenants-in-chief for the whole of Northamptonshire.

Northamptonshire lay on the very edge of the Danelaw divide. The shire emerged from a part-English, part-Danish area in the late ninth century; Watling Street, a Roman road, had marked the north-east boundary of the English territory from the time of King Alfred's peace with Guthrum in 878. The shire was not formally organised around the town of Northampton until the early eleventh century.

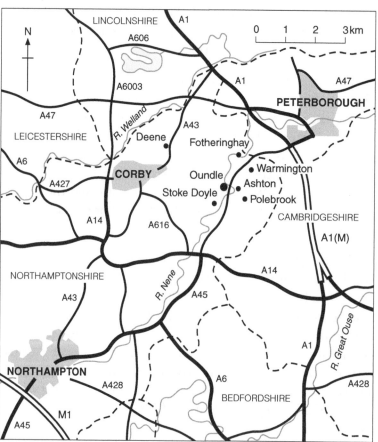

Map of Oundle near Peterborough

The vicinity of Oundle did not escape the political events of the Norman Conquest. The Saxon abbot of

Peterborough, Leofric, died at Hastings, and was replaced by Turold, a Norman monk, in 1069. However, Peterborough was caught up in the Ely rebellion of 1070–71 when Hereward raided the abbey, burning and looting the church and the town – apparently out of loyalty to the Church – before Turold could get there. After his arrival with 160 heavily-armed Frenchmen, Turold restored the church and the king dealt with the Ely rebels.

Domesday Book records 326 villages in Northamptonshire, with a population of some 30,000. The most populated area of the shire was the Nene Valley, where values had doubled since 1066, and where Oundle was situated. There were ironworks at Corby and Gretton and smiths at Deene, Green Norton and Towcester. Water-power was essential for industry and food production; 155 manors had watermills. There were markets at Higham Ferrers, Kings Sutton and Oundle, a castle at Rockingham and a castle built at Northampton soon after 1086.

Oundle lay in the Hundred of Polebrook and the manor of Oundle in 1086 also had land in nearby Thurning and Stoke Doyle. The evidence suggests that Oundle was a large village that was thriving after the Conquest, increasing in value greatly from 5 shillings to £11 with a population of some 150–200, judging by the heads of households listed as villagers (villeins) and smallholders (bordars). The many other peasants without ploughs were of course not listed, as Domesday Book is chiefly interested in what people are worth. The mill, the woodland, 'when stocked', and the market all yielded money for the king and provided the base for the local economy.

The manor of Oundle was not 'subinfedated' by 1086, that is, granted out from the Abbot of Peterborough to any knight or lesser lord, but instead appears to have been held directly by the Abbot in demesne.

Compared to neighbouring villages, such as Ashton and Warmington, which also had mills and a similar population, the only aspect of Oundle that was to mark it out as a future place of greater settlement – and the town that it has become today – was the market, which gave a place great importance at that time. It was Fotheringhay, five miles to the east of Oundle, that was to assume great political significance later in the Middle Ages. In 1086 it was held by Countess Judith, daughter of William I's half-sister and Lambert, Count of Lens, widow and heiress of Earl Waltheof. A motte-and-bailey castle was constructed at Fotheringhay and the king hunted in the forest there. It was also here that the dukes of York formed a major power-base in the fifteenth-century and where the future Richard III was born.

CONCLUSION: A SOCIAL REVOLUTION?

The greatest effect the Norman Conquest had on English society was the total replacement of the Anglo-Saxon ruling class. Not only was the Godwinsson royal family wiped out, but the earls were replaced by cousins and friends of the Conqueror. The landowning class of thegns were dispossessed, that is, those who had survived the three battles of 1066 and the rebellions of 1067–72. They were replaced by a new class of Norman landholder: the knights, who held their lands in return for military service and were bound to their lords by a value-system of oaths and ceremonies alien to England. This social system, known as feudalism, was by no means complete by 1100 and varied from place to place. For the majority of the population, however, the social structure remained largely unaltered, though the building of castles and expansion of towns changed the landscape. The king's devastating raids in the north created famine and widespread misery, but evidence from Domesday Book shows an increasingly wealthy and prosperous England twenty years after the battle of Hastings.

SUMMARY QUESTIONS

1. To what extent was feudalism a new concept to England?

2. Was the Norman Conquest a good thing for the people of England?

Bishoprics A bishopric was the area of authority of a bishop (otherwise known as a diocese), whose base was the cathedral church (meaning 'seat' of the bishop). The first bishoprics emerged in England in the sixth and seventh centuries. The chief bishops were the archbishops of Canterbury and York.

Monasteries This was the general term given to the residential communities of monks and nuns, who dedicated their lives to God and took oaths of chastity and poverty. More specifically, an abbey was a large church with accommodation for the monks or nuns, cloisters, land for farming and a great hall. A priory was a smaller version. Abbeys and priories could have 'mother' houses which controlled them and 'sister' houses which shared the same foundation grant. Many thousands of women were nuns, drawn chiefly from aristocratic society and well educated.

Nunneries Many noble women were educated in abbeys and priories. For example, the nuns at Wilton Priory educated Edith Godwinsson.

Corrupt Evil or morally depraved, or willing to act for money or personal favours.

CHAPTER 7

The Anglo-Norman Church

INTRODUCTION

The Christian Church lay at the heart of the medieval world. Not only was the presence of God very real to ordinary people, but the Church had become a wealthy, politically powerful institution. The Church, with its **bishoprics**, **monasteries** and **nunneries**, was a major landowner in England. Its land was held permanently, and could not be granted away or sold. Land was power: the bishops and abbots were educated men, often at the centre of government, formulating policy and controlling the provinces. Therefore the relationship between William I and William II and the English Church was a very important one, as it was the key to the good government of the Anglo-Norman realm. Consequently, the impact of the Norman Conquest on the English Church was drastic and long-lasting.

WHY WAS THE ENGLISH CHURCH IN NEED OF REFORM?

When William I began to raise an army to conquer England he appealed to Pope Alexander II to support his claim. This was not only because Harold was a perjurer and usurper in Norman eyes, but also because William presented the Church in England as **corrupt** and in need of reform.

The Normans accused the English clergy of abusing their Church. These abuses came in several forms:

- Simony – the selling of Church posts.
- Nepotism – the securing of posts for relatives and friends.
- Pluralism – the holding of more than one office at once.
- Clerical marriage – priests were supposed to be celibate (to refrain from sexual intercourse), but many priests had wives or mistresses.

Reform in Europe

The inspiration to reform the Church of these abuses came from France, where clerical abuses were just as bad as they were in England. The Abbey of Cluny was the starting point for reforming ideas and Pope Leo IX took up these ideas in 1048. The greatest reforming pope was Gregory VII, who clashed with William I. In 1066, Duke William of Normandy claimed to be at the head of these reforms in Normandy, a claim that was generally accepted, and so it was natural enough for the Pope to bless his standard and for the duke to ride into battle at Hastings with the papal banner at the head of his troops.

HOW CORRUPT WAS THE ENGLISH CHURCH BEFORE 1066?

The clerical abuses described above were common in the English Church. Furthermore, the Archbishop of Canterbury, Stigand, was a notorious abuser of clerical privileges. He was both bishop of Winchester and archbishop; several bishops in England refused to be consecrated by him and Harold Godwinsson made sure that he was crowned by Archbishop Ealdred of York, and not by Stigand.

However, the English Church under Edward the Confessor, a very pious man, is not to be held in too low regard. The bishops included the saintly and famous Wulfstan of Worcester, and the English bishops were present at some of the great continental councils, and would therefore have been very aware of the reforming ideas from Cluny and the papacy. Relations with the papacy were good.

WHAT WAS THE IMPACT OF THE CONQUEST ON THE CHURCH?

Even though the pre-Conquest Church was no more corrupt than those on the continent, the Church was drastically affected by the Conquest. Just as a new aristocracy replaced the English earls and thegns, so a new Norman-French aristocracy replaced the English bishops and abbots. Furthermore, some of the English dioceses were altered and many new cathedrals, abbeys and monasteries were built in the period 1066–1100.

- **The bishops** In 1070, Stigand, pluralist bishop of Winchester and archbishop of Canterbury, was finally removed from his offices. Others went with him, including his brother, Aethelmaer of Elmham, Aethelric of Selsey, closely associated with Stigand, and Leofwine of Lichfield, who was married. All three left office in 1070: the first two were deposed (removed) and Leofwine resigned. When Ealdred of York died in September 1069, the way was open for the king to make a new appointment: Thomas of Bayeux. By 1080, Wulfstan of Worcester was the only English bishop left; all the others were either Norman or French. These new bishops were hard-working, intelligent and sometimes brutal men, utterly loyal to the Conqueror and his governance of England.

- **The dioceses** Not only were English bishops replaced, but some of the locations of the cathedrals of the Anglo-Saxon dioceses were moved by the Norman bishops. The new Norman pattern was to base the dioceses in cities, rather like the new, smaller, earldoms. Those dioceses affected included Lichfield, based first in Chester and then in Coventry; Sherborne to Old Sarum (Salisbury); Selsey to Chichester; Elmham to Thetford and then Norwich; Dorchester to Lincoln and Wells to Bath. These dioceses were then divided into archdeaconries and the archdeaconries subdivided into rural deaneries. All these made for a more coherent, strictly hierarchical Church.

- **Archdeacons** With the reorganisation of the dioceses came the new territorial responsibility of the archdeacon.

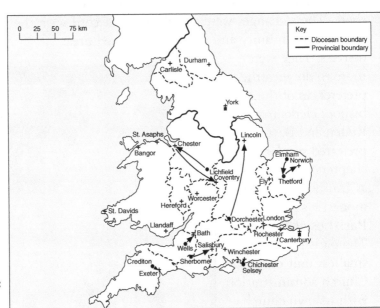

The English dioceses after the Norman Conquest, showing movement of some of the sees

This position had existed before 1066 but was not attached to the archdeaconry. By the early 1070s archdeacons were found in several English dioceses; by 1089 they were almost universal. Within a century the archdeacon was the central figure of diocesan discipline and soon came to preside over the diocesan courts.

- **New cathedrals** As well as moving the diocesan centres to the towns, replacing English bishops with Norman bishops, the Norman bishops set about rebuilding or building from scratch massive cathedrals constructed in a very distinctive **Romanesque** style of architecture. By the end of the eleventh century most of the larger English churches had been pulled down and were being rebuilt in this new style, including cathedrals at Winchester, Canterbury, Durham and Gloucester.

- **Monastic cathedrals** Four cathedrals in Anglo-Saxon England (Canterbury, Worcester, Winchester and Sherborne) had monks instead of **canons**. At Winchester, the new Norman bishop, Walkelin, who was not a monk, attempted to impose canons on the cathedral, but failed. At Sherborne, change prevailed: Bishop Osmund, a **secular** canon, reshaped the community as a secular chapter when it transferred to Salisbury. But new monastic chapters were created after the Conquest at Rochester, Durham and Norwich; and Bath became monastic when the bishop of Wells moved there, as did Coventry when Lichfield was transferred there. These changes were not always in accord with the existing community and sometimes caused great distress. They were more to do with the preferences of the new bishop: clerks from Rouen and Bayeux preferred secular chapters; monks such as Lanfranc preferred a monastic structure.

- **Parishes and priests** The parish was the smallest unit of Church administration with its own church and clergy. Domesday

Bishop Walkelin's new cathedral at Winchester had, and still has, the longest nave in western Europe

Book records around 2000 churches. This figure represents only a small fraction of the churches that are known to have existed at this time. The eleventh and twelfth centuries witnessed a massive surge in church-building, but this had begun before the Conquest. Furthermore, the great majority of parish priests continued to be of English descent. They were only slightly affected by the Conquest because they were of low social status (about that of a villein) and of only rudimentary education; many of them remained married, despite attempts at reform.

WHAT WERE THE ACHIEVEMENTS OF ARCHBISHOP LANFRANC?

At the head of the new foreign bishops and abbots was a new archbishop of Canterbury, Lanfranc, an Italian from Pavia. Lanfranc was already famous as a lawyer and a teacher. He was a monk at Bec and was abbot of St Stephen's, Caen, at the time of his appointment to Canterbury. He was one of the closest advisors of the Conqueror and often acted as regent during his absences in Normandy. His role as a great statesman continued until his death in 1089, after he had helped to establish William II on the throne.

The primacy of Canterbury

Lanfranc's first achievement that marked him out as a great statesman and leading advisor to William I was establishing Canterbury as the prime ecclesiastical office in England, over and above the other archbishopric, York. This, particularly in the light of the northern rebellions and the traditional independence of the north, was important to the king's government. Thomas of Bayeux, the new archbishop of York, however, was not at all pleased to submit to Lanfranc. Lanfranc, encouraged by the monks of Canterbury and forged documents, pressed the traditional English case for the primacy of Canterbury. The king initially supported Thomas but backed Lanfranc, and at the Council of Winchester in 1070, Thomas formally recognised Lanfranc as **primate** of England and ceased his claims to power over the three dioceses of Lincoln, Lichfield and Worcester. In 1072, in return for this, Thomas was placed in charge of the Scottish Church. Lanfranc's primacy was never recognised by the Pope because it gave him

KEY WORD

Primate The chief minister of the Church in England. From 1070 onwards, this has always been the Archbishop of Canterbury.

independence within England at a time when the popes were trying to limit the power of the archbishops and bishops in the Church. Lanfranc, however, was seen as primate in England and he asserted his rights over Scotland and Ireland, as primate of all 'Britain'.

The Councils

Lanfranc used great council meetings to enact these changes in the new, Anglo-Norman Church. Stigand was deposed at the council of 1070. Councils were held in 1070 (Winchester), 1072 (Winchester and Windsor), 1075 (London), 1076 (Winchester) and at least three more councils were held in the period up to 1087. Legislation such as the banning of clergy marriages, compulsory celibacy for priests, the moving of cathedrals to the cities and the formal organisation of the parish served by a single priest dependent upon a single church were passed at these councils.

The Church and the law courts

It was at Lanfranc's third council at Winchester in 1076 that courts of ecclesiastical jurisdiction were established in England. This had royal sanction. Prior to the Conquest, the clergy had to have their case heard in the hundred courts (a hundred was the smallest administrative area within a shire) by bishops and archdeacons. Now, they would be heard in episcopal (bishop's) courts, free from all lay interference. However, the shire courts did continue to hear such cases. Episcopal courts (also called 'synods') were not new in the English or Norman Church. The synod and shire court – bishop and sheriff – worked alongside one another. Synods were useful tools of reform and Lanfranc ordered regular synods to be held in each diocese.

The king may have sanctioned the creation of such synods, but whenever William's political authority was threatened, he acted ruthlessly. The arrest of his half-brother, Odo, Bishop of Bayeux, illustrated this. Odo proposed to withhold his knights from the king and to intervene in papal affairs but William arrested him, not as bishop but as Earl of Kent. William kept him imprisoned until he lay on his deathbed in 1087. The greatest test, however, of Church and state boundaries of jurisdiction came with the trial of William of Saint-Calais in 1088 (see below, page 93).

KEY EVIDENCE

Extract from a letter from Lanfranc to Herfast, Bishop of Elmham (c. 1077) This letter shows how Lanfranc intervened in the behaviour of his bishops. In this case, there is evidence for some rather slack morals of the bishop.

'Give over dice-playing, not to speak of graver misconduct and worldly sports, in which you are said to waste the whole day. Study theology and the decrees of the Roman pontiffs, and give special attention to the sacred canons.'

KEY EVIDENCE

Writ of William I (1072) concerning Church courts 'Wherefore I order, and by my royal authority I command, that no bishop or archdeacon shall henceforth hold pleas relating to the episcopal laws in the hundred court; nor shall they bring to the judgement of secular men any matter which concerns the rule of souls; but anyone cited under the episcopal laws in respect of any plea of crime shall come to the place which the bishop shall choose and name ...'

WHAT WERE WILLIAM I'S RELATIONS WITH THE PAPACY?

When William led his army into battle at Hastings he had with him the papal banner and the blessing of the Pope for his expedition. However, by the end of his reign, relations with the Pope had cooled considerably. This was due to William's desire to maintain independence from the Pope and the increasing reforms within the papacy itself.

The piety of William I

The two popes who had dealings with William were Alexander II and Gregory VII. They both praised William as a righteous king. Good relations between king and pope were an advantage. William needed support in his new kingdom and the popes, especially Gregory VII, needed support to expand papal power, which led them into conflict with the rulers of France and Germany in what is known as the **Investiture Contest**. In 1070, papal **legates** visited England, re-crowned William, deposed a number of English bishops and approved the decrees of the councils of Winchester and Windsor. Many of the new bishops and abbots were men of intellectual and moral quality, and the letters from Pope Gregory VII to William illustrate the warmth between them. Although much of William's genial relations with the popes were based on political opportunity, he seems to have been a genuinely pious man. He founded an abbey on the site of the battle of Hastings and he and his wife Matilda founded two abbeys in Caen.

Pope Gregory VII and William I

Gregory VII was one of the most forthright and determined men to occupy the papal throne. In his ambition to force the rulers of Europe to recognise the **temporal** as well as the **spiritual** power of the papacy, he actually ended his life in exile and in defeat. Although he never came to blows with England, his aims toward England were:

- to enforce the regular attendance at Rome of the English bishops
- to establish a claim of loyalty to the papacy from William.

Both Gregory and William had steely personalities and neither backed down on these issues. Gregory demanded

KEY THEME

Investiture Contest This stemmed from the reforms from Cluny in the mid-eleventh century, which led the papacy to free the Church from lay control, particularly the right of kings and princes to select and invest bishops and abbots with their office. Pope Gregory VII clashed with the Emperor of Germany over this and died in exile. The issue of investiture was certainly an issue in England but did not bring English kings into similar dispute with the papacy.

KEY TERM

Legate A member of the clergy who represents the pope.

KEY WORDS

Temporal Anything relating to worldly affairs and secular business.

Spiritual Relating to religious and ecclesiastical affairs.

that English bishops came to him at Rome in a series of letters starting in 1079 and ending in the near-dismissal of Lanfranc from his position as archbishop of Canterbury. Lanfranc himself only ever went to Rome once, in 1071, and very reluctantly. Many of the threats from the pope never materialised and William handled those that did with great caution.

In 1080 Gregory demanded that William should do him fealty in respect of the kingdom of England. Part of this was papal pay-back for the support Alexander had given William for his invasion in 1066. The Pope asserted that William had promised to do fealty for the kingdom in return for the papal support. In 1080, however, William utterly denied this in a letter to Gregory, see right:

After such a decisive and explicit refusal to acquiesce to the Pope's demands, no further request was made by Gregory. Indeed, he became embroiled in terrible difficulties with the German Emperor Henry VI, who in 1080 elected his own 'anti-pope', Clement III. William I and Lanfranc cleverly played off the two popes against each other, neither recognising or condemning Clement, but using the papal **schism** to avoid papal directives.

William I did agree to one of Gregory's demands, however, and that was the payment of Peter's Pence, the ancient tax payable by monarchs to Rome. William made it very clear that by paying this he offered no other obligation to the Pope regarding fealty or submission of any kind.

WILLIAM II AND THE CHURCH

William Rufus was no less determined than his father to deny the Church any further control over his political power in England. But Rufus lacked the caution and wisdom of his father, and also the personal piety. He sought to maintain royal power over the wealth and power of the Church, and this he largely achieved.

The difficulty with Rufus is that all the writers of the time were prejudiced against him. He comes down to us as not at all devout, but a blasphemer. The monks hated him because he was notorious for delaying the appointments of bishops and abbots to vacant posts, during which time he took the Church income. At the time of his death in 1100

KEY EVIDENCE

Extract from a letter from William I to Pope Gregory (1080) 'I have not consented to pay fealty, nor will I now because I never promised it, nor do I find that my predecessors ever paid it to your predecessors.'

KEY THEME

Schism A division between two parties due to political or ideological differences. Throughout the Middle Ages there was rivalry for the election of popes. Kings and emperors had their own favoured choices and put forward an 'anti-pope' to oppose the pope in Rome.

many bishoprics and abbeys remained vacant. The king took the income from these churches, even putting the monks at Canterbury on very small rations. Rufus also sold Church offices, including Durham (to Ranulf Flambard) and refused to allow Church councils.

The trial of William of Saint-Calais (1088)

During the rebellion Rufus faced when he took the English throne (above, pages 49–51) one of the Anglo-Norman rebels included William of Saint-Calais, Bishop of Durham. The king confiscated the Bishop's property but any attempts to put the bishop on trial were rebuffed. The bishop would not submit to the judgement of laymen in a case involving his bishopric; if there was to be a trial, it should be in his own province, by his fellow bishops and according to ecclesiastical law. Lanfranc, however, along with the Archbishop of York and all the bishops and the barons, claimed that the bishop should plead and submit to the king's judgement in the king's court, as a baron.

William of Saint-Calais refused, but the king's court, composed of barons, bishops and royal servants, proceeded to judgement and the bishop's estates were **forfeit**. Under pressure, the bishop surrendered his castle and left the country. The Pope, Urban II, directed the king to restore the bishop and to send his accusers to Rome for lawful settlement of the case. Rufus ignored this. However, Saint-Calais returned to England in 1092 and made his peace with Rufus.

The trial of William of Saint-Calais illustrates the precariousness of the Anglo-Norman Church settlement. The customs of England and Normandy were against the bishop but his case was based upon canon law, the universal law of the Church. In the twelfth century this was to cause far greater difficulties between Church and state.

Rufus and the papacy

William II continued the anti-Gregorian policy his father had begun. After Gregory's death in 1085, the new pope, Victor III, ruled for a year and had no contact with England. His successor, Urban II, was not recognised by Rufus until 1095, and then on condition that papal legates could only enter England by royal consent.

KEY WORD

Forfeit To lose or be deprived of lands or offices or a privilege as a penalty for wrongdoing.

KEY EVIDENCE

From the trial of William of Saint-Calais, 1088

'"No further delay can be tolerated," said Lanfranc. "When judgement is pronounced in this court, it is necessary that in this court it should be either accepted or answered. You must therefore accept the court's verdict, or, in this place, show good reason for refusing to do so."

'The bishop replied: "Without doubt I appeal against this judgement, and I propose to sustain my appeal at Rome, both because it is my duty to do so, and because in that court justice and not violence prevails. And since from fear of the king not one of you dares to testify on my behalf, I call as my witness the written law of the Church, which assures me that I ought to go to Rome, and that the final verdict in this case ought to proceed from the Roman pontiff."'

WHY DID WILLIAM II FALL OUT WITH ARCHBISHOP ANSELM?

The catalyst for Rufus's recognition of Pope Urban II was the appointment of Anselm as archbishop of Canterbury. The archbishopric of Canterbury had been vacant since the death of Lanfranc in 1089. Early in 1093, Rufus fell seriously ill. Thinking that he was dying, he attempted to resolve the scandalous vacancy by appointing Anselm, Abbot of Bec. Anselm was a pupil of Lanfranc, a monk and a scholar of wide renown. He refused the offer. The king, thinking he would die and be punished by God for not appointing an archbishop, insisted; the bishops begged, and finally the staff was forced into Anselm's monkish hand and the ring pushed onto his finger. Then the king got better.

The academic monk and the red-haired, short-tempered son of the Conqueror were never going to get on. Anselm immediately requested the return of all the possessions of the archbishopric of Canterbury, that the king should trust all things spiritual to his counsel and that he should be allowed to recognise Urban II as the pope, and not Clement III. As abbot of Bec, Anselm had acknowledged Urban as pope, and as archbishop he could not change his mind. These issues arose periodically until 1094, when the king openly declared his loathing for the archbishop before setting off to Normandy for a year.

What was decided at the Council of Rockingham (1095)?

On the king's return from Normandy, Anselm again raised the issue of the pope. Without recognition of Urban, Anselm could not go to Rome to receive his **pallium**, and he could not hold councils or consecrate a bishop. In February 1095 Anselm put before an assembly of bishops and barons the question as to whether obedience to the pope was compatible with the loyalty he owed to the king. The bishops urged Anselm to accept the royal will, because they were men who owed their livings to the royal chapel and were administrators and not theologians. William of Saint-Calais even suggested that Anselm should be removed from his post. Nothing was resolved at the council after four days of debate.

Stalemate

The king, however, plotted to get rid of Anselm. He sent two chancery clerks on a secret mission to Urban, offering to recognise him as pope in return for the deposition of Anselm. The clerks would bring back a pallium, which Rufus could give to someone more amenable. This was carefully concealed from Anselm. The cunning plan backfired badly: the clerks returned with Cardinal Walter of Albano, who declared that no legates or papal letters were to be sent to England without the king's consent. This substantial privilege moved Rufus to proclaim Urban as the rightful pope. Confident of victory, he then demanded the removal of Anselm, but the Cardinal refused. Anselm was triumphant and received his pallium from the altar of his cathedral in May 1095.

The king was now stuck with an archbishop he openly disliked and whom he had obviously attempted to deceive; in trying to get rid of Anselm he had recognised the very pope Anselm wished him to recognise. Anselm had been humiliated but emerged ultimately victorious.

Two years later king and archbishop argued again. Anselm requested permission to go to Rome; Rufus refused. Finally, Anselm went anyway, in November 1097, and in doing so, forfeited his archbishopric. Anselm was received with great honours in Rome. Rufus was threatened with excommunication but Urban could not afford to carry out his threat. The situation between Rufus and Anselm was only resolved by Rufus's death in the New Forest in August 1100.

HOW DID THE MONASTERIES EXPAND UNDER THE NORMANS, 1066–1135?

The impact of the Norman Conquest on the Anglo-Saxon monasteries was massive. 'Devastation' and 'reform' are the two words that sum up what happened to the monasteries in the decades following 1066, followed by the total replacement of English abbots by foreign abbots and the rebuilding and expansion of new monasteries.

Devastation

The chroniclers talk of seizure of lands and treasure and high taxes, depredations confirmed in Domesday Book. The new sheriffs, most notoriously Urse of Worcester and

Tintern Abbey, founded in 1131 as the first Cistercian Abbey in Wales

Picot of Cambridge, took much land and treasure was shipped to Normandy. The 'Normanisation' of English monasteries was part of the colonisation process, along with the building of castles and the submission of the English boroughs (towns). The great example of this is to be found on the Welsh borders, at Brecon. Here, in 1093, after a great victory over the Welsh, a Norman warlord named Bernard de Neufmarché founded a dependent priory of the Conqueror's great abbey of Battle, as a similar statement of conquest.

Reform

Hand in hand with this process of Normanisation was the collaboration between English and Norman reformers in the monastic revival. They used long-dead English saints, such as Cuthbert at Durham and Edmund at Bury, to justify preserving the monks' lands and to attract pilgrims. Even though Latin gradually became the official language of the chronicles and histories, the new writers still wrote lives of English saints. At Peterborough, Canterbury and Worcester, the writing of *The Anglo-Saxon Chronicle* continued, still in the vernacular.

The most remarkable joint venture between English and Normans was the revival of monasteries in the north of England. A Norman knight, Reinfrid, and an English monk from Winchcombe, Ealdwin, were authorised by the great Ethelwig of Evesham to form a mission in the north following the devastation of the winter of 1069–70. The

Norman bishop of Durham, Walcher, gave them the church at Jarrow and Earl Waltheof gave them the church of Tynemouth. Many followers, French and English, soon joined Reinfrid, and Ealdwin and Walcher transferred the community to Durham.

Reform with the English monasteries found inspiration from abroad, particularly from Cluny, the source of so much papal reform in the second half of the eleventh century. Norman abbeys such as Jumièges and Fécamp had themselves been under the influence of Cluny and in turn they influenced English monasteries.

What happened to the Anglo-Saxon abbots?

Many of the greater abbots showed hostility to the new king. Harold Godwinsson's uncle, Aeflwig, abbot of the New Minster at Winchester, was killed at Hastings; Leofric of Peterborough, cousin to Edwin and Morcar, died of wounds sustained at Hastings. Abbots of Canterbury, Glastonbury, Tavistock and Winchester were all suspect in their loyalty to the new regime.

William I dealt with these men by removing them from office. Within six years all the above-mentioned abbots were gone, replaced in every case by men from Normandy. Of the twenty-one abbots present at the council of London in 1075, thirteen were English; only three of these remained in office in 1087.

The new Norman abbots brought with them family and friends. Lanfranc brought monks from Bec to Canterbury; new foundations at Shrewsbury, Chester, Brecon and Monmouth were colonised by monks from Sées, Bec, Battle and Brittany. On the whole, however, the influx of foreign monks was gradual and piecemeal.

New abbeys and monasteries, 1066–1135

As with cathedrals, the Normans built new monasteries, which stamped the imprint of the new regime firmly on the geopolitical landscape of Anglo-Norman England. The new landlords of England endowed Norman abbeys with land and wealth from English churches and founded new establishments in England. The Conqueror's example at Battle Abbey was followed by the earls of Chester and

Shrewsbury (Benedictine) and William de Warenne at Lewes (Cluniac).

The connection with Cluny as a source of inspiration for the reform of English monasticism continued well into the twelfth century. William II founded one monastery, at Bermondsey, and this was Cluniac; Henry I (1100–35) refounded the abbey of Reading and filled it with Cluniac monks from Lewes. Henry I funded the completion of the great **nave** at Cluny in 1132 and set up an annual contribution of 100 marks of silver. Henry I's nephew, Henry of Blois, was a monk at Cluny and became abbot of Glastonbury in 1126.

KEY WORD

Nave The long, rectangular part of a church, where the congregation sits.

Augustinians, Cistercians and Gilbertines

The number of Cluniac houses in England never rose above around thirty. But the job was done; reform bred reform, and the Augustinian canons, who set a stricter standard of life, were established in England in the 1090s at St Botolph (Colchester), St Mary (Huntingdon) and St Gregory (Canterbury). These foundations were soon followed by houses scattered around England, particularly in East Anglia and south-east England. The church of the priory at Carlisle became in 1133 the cathedral with a chapter of Augustinan canons.

The Cistercians had a more powerful impact on English monasticism. The monastery of Cîteaux in the duchy of Burgundy was founded in 1098 and given great popularity by St Bernard, who joined it in 1112. It was the constitution of an Englishman, Stephen Harding, the third abbot (1109–33), which gave the order its famous uniformity and austerity. The first Cistercian abbey in England was Waverley, Surrey (1129), but the most famous abbeys were in Yorkshire, at Rievaulx, Fountains and Kirkstall. These abbeys flourished and prospered, becoming great agricultural and economic enterprises, as well as political centres of power in twelfth-century England.

The single English order founded during this Norman period of monastic revivalism was the Gilbertine order, founded by Gilbert, priest of Sempringham. In 1131, Gilbert provided a building attached to his parish church for pious women. Lay sisters and brothers were added to do domestic and agricultural work, and canons to serve the community as priests, working on the model of the abbey of Fontrevault (Anjou, France). This revived the double monastery for men and women, but the Gilbertines remained an English order; the vast majority of their communities were in Lincolnshire, and they did not spread to the Continent.

CONCLUSION: A NEW CHURCH?

The Norman Conquest had a great impact on the English Church in the following ways:

- Virtually all the English bishops and abbots were Norman or French by 1100.
- Many English cathedrals were moved to new towns and built in the Romanesque, or Norman, style.
- Archdeacons became central figures in the administration of the bishoprics.
- Lanfranc asserted the primacy of Canterbury.
- Lanfranc's councils established the independence of ecclesiastical law courts.
- Both William I and William II resisted papal intervention in their Church affairs but avoided open conflict with the papacy.
- The Cluniac reforms found their greatest expression in England in the monastic revival following initial devastation, influencing other new orders to spread throughout the country.

SUMMARY QUESTIONS

1. Assess the importance of Lanfranc's career to the English Church.

2. How successful was the anti-Gregorian policy of William I and II?

3. Why and how did the monasteries expand in England, 1066–1135?

AS ASSESSMENT SECTION

SOURCE-BASED QUESTIONS IN THE STYLE OF AQA (THE NORMAN CONQUEST: BRITAIN, 1060–1087)

Source A:

From *The Anglo-Saxon Chronicle,* 1069.

He had castles built
And poor men hard oppressed.
The king was so very stark
And deprived his underlings of many a mark.

Source B:

From a writ, 1077, from William I to his barons.

Summon my sheriffs by my order and tell them from me that they must return to my bishoprics and abbacies all the demesne, and all the demesne-land which my bishops and abbots, either through carelessness or fear or greed, have given them out of the demesne of my bishoprics and abbacies.

Source C:

From a record of judgement given by William I, around 1086.

King William held a court at Laycock, a manor of William of Eu, and there decided a plea concerning the claims which William of Braose had made respecting the abbey of Holy Trinity. The trial lasted one Sunday morning until evening, and there were present with the king his sons and all his barons.

Source D:

Account of the Domesday Inquisition, by Florence of Worcester (1118).

King William caused all England to be surveyed: how much each of his barons possessed; and how many enfeoffed knights; and how many ploughs, villeins, animals and livestock, each one possessed in all his kingdom from the greatest to the least; and what dues each estate was able to render.

(a) Study Source D and use your own knowledge.
     What is meant by the phrase 'enfeoffed knights'?   *(3)*

How to answer this question
- Provide some explanation which answers the question.
- Refer to the source to back up what you are saying.

Style

Here is an example of the style you should use:

Domesday Book was commissioned by William I late in 1085 to ascertain who held what land and how much it was worth to him in taxation. 'Enfeoffed knights' were those who had been granted land by the barons (the tenants-in-chief) and usually held their land by military service.

> (b) Study Sources B and C. How valuable are these sources in helping our understanding of the nature of William the Conqueror's government?   (7)

How to answer this question

When answering a question about the value of a source you should try to avoid generalisation about the source and you should concentrate on more than just its content. You should ask yourself at least some of the following questions:

- What is the nature of the source?
- Who is the author of the source?
- What is the purpose of the source?
- Has the author deliberately distorted the evidence?
- What are the limitations of the source?

Style

To gain top marks you need to ensure that you cover both sources. Here is an example of the style you might use:

Source B is valuable in understanding the nature of William's government because it is a writ, which was a document formulated by the chancery, the king's writing office. The source reveals that the king was keen to restore law and order after the military occupation of the country. The source is, however, limited in that it only deals with one particular event during the period. Source C is also valuable because it informs us that the king was actively involved with legal disputes, with his family and his barons acting as chief advisors. Source C is limited in that this is only one law case where the king was present, and he may not have been present at all law cases.

> (c) Study Sources A, B, C and D and use your own knowledge.
> How far do you agree with Source A that William I had 'poor men hard oppressed' during his government of England?   (15)

How to answer this question

You are asked to give an analytical answer to this question. The main focus of your answer must be on how William I and the Normans treated the conquered English people and with what effect on Anglo-Saxon society. To be awarded top marks you need to do the following:

- Argue using the sources and your own knowledge.

- Show that you can sustain a judgement throughout the question.
- Show that you understand the context of the judgement made by *The Anglo-Saxon Chronicle*.
- Show that you understand that although the nature of the Conquest was military, William continued to use much of the machinery of Anglo-Saxon government in order to govern effectively.

Plan

Before you start an answer to this question it is important that you write a plan. Your plan should include the main points of argument or analysis that you are going to use in your answer.

Structure

To reach the highest level you need to include the following:

- Introduction, where you briefly explain your main points.
- Argument, where you discuss the brutal and oppressive impact of the Conquest on the English.
- At some stage, your essay will include a 'however' paragraph, where you show the importance of the continuity and legal methods used by William to govern.

Information to use

The question asks you to use your own knowledge and the sources. The following may be used from the sources:

- Source A shows that castles and taxes oppressed the people.
- Source B shows that the sheriffs were out of control in taking land from the Church but that the king was attempting to rectify this.
- Source C shows that the king was keen to use laws to impose order in the country.
- Source D shows that the king wanted to record his new lands and landholders in order to ascertain what money his government would receive.

From your own knowledge you should include the following:

- To a certain extent the English were treated harshly.
- The evidence for this is to be found in castle-building, high taxation, the brutal suppression of rebellions and the replacement of English lords with Norman knights.
- However, William I was eager to prove that he was the legal heir to the throne and he wanted to use Anglo-Saxon laws and customs as much as possible to govern peacefully and without difficulty.
- The evidence for this is found in the use of writs, shires, sheriffs and the making of Domesday Book.

For example, your answer might read as follows:

The views of the Anglo-Saxon Chronicle are valuable because they are contemporary and were written by educated men who received relevant information in the monasteries of York, Canterbury and Peterborough, where they were compiled. However, they were written by Anglo-Saxon monks who had seen the Anglo-Saxon people suffer a great deal under the Normans and so might exaggerate the harsh impact of the

Norman government. The other sources all show to some extent the lengths William went to in order to preserve existing laws and customs. These included the use of the writ, the sheriffs and the shire, all Anglo-Saxon in origin.

EDEXCEL COURSEWORK, UNIT 3C

Your coursework assignments will be divided into two parts:

Part A is based on a response to sources. You will be asked to interpret and evaluate sources in the same manner as Unit 1. There will be 10 marks awarded for this question and a word limit of 500 words. Here is an example of the style of questions asked in Part A:

- How far do the sources support the view in Source A that between the years 1066–1075 England was not just conquered but colonised?

Part B will consist of a question which will focus on the causes/consequences of a major event or development. You will be expected to do the following:

- Write in an analytical fashion in response to the question.
- Show an understanding of the relationship between causes/consequences.
- Where relevant, you should refer to the appropriate views of historians.

Here is an example of the style of questioning in Part B of the coursework:

- To what extent did the Norman Conquest bring to an end Anglo-Saxon government and cause a radical change in society?

Before you start writing your coursework, here are a few tips.

- Do not leave your coursework assignment to the last minute.
- Use your teacher for advice.
- Plan your coursework thoroughly before you start writing.
- Make sure that your written style is concise and to the point.
- Do not exceed the word limit of the coursework.

A2 SECTION: ENGLAND, 1100–1228

INTRODUCTION

The focus of this section is change over a period of time. The main developments and turning points of the period will be covered so that the reader can develop a broad overview of the period and a **synoptic** understanding. This means that the key issues, themes and concepts can be linked and compared.

Charismatic kingship and bureaucracy

The key issues and themes will include how central and local government became increasingly sophisticated and powerful as the Exchequer and justiciars and royal law courts emerged. At the heart lies the character of the kings and how they dealt with new challenges within government. 'Charismatic kingship' – that is, the powerful personalities of the kings – found itself at odds sometimes with the new bureaucratic and legalistic kingship of the twelfth century. The most successful kings were those who used their charisma to harness and control bureaucracy. They included Henry I, Henry II and Richard I, who were able to combine physical presence, brute force and military skill with diplomatic intelligence. The kings with the least charisma who failed to deal with events include Stephen and John, who were bold enough at times to seize the initiative but lacked vision and determination. Both Stephen and John were, to an extent, overwhelmed by emerging social forces not of their own making.

The changing society

Outside the political world, England in the twelfth century underwent change and development. Towns sprang up, forests were cleared, the population doubled and the economy became more attuned towards cash and credit. Cathedrals, monasteries and universities educated a new class of bureaucrats. Laws became standardised and government finances more strictly regulated. The aristocracy became educated and increasingly aware of their legal position and rights from the king.

The making of a nation state

The accession in 1154 of a king of England who came from the centre of France (Henry II), linked England to large parts of France. The conquest of Wales continued; Ireland was invaded and partly settled by Anglo-Norman lords. Scotland was subdued but never quite conquered. The loss of the continental territories forced the monarchy into a tight corner with the baronage, so that the unwritten contract between king and subjects became a

KEY TERM

Synoptic (from Greek *sun* 'together' and *opsis* 'seeing') A way of looking at a subject that draws together the different elements, for example the religious, political and economic aspects of a king's policy.

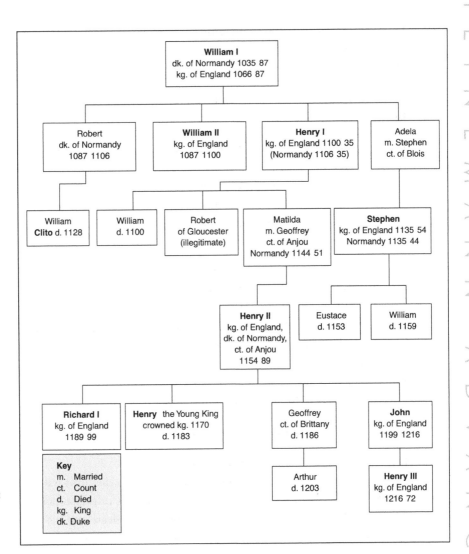

The kings of England, 1066–1216

Key
m. Married
ct. Count
d. Died
kg. King
dk. Duke

matter for open debate and future law. England, already a sophisticated Anglo-Norman state by 1100, was set on the path to representative government and, perhaps, the beginning of a nation state.

CHRONOLOGICAL OVERVIEW

1100   Accession of Henry I, youngest son of William I.
Great developments in finance, justice and administration. A period of peace and prosperity in England.

1106   Defeat of Henry's brother Duke Robert of Normandy unites England and Normandy until 1135.

1110   First written reference to the Exchequer.
Fundamental change in the financial organisation of central government instigated by Henry I and his bureaucrats.

1121 Henry's only son and heir drowned.

A disaster for Henry and the Norman dynasty; this sowed the seeds of civil war.

1128 Oath sworn by barons to recognise Henry's daughter Matilda as his heir.

1135 Death of Henry I; seizure of the crown by his nephew, Stephen of Blois.

A reign dominated by intermittent warfare between the king and his cousin Matilda when certain barons were able to exercise over-mighty powers due to Stephen's weakness and disputed succession and as a reaction to the constraints of Henry I.

1154 Death of Stephen; unchallenged accession (the first since Edward the Confessor in 1042) of Henry II, son of Matilda, great-grandson of William I.

A new dynasty: the Plantagenets. A reign of tremendous energy and achievement in the spheres of justice, administration and finance, as Henry II took up what his grandfather, Henry I, had left in 1135. England became one of many dominions with an absentee king; government had to become more autonomous.

1170 Murder of Thomas Becket, Archbishop of Canterbury.

1189 Death of Henry II; accession of Richard I.

The finances and royal administration were tested to the limit with Richard's long absence on the Third Crusade and his imprisonment. The costs of the crusade, the ransom for the king's release and his castle-building to restore power after his return, were huge for England.

1199 Unexpected and premature death of Richard; accession of John, youngest son of Henry II.

John's accession was challenged by his nephew, who disappeared in John's custody.

1204 The loss of Normandy and the fall of the Angevin 'empire'.

John's abduction of Isabella of Angoulême led to war and ultimately the collapse of his continental possessions.

1215 Magna Carta

John's attempts to persuade an uninterested baronage to reconquer Normandy and his conflict with the papacy led to civil war and the making of the Magna Carta. Magna Carta signalled the beginning of the 'common counsel of the realm' as a political concept.

1216   Death of John: accession of Henry III, his nine-year-old son

A regency council was set up and the civil war ended in 1219.

KEY QUESTIONS

The A2 section of the book will look at the following questions:

1. How did the relationship between the Crown and the nobility change in the period 1100–1216?

2. To what extent was the personality of the monarch a key factor in government?

3. How effective were changes made in administration and justice from 1100 to 1216?

4. How accurate is the assessment of Stephen's reign as an 'anarchy'?

5. Who won and who lost the dispute between Henry II and Thomas Becket?

6. Why did John lose Normandy?

7. How significant was the Magna Carta?

8. To what extent did the Papacy increase its power over the English Crown in the period 1100–1228?

SECTION 1

The reign of Henry I

INTRODUCTION

The crossbow bolt that killed William Rufus in 1100 was a bolt from the blue for the fortunes of the youngest surviving son of the Conqueror. In the absence of his brother, Duke Robert of Normandy, on the First Crusade, Henry had himself crowned and ruled England for thirty-five years; in 1106 he defeated his elder brother in battle, imprisoned him for life (twenty-eight years) and governed Normandy. Henry I was a ruthless, intelligent and charming king, possessed of qualities both his brothers – Rufus harsh and short-tempered, Robert inept and short-sighted – lacked. Henry I's reign witnessed what has been called an explosion of literacy in England; some 400 written acts of his father's reign survive, but 2000 survive from his reign. Distinct offices of government developed under his government: the Church flourished as it never had under Rufus, and England and Normandy were at peace. But if a medieval king's reign is to be measured in the security he leaves his heir, then Henry I failed. His only legitimate son (he had around twenty illegitimate children) drowned in 1120. Henry was forced to push his wilful daughter onto the reluctant barons who, taxed and harassed by the king, repaid him by allowing the king's nephew, Stephen, to seize the throne in 1135. Stephen's ineptitude and the divisions between the barons plunged Henry I's peaceful and prosperous England into civil war.

A *COUP D'ÉTAT* AND ANOTHER DISPUTED SUCCESSION

Henry's speedy coronation sparked another succession crisis. Henry gained power with the help of a few select allies but immediately had difficulties holding onto power. The problem was the same as in 1088, when Rufus became king of England (although by the order of his dying father); some thought that England and Normandy should remain united and that Duke Robert, the eldest son of the Conqueror, should rule both. This reflects the fact that, as yet, there was no hard-and-fast rule of succession. The key point is that Henry did not usurp his brother; being the eldest son of the previous king did not ensure succession, as Robert had already been passed over by Rufus. Certainly Henry's claim to the throne was debatable and caused him grave difficulties in the first year of his reign. The major problem was not that he was a younger son but that most of the Anglo-Norman barons were already homage-bound to Robert, due to an agreement made between Robert and Rufus, excluding Henry from succeeding to Normandy and England.

KEY EVIDENCE

The death of William Rufus, from 'The Deeds of the Kings of the English' by William of Malmesbury (1125) 'The sun was now setting, and the king drawing his bow let fly an arrow which slightly wounded a stag which passed before him. He ran in pursuit, keeping his gaze rigidly fixed on the quarry, and holding up his hand to shield his eyes from the sun's rays. At this instant Walter [Tirel] forming in his mind a project which seemed fine to him, tried to transfix another stag which by chance came near to him while the king's attention was otherwise occupied. And thus it was that ... he pierced the king's breast with a fatal arrow. When the king received the wound, he said not a word, but breaking off the shaft of the arrow where it stuck out of his body, he fell upon the ground and thus made more speedy his own death.'

Henry held onto power in the following ways:

- He acted fast, while his brother Robert was still travelling back from the Holy Land.
- Several eminent court nobles supported him, including the Count of Meulan and Earl Henry of Warwick.
- The Bishop of London agreed to crown him when Henry agreed to recall the exiled Archbishop Anselm, which he did.
- On the day of his coronation, Henry issued promises of good government, pardoning all debts owed to his dead brother and reforming all the bad practices Rufus was accused of. This was sent out to all the shire courts, abbeys and churches.
- The hated and oppressive Ranulf Flambard, a symbol of Rufus's government, was hunted down and thrown into the Tower of London.
- To seal his public relations with the English people even further, the thirty-four-year-old king married Edith, the Anglo-Saxon sister of King Edgar of Scotland and niece of Edgar Atheling. (She renamed herself Matilda, to keep the Anglo-Norman aristocracy happy.) Their children would therefore be descendants of the Old English royal House of Wessex. They married in November 1100.

1106: THE ENGLISH CONQUEST OF NORMANDY

Duke Robert arrived back in Normandy in September 1100. He was annoyed that Henry had taken the throne but did nothing. However, after Flambard escaped from the Tower to Normandy early in February 1101, Flambard encouraged the duke to prepare an invasion fleet.

When Robert began his preparations, Henry began to lose the support of the great nobility in England, including Count William of Mortain, nephew of the Conqueror, William de Warenne, Earl of Surrey, Robert de Bellême, Earl of Shrewsbury and Ivo de Grandmesnil, Lord of Leicester. These were some of the most powerful men in England. The death of Hugh, Earl of Chester, a supporter of Henry, did not help.

In July 1101, Duke Robert took an invasion fleet to England and landed at Portsmouth. Henry was in a far worse position than Harold Godwinsson had been in 1066. He met his brother at Alton, in Hampshire, but the two armies showed no inclination to fight. Archbishop Anselm led the negotiations and Robert accepted £2000 a year to renounce his claim to the throne. The duke returned to Normandy in September.

Henry was not as amiable as his brother Robert. He spent the next five years neutralising his enemies of 1101 and building up new allies. He won over William de Warenne by 1105, and hounded out William of Mortain and Ivo of Grandmesnil. He also outwitted and forced Robert de Bellême to leave

England in 1102, in what was the last baronial rebellion in England for the next thirty-six years.

Henry visited Normandy in 1104 and 1105 with a great show of wealth and power, determined to demonstrate to the Norman nobility and Church that he could be a better ruler of the duchy. Robert realised the deadly game his younger brother was playing and visited England early in 1106 to negotiate, but Henry refused to withdraw from the duchy and took an army there in the spring of 1106. He burned Bayeux and camped at Caen; Robert camped at Falaise, their father's birthplace. Henry then marched out to the castle of Tinchebray and there the two brothers fought a battle that decided the fate of the Anglo-Norman realm for the next thirty years.

Many were appalled at the sight of the sons of the Conqueror fighting over the Anglo-Norman power bloc their father had created almost exactly forty years earlier. But attempts by churchmen to restore peace failed.

The Battle of Tinchebray, 1106

The battle lasted only an hour and was fought with both armies predominantly on foot. However, the issue was resolved by Henry's use of a small but decisive force of cavalry as the two armies became locked in mortal combat. The duke's army panicked and ran; the duke and his leaders were captured. Duke Robert was placed in honourable captivity in Normandy, Wiltshire and Cardiff for the rest of his life; he died, aged eighty-two, in 1134. Henry never claimed to be duke of Normandy (government records still call Robert that in 1130) but he claimed to govern the duchy in the light of his brother's incompetence.

CONTRACTUAL KINGSHIP: A NEW MONARCHY?

The struggle between Henry and Robert had significance for Henry's governance of England in several ways. In return for baronial and ecclesiastical support Henry had to make promises. At his coronation he swore an oath, which for the first time became a 'charter of liberties' as opposed to the vague promises traditionally made by English kings since the tenth century. This was expressed in writing for the first time and was also issued by Stephen and Henry II. Later generations evoked it as a guarantee of the rights of free Englishmen and women against the crown, most importantly when it was cited as a precedent and model for Magna Carta.

There was no actual 'law of King Edward', but this phrase was taken to summarise the entire Anglo-Saxon past and to emphasise its continuity into the Anglo-Norman period. Furthermore, in the charter, Henry claimed that the 'common counsel' of the barons had crowned him. This established the principle, in writing, that the king governed with the support of his barons, not alone.

KEY EVIDENCE

Extract from the 'Coronation Charter' of Henry I (1100)
'I abolish all the evil customs by which the kingdom of England has been unjustly suppressed ... I restore to you the law of King Edward [the Confessor] together with such emendations to it as my father made with the counsel of his barons.'

The king's personality

Although this charter may have set a new precedent, it was chiefly concerned with gaining the support of the nobility and the Church and affirming their rights. These were concerns that any new king had. Much of it had to do with existing customs and traditions. What was very different about Henry's kingship was the man himself: his intellect, charm, ruthlessness, vigour and preference for diplomacy made him very different from his brutish, impatient and warlike brother. A childhood spent as a third son with little or no expectation of an inheritance, followed by thirteen years of dependence on his brothers, punctuated by humiliation, had nurtured a man of supreme patience with an eye for detail that set him apart from his boastful, blustering and inept brothers. Henry brought reconciliation between Crown and Church, peace within England and a measure of stability between England and Normandy. Henry's thirst for control, his energy and prodigious memory inspired some vital fundamental reforms and innovations within the Anglo-Norman government.

The royal household

Under Henry I the royal household underwent change. He did not imitate his father's trend for great ceremonial crown-wearing occasions; he had, after all, been born 'in the purple' (that is, when his father was king of England), and since the Conquest of England was well established by 1100 he did not have the need to publicise his new kingship to the people that William I had. Furthermore, Henry's total lack of expectations as the younger son without an inheritance remained with him in the sense that he was content to do without lavish display. His favourite residence was at Woodstock, Oxfordshire, which did not have a church or any facilities for a major ceremonial event.

Under Henry a 'constitution' or set of rules for the household was drawn up, with allowances for authorised officers and departments. This constitution was written soon after Henry's death in 1135 and illustrates just how well organised and institutionalised the royal household had become; the highest-paid official was the Chancellor, with 5 shillings a day, the lowest was the leader of the bloodhounds, with a penny a day. Chaplains, stewards, constables, chamberlains, butlers, marshals, dispensers (of food and wine), keepers of the cups, fruiterers, cooks, fire-stokers, horn-blowers and huntsmen all had their place in the household and their salary.

The king's route around England was posted in advance so that he could travel freely without having to remain in one place – this would require great expense and organisation. The king used his increasing wealth to build up a larger military section of the household, which became an élite force that formed the core of his army at Tinchebray. Young aristocrats from

Wales, France and Germany were all attracted to the household to learn the art of warfare under Henry I, so great did its reputation become.

'MEN RAISED FROM THE DUST': FINANCE, JUSTICE AND THE BUREAUCRATS

Some time between 1107 and 1108, during the time the king was back in England, Henry, Bishop Roger of Salisbury and Count Robert of Meulan devised between them the idea of the central government accounting office. The king had been taxing his subjects hard since 1100 to pay for his campaign against Robert and a number of thorough surveys into the financial obligations of some counties were conducted after 1107. Henry was not new to extracting large sums of cash from his people; England was wealthy and the mechanisms for collecting the money had been in place since the late tenth century. What *was* new, however, was the centralisation of these financial services and the bureaucracy that went with it.

The Exchequer

The first written reference to the new system was in 1110. This was the Exchequer, so called because of the chequered cloth used as a calculating device in accounting sessions. An abacus was also used, which meant that the sheriffs, who were probably illiterate, could see what was going on. Twice a year, at Easter and Michaelmas (29 September) a team of government officials, known as 'barons of the Exchequer' met with the local officials to collect the dues owed to the king, issue receipts and compile a roll of national income and expenditure.

Before the Exchequer was set up, a system of tallies existed where split hazel sticks were used as receipts for cash. Abacuses were known to have existed in William II's reign and came from Lorraine to England and Normandy. Accounts were gathered at Winchester. Fiscal records were not new either, but the twice-yearly meetings of the Exchequer court session, chaired usually by Bishop Roger of Salisbury, revolutionised the nature of English government. The records, or rolls – later known as 'pipe rolls' because they were stored in pipe-like tubes – were compiled every Michaelmas. They centralised English finances and gave the bureaucrats a new identity. The earliest surviving pipe roll is for the year 1130.

The royal income

The 1130 pipe roll of Henry I shows that the annual royal income amounted to up to £30,000 – more than his father the Conqueror, at £20,000. Henry's problem was the debasement of the currency because of the shortage of silver resulting from expenditure on Normandy. In 1124 the king ordered Roger of Salisbury to have all moneyers (those in charge of coin-making) castrated and deprived of their right hands if they were found guilty of replacing silver in the coinage with cheaper metals. In 1126 he revised the taxation owed by

From the 'Establishment of the King's Household' (1136) 'William Mauduit [chamberlain of the Exchequer] shall have fourteen pence a day and shall live always in the king's household and he shall have 1 fat wax candle and 12 pieces of candle, and 3 packhorses with their allowance.'

Writ of Henry I (between 1100 and May 1118) 'Henry, king of the English, to Roger, bishop of Salisbury, and to the barons of the Exchequer [*baronibus scaccarii*] greeting. Know that I have ratified the gift which Queen Matilda, my wife, gave and granted to the canons of Holy Trinity, London, to wit 25 pounds "blanch" which she gave them from the "farm" of the city of Exeter. And I order you so as to constrain the sheriff that he gives it to them, as you would do this out of my own "farm."'

the county farms and by 1129–30 the sheriffs had to pay extra on top of these taxes. That year two of the king's officials took over eleven shires and offered an extra payment of 1000 marks, which they met in full. Sheriffs under Henry I certainly had less opportunity than before to enrich themselves.

Roger of Salisbury: bishop, chancellor and justiciar

Roger, Bishop of Salisbury, was a key figure in these administrative changes. He rose from obscurity in Avranches, Normandy, to become chancellor under Henry I and Bishop of Salisbury in 1102. Soon after 1107 he became justiciar. The post of justiciar had its precedent in the careers of other great administrative churchmen such as Lanfranc and Ranulf Flambard, but what was different was the huge increase of business under Henry I.

Roger also founded a dynasty of bureaucrats; his son, Roger, became chancellor under Stephen; his nephew, Nigel, Bishop of Ely, Nigel's son, Richard FitzNeal, Bishop of London and Richard's kinsman, William of Ely, all became royal treasurers in turn. Another nephew of Roger's was Alexander, who became bishop of Lincoln. Roger was so powerful under Henry that he was considered second only to the king, but under Stephen he and his family fell from power dramatically. Roger's career perhaps represents what one contemporary chronicler, Orderic Vitalis, described as 'men raised from the dust'.

Royal justice

As well as being credited with raising men 'from the dust', Henry I was also nicknamed 'the Lion of Justice', because of the important procedural developments in royal and criminal justice during the period 1100–35 and his firm application of the law's penalties. Roger of Salisbury, as justiciar, held his court at the Exchequer with justices from the whole realm of England, a group of around six bishops and barons who were acquiring the authority of a regular bench of justices. They heard every type of case in the king's court, particularly disputes over land, the 'common pleas'. Roger sent these colleagues to perambulate the shires, to hear cases. They were thus itinerant and their movements were known as general 'eyres'. On their eyres, the justices heard all pleas of the Crown, forest law, and royal rights.

In 1108 Henry increased the penalties for various offences, making theft and robbery capital crimes and decreeing that false moneyers should be punished by blinding and castration. The king was equally firm in his own household. Under his brother's reign, the arrival of the royal household in the region brought terror and violence, robbing the locals of their food and drink and assaulting the women. Henry I instituted a penalty of blinding and castration for any of his courtiers found guilty of plunder, extortion or rape.

Royal justice was financially beneficial to the king, hence the position of Roger as both justiciar and chief baron of the Exchequer. The itinerant justices gathered the rents of the royal estates and fined those who had failed in their duties. £11,000 came from profits of justice and feudal incidents (such one-off payments, inheritance taxes).

Traditional English laws

Henry also looked back as well as forward. Henry's coronation charter illustrates how interested he was in restoring and maintaining Old English laws and customs. Murder fines, for example, were to be assessed justly, according to the 'law of King Edward'.

Local justice

The sheriffs, Anglo-Saxon in origin, remained at the heart of local justice. Local courts, however, had been subject to serious abuses in the decades preceding Henry I. Ranulf Flambard had been granted authority over the sheriffs by William Rufus and used this authority to enrich himself and the king. Also during the reign of William Rufus, probably at Flambard's suggestion, local justices had been appointed in the shires. Their duties included bringing criminals to justice and prosecuting them in the local public courts. Also at this time archdeacons and rural deans became active as prosecutors in ecclesiastical courts.

All this activity at court and in the provinces resulted in great compilations of the old laws of England under Cnut, Edward the Confessor and William I as well as new laws of Henry I.

Local government

Royal government in the provinces still depended very much on the sheriffs. A strong king was concerned that the sheriffs did not become too powerful and Henry I replaced sheriffs when he saw fit: a sheriff was appointed by the king and could be removed by the king – his office was not a fief. Old families who remained loyal and efficient kept their offices, but new men of high and low social status became established. The shire and hundred courts were the hub of local government. A charter in the first decade of Henry's reign illustrates how keen the king was to retain control over one of his more notorious sheriffs, Urse of Abbetot, and to ensure that those courts retained the traditions they had under Edward the Confessor:

Feudal obligations

In his coronation charter of 1100, Henry I was keen to redress the problems of abuses his brother had inflicted upon his aristocracy regarding their feudal rights and obligations. He promised to assess only just and lawful **reliefs** on inheritances, not arbitrary sums as his brother had done; this stabilised

KEY EVIDENCE

Extract from the pipe roll of Henry I (1130) 'Miles of Gloucester [the Sheriff] accounts for 80 pounds and 14 pence "blanch" for the old "farm" of the shire. He has paid this in the Treasury. And he is quit [free of debt].

KEY EVIDENCE

From the 'Laws of Henry I' 'The judges for the king are the barons of the shire who hold free lands therein. Through them are to be judged the causes of individuals by means of alternate pleadings. But villeins and cottars and farthingmen and those who are base-born and without property are not to be numbered among the judges of the law.'

KEY WORD

Relief An inheritance tax, paid when an heir entered into his inheritance, paid by tenants-in-chief to the king and by tenants to their lords.

aristocratic inheritance by assuring families that their lands would pass to their heirs on payment of a reasonable relief to the king.

The new king also promised something new: he granted for the first time to those who rendered knights service in return for their land, freedom from payment of all gelds and obligations on their estates, so that they could equip themselves with horses, arms and armour.

Not all promises made in 1100 were kept, however. In 1100 the king vowed not to give a widow in marriage without her consent but in 1130, as the pipe roll shows, he fined Countess Lucy of Chester a substantial sum for the privilege of not having to remarry for five years.

Feudal obligation worked both ways. The barons and knights held their land in return for military service organised in quotas, something that had begun in the reign of William I but was quickly becoming very different in practice. Military service was being commuted to money payment before the reign of Henry I. This was called 'scutage' or shield-money, fixed at a pound on the knight's fee. A further complication was the practice of 'subinfeudation', that is, the subdividing of estates, which broke up the knight's fees and therefore led to the disintegration of the knights' service actually owed. It was far easier for the lord to collect a money rent from each of the fractional fees to pay an overall sum to the tenant-in-chief or the king.

WALES AND SCOTLAND

Wales

Under William II, the Norman incursions into Wales continued. By 1100, the eastern and southern parts of Wales were occupied by Norman lordships at Pembroke, Glamorgan and Brecon. Whilst the Normans were largely successful in the south, large parts of Wales, including Gwynedd (north) and Powys (centre) remained under the control of the various Welsh princes. The rising and falling fortunes of Anglo-Norman and Welsh aristocratic families determined the pattern of settlement throughout the twelfth century.

Henry I intervened often in Welsh affairs, launching large-scale invasions in 1114 and 1121, and making and breaking alliances and families. He dispossessed the Montgomery family, who were earls of Shrewsbury, and made his illegitimate son Robert earl of Gloucester in 1122 and lord of Glamorgan, and thus one of the dominant political powers of southern Wales.

Scotland

Relations with Scotland were far more peaceful under Henry I. William I had brutally subdued the north of England and invaded Scotland in 1072 when he received King Malcolm's submission. In 1091 his son William

Rufus took an army into Scotland and again received Malcolm's submission. But after Malcolm's death in 1093, peace predominated between England and Scotland until 1136. Malcolm's son David was king of Scotland from 1124 to 1153; he was also earl of Northampton and a favourite of Henry I, who had married his sister. David was an Anglo-Scottish nobleman long before he became ruler of Scotland.

DYNASTIC DOOM: THE WHITE SHIP DISASTER AND EUROPEAN ALLIANCES

For all but the first two years of the thirty-five-year reign of Henry I, England was at peace; for twenty-seven of his twenty-nine years in Normandy there was peace in the duchy. This was achieved first by the capture and life-imprisonment of Duke Robert in 1106, but also by Henry's indefatigable efforts in forming diplomatic alliances with the neighbouring regions of Maine and Anjou and peace treaties with the king of France in 1113 and 1120.

Disaster struck, however, in November 1120 when the king's only legitimate son, William, drowned off the coast of northern France, near Barfleur. November was not necessarily a dangerous time to cross the Channel, and the sea was calm that evening, although there was no moon. The king's son was with his half-brother and sister and many younger members of the nobility. Apparently they urged the captain to race the king's ship and promised extra rations of wine; by all accounts, both crew and passengers were drunk. As the ship cleared the harbour and turned north to Southampton, the captain misjudged the position of the reef known as the Raz de Barfleur, which stove in the bottom of the ship. The ship capsized and only one man out of the 300 passengers survived the freezing night.

The death of the heir to the throne was a personal and national catastrophe. The young man was of age and had made a good name for himself; his mother was of the Old English royal line and represented the union between Norman and Saxon. The English aristocracy gave him their support; the monks approved of the ancient lineage. No one dared to tell the king on the first day back in England, and when Count Theobald of Blois had a young boy throw himself at the king's feet and tell him of the disaster, Henry fell to the ground, overcome with anguish. He had lost two sons, a daughter, his only heir to the kingdom and his peace alliances were shattered.

Henry's women

It has to be one of the great ironies of Henry's personal life that of all the children he fathered – more than any other king of England (two legitimate children, eight illegitimate sons, eleven or more illegitimate daughters are known) – he had only one legitimate son and heir who died young. Henry

KEY EVIDENCE

The sinking of the White Ship, from 'The Deeds of the Kings of the English' by William of Malmesbury (1125)

'Wherefore these rash youths, who were flown with wine, launched their vessel from the shore although it was now dark. She flew swifter than an arrow, sweeping the rippling surface of the deep, but the carelessness of her drunken crew drove her onto a rock, which rose above the waves not far from the shore. All in consternation rushed on deck, and with loud cries got ready their boat-hooks in an endeavour to force the vessel off, but fate was against them and brought to naught their efforts.'

was a father long before he succeeded to the throne; during the reign of his brother Rufus he fathered several children, all with English women.

Henry's Anglophilia was well known by the time he took as his wife Edith, daughter of Malcolm III of Scotland and niece of Edgar Atheling. At court, the French nobility mocked the royal couple as 'Godric and Godgifu'. But the support of the English landowners in 1100 and 1106 was crucial; he let the ageing Edgar Atheling retire with grace after his capture at Tinchebray (and a lifetime of being on the wrong side); three of Edith's other brothers, Edmund, Alexander, and David, were successively kings of Scotland during Henry's reign. His marriage to Edith provided a solid internal power-base; furthermore, the woman herself was highly educated, saintly, and took an active interest in government, encouraging the poets, musicians and scholars who flocked to Henry's humane court following the end of his brutal brother's court.

Marriage alliances

Henry ensured that his illegitimate offspring were cared for and educated. Henry's eldest natural son, Robert, became earl of Gloucester, chief supporter of his half-sister, Matilda, in the wars against Stephen. They provided useful political marriage alliances. The natural daughter who died on the White Ship, Matilda, was married to the powerful Count of Perche, Rotrou; the natural son who drowned, Richard, was Lord of Breteuil in his wife's name, a vast Norman lordship. All in all, Henry arranged the marriages of eight or nine of his natural daughters to princes or great nobles (including Alexander, king of the Scots and Conan, Duke of Brittany), all of whom ruled lands of strategic importance to him.

The king reserved the greatest marriage alliances, however, for his legitimate children. In 1119, after six years of negotiations, Prince William had married Matilda, daughter of the powerful Count Fulk of Anjou. The girl's **dowry** included the overlordship of the county of Maine and a string of important border castles. This was a keystone in Henry's policy of securing the Normandy frontiers and of acquiring allies against the perennial enemy, the king of France. In 1109 Henry's legitimate daughter, Matilda, had been **betrothed** to the German Emperor, Henry V; they married in 1114. This Anglo-German alliance gave Henry a powerful force to the east of France, something he drew upon in a war of 1124.

William 'Clito'

Henry I's careful planning and diplomacy were constantly under pressure from the greatest thorn in his side, which dominated Norman-French politics from 1106 to 1128. This thorn was the person of William 'Clito' (the Young), son of Duke Robert and grandson of the Conqueror who some saw, in the absence of his imprisoned father after Tinchebray, as the rightful duke of Normandy and king of England.

KEY WORDS

Dowry The dowry (or 'dot') was the sum of money or gift of land and possessions a girl's father offered to the groom.

Betrothal Medieval marriages amongst the upper classes were almost all arranged. The betrothal was more than just an engagement; it was marriage by proxy, that is, a ceremony that was as binding as the marriage itself. Betrothals could occur at any age but the marriage would not be consummated (sexually active) until the bride was usually fourteen or more, though twelve was not unusual.

William Clito was four years old when his father was captured at Tinchebray. Henry placed him in the custody of Duke Robert's illegitimate daughter and her husband, but in 1110 felt that the boy might become a focus of rebellion. Unusually for Henry, his agents bungled the capture of the boy and he was smuggled out of the duchy. After 1112 he found safety at the court of Baldwin of Flanders, son of the crusading count and friend of Duke Robert and was knighted by the Count in 1116 at the age of fourteen.

King Louis VI of France

By far the most powerful patron of William Clito was the king of France, Louis VI, of the ruling Capetian French dynasty. He became king in 1108 and immediately flexed his muscles. There were border confrontations and disputes between Louis and Henry until 1124, when some sort of lasting peace was established. The key bases of power were Normandy, Anjou, Blois-Chartres (where Henry's nephew, Count Theobald was ruler) and the Vexin, the Norman-French border on the Seine. During this period of time the rulers constantly manoeuvred back and forth, seeking advantages over one another.

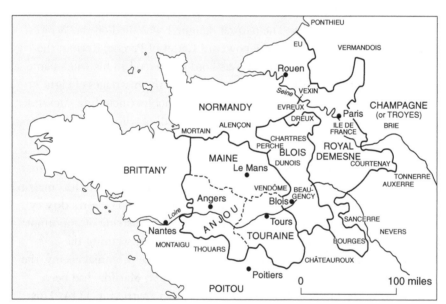

North-west France c.1120 showing the neighbouring lords of Henry I

Maintaining the peace

Several key events occurred in this time, which enabled Henry to maintain the peace on his Norman borders:

- In 1112 Robert de Bellême, Henry's old and most hated enemy, was arrested and sentenced to life imprisonment. He was a major threat to Henry on the Normandy-Anjou borders and a supporter of Clito and Louis.

- In 1113 Count Fulk of Anjou sought peace with Henry and betrothed his daughter to Prince William, Henry's son and heir.
- That year Louis of France also sought peace, recognising that Henry had successfully set up a line of buffer states around the fringes of Normandy, with allies including Count Robert of Meulan and Count William of Evreux, Henry's cousin.
- In 1118 the deaths of Robert of Meulan, William of Evreux and Edith, the Queen, shook Henry's regime badly; William of Evreux's heir, Amaury, was a loyal baron of King Louis.
- Very suddenly, internal order in Normandy collapsed; Count Baldwin of Flanders invaded in the name of Clito. Theobald of Blois-Chartres remained loyal and Henry married his son to the daughter of Fulk of Anjou to secure support.
- When Louis invaded in 1119 the two kings met in battle, at Brémule. This was a major defeat for Louis. William Clito escaped on foot. Baldwin of Flanders died of a head wound in a tournament soon afterwards.
- In October 1119 Henry put a seal on his triumph when Pope Calixtus II arrived in France. Louis and Clito protested at Henry's dispossession of Duke Robert; Calixtus, known as Guy of Vienne before his papal election, was a great-grandchild of Duke Richard II of Normandy, and so was Henry: the Pope urged peace between England and France. Prince William did homage for Normandy to Louis and Clito was ignored.

And so it was that Henry returned in triumph to England after four years abroad with all his court and his son and heir in November 1120, only to experience the disaster of the sinking of the White Ship.

THE ISSUE OF THE SUCCESSION

The death of Prince William was a dynastic disaster. For the third time since the Conquest, England and Normandy were faced with a succession dispute. Anglo-Norman court politics in the period 1125–35 were fixated on the succession to the king. There were several possibilities:

- Some now believed that Henry would have to recognise his nephew William Clito as king and duke of the Anglo-Norman realm. William Clito, a mature man in his mid-twenties, was still regarded by many as the proper heir to the throne; he was grandchild to the Conqueror and if the rule of primogeniture was followed, he had a better claim than Henry himself. He enjoyed widespread support and affection. Fulk of Anjou demanded his daughter back and with her, Maine; when Henry refused, Fulk joined a new pro-Clito alliance.
- Seeing that Henry was set against recognising Clito as his heir, his barons advised remarriage. Henry chose Adeliza of Louvain.
- Henry had other nephews: Count Theobald of Blois and his younger brother Stephen, sons of his sister Adela and grandsons of the Conqueror.

- Another possibility was Henry's first-born and favoured son, Robert, Earl of Gloucester. But Robert was illegitimate and no matter how highly regarded he was, he was a bastard; times had changed since his bastard grandfather, William the Conqueror had become first duke of Normandy and king of England.

A new marriage and false hopes

Once set upon a course of action, Henry did not waste time. In February 1121, aged fifty-three, the king married his teenage bride, Adeliza, daughter of Godfrey, Count of Louvain and Duke of Brabant. She was carefully chosen: she was a beautiful young woman (always a consideration for Henry), a descendant of Charlemagne whose father ruled lands strategically placed between Flanders and north-western Germany and who was a close associate of the Emperor Henry V, son-in-law of Henry I of England.

Unfortunately for Henry, they had no children. Adeliza went on to have sons and daughters with her second husband and Henry fathered a daughter with the teenage daughter of his late friend Robert of Meulan. The childless marriage only strengthened William Clito's party.

The last rebellion, 1123–24

It was a son of Robert of Meulan who in 1123 instigated the last Norman revolt against Henry. Waleran ruled the largest part of central Normandy and opened negotiations with Clito so that he could keep in with both sides. Henry's spies were in on the plotting from the start and he was able to track the rebels and foil their plans. But matters grew worse when Fulk of Anjou married another of his daughters to William Clito, promising Clito the county of Maine. Henry had planned this for his own son and now had to watch while the alliance ranged against him. The threats vanished, however, when Waleran was captured after a pitched battle between his troops and Henry's household men.

The oath to Matilda and marriage to Geoffrey of Anjou

The death of the Emperor Henry V in 1125 removed one possible contender to Henry I's throne. Emperor Henry's marriage to Matilda had been childless and the young woman returned to the court of her father, Henry I, in Normandy in 1126. Henry then set about making his daughter Matilda his successor. Henry did this in two ways:

- He arranged a marriage between Matilda and Geoffrey, son of Fulk, Count of Anjou. This continued his pro-Angevin policy.
- He held a ceremony at court where the barons and bishops of England took an oath to support Matilda's succession at his death.

Geoffrey and Matilda married in 1128 and one month later William Clito died of wounds sustained in the battle with Henry's men. Henry's succession took a turn for the better. Married life between Geoffrey (a teenager) and Matilda (in her late twenties) was not smooth and there are indications that Geoffrey expected to be crowned alongside Matilda on his father-in-law's death. In September 1131 the couple were reconciled, and a council at Northampton was asked to swear faith to Matilda as heir to her father – Geoffrey was not included. In March 1133 Matilda had a son, Henry, and it was the king who lifted his grandson from the font at his baptism and gave him his own name. Just over a year later, Matilda had a second son, Geoffrey, and the succession through Matilda seemed more assured.

CONCLUSION: A SURFEIT OF LAMPREYS AND A LEGACY OF CONFLICT

In November 1135 Henry became gravely ill and died in his hunting lodge in Normandy. He was of sound mind and body and his death was unexpected, even though he was in his sixty-eighth year. One chronicler tells us that the king ignored his doctor's orders and ate a dish of lampreys (eels); others simply state that he fell ill whilst hunting, confessed his sins and died, his bastard son Robert at his side. He left money to pay his household wages, orders that he should be buried at Reading and that his daughter should succeed to all lands on both sides of the Channel.

Henry I's achievements were great. He ensured thirty-five years of peace in England and re-united England with Normandy after 1106. He was then able to make far-reaching financial and legal reforms in government, which laid the foundations for change throughout the twelfth century. His failure to leave a male heir, however, was nearly the undoing of all his successes. When he died, his daughter was not at his side. Matilda was in a dispute with her father concerning some castles in Normandy. When the king's body arrived in England it was greeted by the new monarch and this was not Matilda but her cousin, Stephen of Blois, crowned in December 1135. As a result of this, everything Henry I had worked for was shattered into a thousand pieces, and England was plunged into uncertainty, dispute and division for the next nineteen years.

Was the reign of King Stephen a period of 'anarchy'?

INTRODUCTION

England faced another succession crisis in 1135; the fourth out of four successions since 1066. But Stephen moved so swiftly that no war or rebellion broke out in 1135. His rival was an unpopular woman, and it looked at first as if peace would prevail. But war broke out in 1139 and raged intermittently until 1147; it split the nation. England had been at peace since 1072, but now witnessed sieges and battles. The king was captured and ransomed. The Londoners rejected his rival. This chapter will look at how this situation came about and its consequences for law and order in England.

WHY WAS STEPHEN ABLE TO TAKE THE THRONE?

- The series of *coups d'état* since 1066 had prevented a sound procedure of succession from developing.
- All the chroniclers admit that Stephen was Henry I's favourite nephew. Henry enriched Stephen, granting him the county of Mortain in western Normandy and vast estates in England.
- Furthermore, Henry arranged for Stephen to marry Matilda, niece of the late Queen Matilda, which would have made their offspring descendants of the Old English ruling house, a fact that cannot have been lost on Henry.
- Stephen, like Henry when he took the throne in 1100, was in the right place at the right time, sailing immediately from Wissant (Boulogne) to England.
- Stephen was at liberty to move, unlike many of the barons at court, who were bound by a solemn oath to stay in Normandy until the king was buried properly.
- He gained the support of Roger of Salisbury, justiciar, Henry of Blois, Bishop of Winchester (his brother) and Archbishop William of Canterbury. These were some of the most powerful men in the kingdom, and all had resisted Matilda's succession in 1126 and the Angevin marriage alliance.
- They justified their decision by claiming that the oath was invalid because the king had imposed it on them; furthermore, one story came out that the king had released his nobles and bishops from the oaths as he lay dying.

KEY PERSON

Stephen of Blois Born around 1096, the younger son of Adèle, daughter of William the Conqueror. His father, Stephen, count of Blois, was killed fighting in the Holy Land in 1102. In 1113 Stephen went to England for the first time and spent the next twenty-two years in the court of his uncle, Henry I. He established himself as a capable soldier and his marriage to Matilda, daughter and heiress of the Count of Boulogne, placed him at the forefront of the Anglo-Norman magnates in terms of power and wealth. He was considered to be an honourable and pious man, and the obvious choice after Matilda.

KEY THEME

Anarchy Unlimited, widespread political and social chaos; the total breakdown of law and order and the complete failure of the routines of government.

- Stephen had the support of London, too. The Londoners, who had been harshly taxed by Henry, claimed their ancient right to choose the king in times of danger. Stephen was well-known in the city and was a patron of two churches, St Martin-le-Grand and Aldgate Priory. London, as we shall see, was crucial to the struggle between Stephen and Matilda.
- Matilda was a woman, and that made it very difficult for twelfth-century society to accept her as a ruler in her own right.
- This was compounded by the fact that Matilda was married to an Angevin, the traditional enemy of Normandy; thus the count of Anjou, in his wife's name, would be virtual ruler of England and Normandy.
- Matilda's position was further weakened by the fact that her father had not provided her with a landed power base in England or Normandy. She did not have control of a single castle – she was quarrelling with her father over this at the time of his death.

Stephen went to Winchester where he was given the keys to the treasury, and from there he was crowned on 22 December 1135. Ten days later he carried the coffin of his uncle at the royal funeral at Reading.

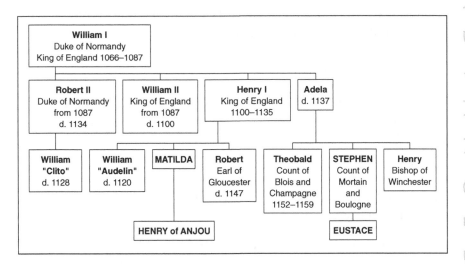

Stephen's genealogy

HOW DID STEPHEN SECURE HIS HOLD ON THE THRONE?

All that Matilda and Geoffrey accomplished on hearing of Stephen's triumph was the seizure of several border castles north of Maine. The majority of the Norman barons refused to accept them. However, Stephen needed to gain international recognition and to ensure that Matilda was well and truly out of the running. Much of this was due to the activities of Stephen's brother, Henry, Bishop of Winchester:

- Henry gathered testimonials from the bishops of England and Normandy, King Louis VI of France and Count Theobald of Blois (their elder brother).

- A high-powered embassy was sent to Pope Innocent II in Rome and persuaded him to accept Stephen's claims.
- The Pope sent a letter endorsing Stephen, which was circulated around England and Normandy.
- Stephen's advisors claimed that Stephen had quelled the potential breakdown of law and order following the death of King Henry (this was an exaggeration and was to backfire on Stephen when his own reign slipped into disorder).
- Stephen went north after Henry I's funeral and made his peace with King David of Scotland (his wife's uncle). David had recently occupied Cumberland and Northumberland. Stephen's impressive army funded from the vast treasury built up by Henry I sufficiently impressed David.
- Stephen held his Easter court at Westminster in 1136; his wife was crowned and a great banquet was held and gifts were given out; the barons swore oaths of allegiance to him.
- Stephen confirmed the liberties of the Church, granted pardons, and allowed barons to divide up their estates when they left several daughters as heirs.
- Stephen visited Normandy in March 1137; after meeting his brother the count of Blois, he met the king of France on the border, who recognised him as the king of England and accepted homage from Stephen's ten-year-old son Eustace for Normandy.

WHY DID STEPHEN LOSE THE SUPPORT OF EARL ROBERT?

The key to the security of the entire Anglo-Norman realm lay in Normandy; Stephen failed to appreciate this. He raised a large force to crush the Angevins but his army, containing large numbers of Flemish mercenaries, fell out with the Normans, and he achieved only a three-year truce. When Stephen left for England, never to return again to Normandy, he left behind Robert, Earl of Gloucester.

Robert claimed that the oath he had sworn to Stephen in 1136 was conditional; he had only sworn fealty to Stephen if the king continued to be faithful to him. Furthermore, he decided that his oath had been unlawful, given the oath he had sworn to Matilda in 1126 and Stephen's seizure of the throne in 1135. It is possible that Robert only supported Stephen in 1135 by default; he could not at that time support Matilda because she was in the middle of border warfare with her own father, Henry I.

The influence of Waleran, Count of Meulan

Waleran's prominence at Stephen's court squeezed out Bishop Henry and Earl Robert and possibly engineered the downfall of Bishop Roger of Salisbury and his family. Waleran, son of the great Robert of Meulan, was an identical twin (his younger twin brother, Robert, was earl of Leicester). He had vast estates in England (where he was count of Worcester) and in

KEY EVIDENCE

From a Charter of Stephen addressed generally (1136)
'I allow and concede that jurisdiction and authority over ecclesiastical persons and over all clerks and their property, together with the disposal of ecclesiastical estates, shall lie in the hands of bishops … I will observe good laws and the ancient and lawful customs in respect of pecuniary exactions for murder and pleas and other causes, and I command them to be observed.'

Normandy. The Beaumont twins had a vast network of kinship connections: William de Warenne, earl of Surrey, was a step-brother; the earl of Warwick a cousin; the earl of Northampton a son-in-law, and the earl of Pembroke a brother-in-law.

Loss of support from the bishops

Stephen sent Waleran ahead to Normandy in 1136 to establish peace in his name. Waleran was by now the king's son-in-law, having been betrothed to Stephen's two-year-old daughter; he was also a cousin of Louis VI of France. After the failure of the summer campaign against Anjou, Bishop Henry, the king's brother, fell out of favour, and it was Waleran who accompanied the king back to England. In 1139 Stephen began to arrange the marriage of his son Eustace to the sister of King Louis of France and it was Waleran who acted as ambassador to Paris. In June of that year a court conspiracy sponsored by Waleran brought about the downfall of Bishop Roger of Salisbury. Roger was suspected of awaiting the arrival of Earl Robert and, following a street brawl involving the bishop's men, he and his family were arrested, and their castles seized.

Although some thought that Roger of Salisbury was too powerful and should not hold castles, the Church was bitterly offended at the way the bishop and his family were treated. Stephen now began to lose the sympathy of the Church. Stephen's brother, Henry of Winchester, now a papal legate, attempted to find common ground, but failed. See pages 214–15 for Stephen's relations with the Church.

Rebellion in England and the return of Robert and Matilda

The timing of the loss of support from the Church was crucial, for it was in September of 1139 that Earl Robert and Matilda landed in England. Rebellion had broken out across England after Robert's **defection** the previous summer, but Stephen had crushed them all in a brilliant campaign. When Matilda came in person to England, however, all the grievances and discontent had a focus: rebellion now became **civil war**.

WALES AND SCOTLAND
Wales

Henry I's achievements in Wales and Scotland were largely destroyed after his death. In the years following 1136 the Welsh reconquered Norman castles in Carmarthen, Oswestry and Mold. The southern areas of Cardiff and Newport continued to be heavily Anglicised but the upland valleys of the north remained strongly Welsh. The barons under Stephen were too concerned with the politics of England to make war against the Welsh.

Scotland

In Scotland, the situation after 1135 was plunged into open conflict. King David I, brother-in-law to Henry I, was entirely committed to Matilda's cause, not to Stephen's. He invaded England after Stephen's coronation and seized Carlisle, which remained a chief seat of power until his death in 1153. In 1138 David was defeated at the Battle of the Standard, but managed to gain control of Cumbria, so weak was Stephen's position. David's greatest gain was Northumberland, which Stephen granted to his son Henry in 1139. David's wife was the daughter of Earl Waltheof of Northumberland, executed for his (minor) part in the 1075 rebellion. David's son Henry held the earldom, with his base at Corbridge, until his death in 1152, when it passed to his younger son, William.

The succession crisis of 1135 caused paralysis and retreat in Wales and outright loss of English territories to the Scottish, altogether a major reversal on the Norman advances made since 1066.

'WHEN CHRIST AND HIS SAINTS SLEPT': A TIME OF ANARCHY?

Much has been made of the rest of the reign of Stephen as a time that historians once called 'the anarchy' when the barons fought out their private feuds across the kingdom. In fact, Stephen retained control over much of his kingdom; the core of the rebellion remained in Herefordshire, Gloucestershire and Somerset. Here the fighting was fiercest, as it was here that Earl Robert headed the Angevin party in England, along with Flemish and Welsh mercenaries. Stephen could damage and contain the rebels, but could not eradicate them.

Ranulf of Chester and the battle of Lincoln (1141)

Stephen's determination to close with his enemies led to the greatest catastrophe of his reign. Pitched battles in medieval warfare were very rare, precisely because they could be decisive, as at Hastings and Tinchebray. For that reason, medieval rulers and rebellious barons preferred besieging castles and skirmishing, where an advantage could be forced without taking a great risk. But in Stephen's situation, with the continuing festering sore of rebellion and betrayal in his kingdom, a pitched battle could solve the situation once and for all.

The immediate cause was the seizure of Lincoln Castle by Earl Ranulf of Chester. Ranulf was a powerful baron but wanted to extend his powers into Lincolnshire. One contemporary source says that Ranulf ruled nearly a third of the country; he was Earl of the great earldom of Chester; he had inherited large estates in Lincolnshire; his half-brother, William de Roumare, was Earl of Lincoln. Ranulf also wished to recover the barony of Carlisle which his father had held and which Henry I had granted away to the son of the king of Scotland.

Before Christmas 1140, Stephen met Ranulf and agreed for the earl to keep the castles of Lincoln and Derby. But when the Bishop of Lincoln sent a message in January 1141 telling the king that the earl and his family were in the city without a strong garrison, Stephen took his chance, storming north so suddenly that Ranulf fled the castle at night, leaving his family behind.

As he retreated to Derby, Ranulf summoned aid from his father-in-law, who happened to be Robert, Earl of Gloucester. The two earls met in Leicestershire with a large force and marched on Lincoln and offered battle. Stephen, eager to accept, marched out of the town, even though his army was smaller than the rebel army. The royalist cavalry charge on the Welsh infantry failed and the king was then surrounded by the main English rebel army. Dismounted, the king fought bravely with his axe until it broke and then with his sword. His bodyguard were either killed or captured and he was taken prisoner. The battle lasted only about an hour.

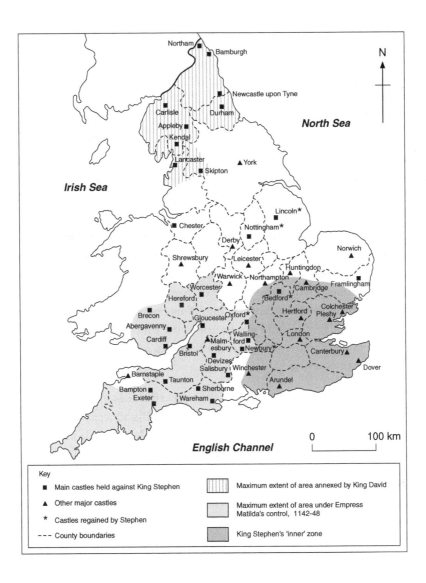

The civil wars of Stephen

Key

- ■ Main castles held against King Stephen
- ▲ Other major castles
- * Castles regained by Stephen
- - - - County boundaries

||||| Maximum extent of area annexed by King David

Maximum extent of area under Empress Matilda's control, 1142–48

King Stephen's 'inner' zone

WHY WAS MATILDA NOT CROWNED QUEEN OF ENGLAND?

Stephen spent the night under guard in Lincoln Castle, then went to Gloucester Castle and finally to Bristol Castle, where his triumphant cousin Matilda ordered him to be kept in chains. But before the year was out, he was released and Matilda's forces were in disarray.

It has been suggested that Matilda lost support because she was a woman in power in an age when women were expected to be subordinate. Other medieval women wielded great power and were not treated in the same way as the sources treat Matilda (for example, Matilda's own mother and grandmother, both Matildas, had wielded real power at the courts of Henry I and William I during their monarch's absence, and Matilda's aunt, Stephen's mother, Adela, governed Blois in the long absence of her crusader husband). However, these women were queen consorts who held office by virtue of their husbands' position; Matilda's situation was different.

Matilda lost her advantage over Stephen after Lincoln for three reasons:

- Baronial loyalties were divided.
- The personality of Matilda.
- The achievements of Queen Matilda. The concept of a queen ruling in her own right (as queen regnant) was foreign to conteporary minds.

Baronial loyalties

After the battle of Lincoln, Stephen's position was by no means hopeless. Waleran of Meulan had escaped the field of battle to Worcester; William of Ypres, the great mercenary captain, was in London with the Queen, and William Martel, the king's steward, was in Sherborne. Neither Ranulf, Earl of Chester or David, king of Scotland, added their forces to those of Matilda (or the 'Empress' as she was known from her days as wife to the emperor Henry V of Germany). After the disaster of Westminster, Bishop Henry (who said that he only allowed the Empress into Winchester to be in a better position to help his brother) did not return to the Empress's side. Only five bishops were in regular attendance on the Empress, and the magnates were her uncle and half-brothers.

There were defections, however; in June, the powerful East Anglian barons Geoffrey de Mandeville, Aubrey de Vere and Hugh Bigod went over to Matilda; in July, Waleran of Meulan defected, but only to save his lands in Normandy, to which he returned shortly afterwards.

The personality of Matilda

Matilda was a woman of fierce and harsh temperament. She played on her imperial status; she lacked judgement and flexibility. She openly lost her temper at court and she threatened men who ought not to have been

The Battle of Lincoln, from 'The History of the English', by Henry of Huntingdon (1141) 'Then a fresh shout arose and every man rushed at the king while he in turn thrust back at them all. At length his battle-axe was shattered by repeated blows, whereupon he drew his trusty sword, well worthy of a king, and with this he wrought wonders, until it too was broken. At sight of this, William de Cahaignes, a very valiant knight, rushed upon him and, seizing his helmet, shouted with a loud voice, "Hither, all of you, hither, I hold the king." Everyone flew to his aid and the king was taken prisoner.'

threatened; she chained and confined Stephen for almost a year, which Henry I and William I – both brutal men in their time – had avoided doing to their captives – and she lost the support of London, which proved crucial to her coronation. Due to the fact that she was a woman, she was criticised more harshly by the author of the *Gesta Stephani*.

In the spring of 1141 the Empress Matilda entered Winchester and stated that she was now queen of England. But political reality in the twelfth century was that nobody was king or queen of England until they had been crowned. The bishops insisted that she call herself 'Lady of England and Normandy'. In June the Empress moved her army to St Albans and then occupied the Palace of Westminster. Queen Matilda, wife of Stephen and resident in the Tower of London, moved south, into Kent.

Empress Matilda then offended and alienated so many around her that when she dismissed the delegation from the city of London, those still loyal to Stephen rang the city bells and invited Queen Matilda back into the city. As the London mob stormed the palace, the Empress had no choice but to flee.

The achievements of Queen Matilda

It was to be the other Matilda who proved to be the better woman. As niece of King David of Scotland, Queen Matilda claimed descent from Ethelred II of England, just as her cousin the Empress did; Queen Matilda's father and uncle were also famous crusaders, the latter having been proclaimed king of Jerusalem in 1101. Stephen's queen spent the year 1141 rallying the bishops and the barons to her cause, reminding them of the king held in chains and of her son's rights.

The queen based herself in London, where the city fathers were divided as to what to do. After the queen was forced to leave, when the Empress took her army to Winchester, the queen and William of Ypres seized their chance to give the bishop a lesson. The queen cut off the Empress's forces in the city and although the Empress escaped, Earl Robert was captured.

THE RETURN OF THE KING AND THE END OF THE CIVIL WAR: 1141–47

Matilda's cause was lost without Earl Robert. In order to negotiate his release, the Empress was forced to exchange him for Stephen in November 1141. Stephen appeared in state with his queen at Canterbury, where he held his Christmas court. Almost a year in jail had taken its toll, however, and the king fell gravely ill in the spring. Devon and Cornwall and most of Normandy were in the hands of the Angevins. In the summer, however, the king recovered and moved with speed to Dorset, seizing Wareham, an important Angevin port, then striking north to Oxford, where he trapped the Empress. Matilda escaped but Oxford was taken by Stephen, thus keeping the Angevins back beyond the Cotswolds.

Geoffrey de Mandeville and the 'Anarchy'

1143 was not a good year for Stephen; he and his troops were surprised at Wilton in Wiltshire and had to flee for their lives. William Martel was captured and Stephen had to hand over Sherborne Castle to secure his release and accept a truce. Robert of Gloucester now dominated the territory from Bristol to the Dorset coast.

To make matters worse, Stephen then provoked the wrath of one of his own barons, Geoffrey de Mandeville. The situation was similar to that of Ranulf of Chester; another 'overmighty' subject having too much power, wanting more and then rebelling. Neither was necessarily motivated by loyalties either to or against Stephen. Personal gain seems to have been the main factor.

Geoffrey de Mandeville had been made earl of Essex by Stephen in 1140, but allied himself first to the Empress after the Battle of Lincoln and then to the queen after Matilda's failure to become queen. Each time he swapped sides he gained more cash, land and offices; by 1143 he was sheriff and justiciar in three counties and Constable of the Tower of London, a crucial post. In September of that year Stephen arrested him at St Albans on suspicion of plotting to rejoin the Empress. Geoffrey surrendered the Tower and his Essex castles but then went on a prolonged spree of violence in Cambridgeshire and the Fens until the summer of 1144. He ransacked and burned Cambridge, turned Ely into a fortress, made the Abbey of Ramsay a military headquarters and inflicted death and destruction on the surrounding population; famine followed. Stephen was unable to get to him in the Fens and only a mortal wound from an arrow ended the violent career of Geoffrey de Mandeville.

In 1892 the historian J.H. Round produced a book on Geoffrey de Mandeville. He was portrayed as the king's arch-enemy, out for everything he could get, typical of the barons of the time. But Geoffrey's career was by no means typical of Stephen's reign. His activities only affected a small area. Furthermore, he made no attempt to join the forces of the Empress.

Stalemate and the death of Earl Robert (1147)

Both sides were short of resources and found that people simply did not want to fight. Stephen knew that he had to capture Gloucester to strike at the heart of the Angevin party; he was close in 1146, and a peace conference was held, although nothing came of it.

Then in October 1147, Earl Robert died. This was the end of Empress Matilda's cause. She did not stay in England longer than four months, but left for Normandy, never to return. The civil war in England was over. The West Country remained an Angevin stronghold, which formed a future launch pad for Matilda's son, Henry.

SECURING THE SUCCESSION: EUSTACE OR HENRY?

After 1147 the issue was not whether Matilda would become queen but whether her son Henry would succeed Stephen, instead of Stephen's son Eustace. For the last six years of his reign Stephen struggled to pass on his dynasty to his son. Eustace came of age in 1147, aged 21, was knighted by his father and invested with the county of Boulogne. Eustace was a capable young man of military experience and some diplomatic wisdom. He knew that to ensure his succession he would have to either capture or kill his opponent, Henry, son of the Empress. Eustace attempted this in 1149, when Henry met King David of Scotland at Carlisle and rode back via the Cotswolds into Angevin territory in the West Country. Henry escaped the ambush but contemporaries were well aware of the competition between the two young men.

Stephen pursued two policies to ensure Eustace's succession:

- Crowning his son in his own lifetime.
- Forming anti-Angevin alliances in Europe.

Both policies failed. The custom of crowning the heir was common in France but unknown in England; even so, it was a realistic prospect for Stephen. However, the Church refused to comply, citing the ambiguity of Stephen's own coronation. Archbishop Theobald of Canterbury flatly refused to crown Eustace.

Stephen's second plan, an Anglo-French alliance against the Angevins, was agreed in 1151. Count Eustace struck deep into Normandy in the summer of 1151, getting within 20 miles of Rouen, but the king of France, Louis VII, fell ill in Paris and dismissed his army.

Disease and deaths

The period 1151–53 saw the deaths of many leading nobles and rulers in north-west Europe, possibly following the devastating famine of 1150 and its ensuing diseases. In September 1151, Geoffrey of Anjou died, leaving his son Henry the duchy and county of Anjou. But if Henry could not now leave his new territories safely to pursue the crown of England, any hopes Eustace had of exploiting this were dashed with the death first of King Louis's minister, Abbot Suger, then of Eustace's uncle, Count Theobald of Blois-Chartres, and finally of Queen Matilda, in 1152.

Fiasco at Wallingford and the death of Eustace

Early in 1153 Duke Henry landed again in England and found great support in the West Country; Stephen discovered the unpleasant fact that people did not want to fight against Henry.

August 1153 saw the final and decisive confrontation between Duke Henry and King Stephen outside Wallingford Castle. The king outmanoeuvred the young duke but his sword broke in his efforts to finish off the Angevin. The king's army refused to fight and instead opened negotiations. In a fury, Count Eustace rode to Cambridge, but was struck down by disease and died within a week.

Peace and reconstruction within the realm

In November 1153 Stephen recognised Henry as his adopted son and heir in a treaty signed at Winchester. Henry in turn allowed Stephen to remain on the throne for his lifetime. Henry left for Normandy in the spring of 1154 and in England peace had begun in earnest; Angevin barons paid in accounts to the Exchequer and the West Country obeyed the king's law once again. Stephen held a great court at York and impressed upon the northern barons that the heady days of Ranulf of Chester were over. In October the king was in Kent, discussing the return of Flemish mercenaries to Flanders when he fell ill, probably with dysentery, and died.

CONCLUSION: WEAKNESSES, MISTAKES AND 'ANARCHY'

The civil wars of Stephen's reign could be seen as a result of his weaknesses and mistakes or as a reaction to the merciless grip of Henry I and his leaving a daughter as his heir.

Weaknesses or piety?

Stephen (and no other English king) was referred to by later twelfth-century writers as *rex piissimus* 'most pious king'. He was deeply devout by contemporary standards; he had an Augustinian father confessor licensed to hear him by the archbishop of Canterbury. Many of Stephen's actions were motivated by piety. Such piety might be seen as weakness by modern generations. For example, in 1138 he avoided besieging Ludlow, which was commanded by a woman. When he trapped the wives of the earls of Chester and Lincoln in the castle of Lincoln in 1141, he let them go. In 1152, when besieging Newbury Castle, he had with him as a hostage the son of the rebel John Marshal, five-year-old William. Urged by the barons to kill the boy to make an example, Stephen refused. Instead, he took the boy on as a page and that boy rose to become one of the great twelfth-century magnates (see below, pages 204–9). Stephen was a chivalrous king. He was a successful military commander and a brave man; he was pious and generous. He allowed honourable enemies to go into exile or to go free, and only in one case did he execute opponents who surrendered.

> ### KEY EVIDENCE
>
> **Charter of Stephen describing the 'Treaty of Winchester', 1153**
> 'Know that I, King Stephen, have established Henry, Duke of Normandy, as my successor in the kingdom of England, and have recognised him as my heir by hereditary right; and thus I have given and confirmed to him and his heirs the kingdom of England.'

That said, contemporaries also spoke harshly of Stephen's weakness as a ruler. 'In King Stephen's time justice was banished from the kingdom and everything open to plunder' wrote one chronicle. 'He was soft and easy-going and did not justice', proclaimed *The Anglo-Saxon Chronicle* for the year 1137.

Mistakes

Stephen was also subject to several serious failures of judgement. He misjudged the issue with Roger of Salisbury and his family. He was influenced by a court faction with its own vested interests and lost the support of the senior clergy as a result. His arrest of Geoffrey de Mandeville, again influenced by vested interests in the royal court, led to Geoffrey's rampage through East Anglia.

Comparisons with Henry I: perceptions of civil unrest and 'anarchy'

Stephen's actions against members of the clergy and aristocracy were not unprecedented. Henry I had acted in a similar way. Contemporaries agreed that Roger of Salisbury was far too powerful. What made it difficult for Stephen was that his kingship was undermined by the civil unrest of his reign.

Contemporaries bemoaned the state of the country during the fighting. Of the fourteen sources that describe the reign, only six were contemporary and of those, only two describe the entire reign. The other four cease by 1142. The two contemporary sources that describe the entire period were written by Robert, Bishop of Bath and Wells (the *Gesta Stephani* 'Deeds of Stephen' – the most important source and close to Stephen) and by Henry, Archdeacon of Huntingdon (*History of the English*), who distrusted Stephen and disliked Matilda. Both these sources had two different local perspectives and both talk about the horrors of the wars.

The extent of these horrors has been much debated by historians. Large amounts of land in the south-west, the north and the Midlands were recorded as 'waste' in sheriff's accounts between 1154 and 1160. This was where the fighting had taken place in Stephen's reign. So unruly and brutal had this been that the period has been termed an 'anarchy' by historians. Society and order collapsed as every man scrambled for power. The state of coinage is often used as evidence for the breakdown of centralised government in certain regions during Stephen's reign. After 1140, the centralised system with its national distribution of standard official dies from London broke down. Mints at Bristol, Cardiff, Swansea, Oxford and Wareham struck coins in the name of the Empress.

The word 'anarchy' is a powerful word and is wrongly used for the reign of Stephen. Contemporaries did not use this word. A nineteenth-century historian and bishop, William Stubbs, used it first in 1867. To Stubbs, Stephen was a weak king, unable to control the forces of feudalism. J.H. Round, writing in 1888, followed this, calling it the 'anarchy', and wrote in 1892 that Stephen was at the mercy of an unscrupulous aristocracy.

Only in the last twenty-five years has the dominance of the word 'anarchy' been challenged. 'Waste' may simply have recorded land not assessed for taxation, rather than damaged land, or it may have signified that the taxpayers could not be established on those lands. Professor David Crouch argues that 'time and time again throughout the conflict they [those fighting] showed themselves willing to discuss peaceful solutions … at no level did the conflict involve the dissolution of the social or political order'. Stephen's struggles with the aristocrats had more to do with his personality – his piety, his chivalry and his poor judgements – than with the forces of feudalism out of control.

Government did not break down completely in Stephen's reign. The Exchequer continued to function and coins were minted. The great barons did not change sides as often as used to be believed, and only then reluctantly. The great test for an 'anarchy' in Stephen's reign is to be found in the first years of the reign of Henry II. If England had been so devastated by warfare and government so limited by feudal barons, then how was it that peace was established and that the government functioned smoothly within two years?

SECTION 3

The reign of Henry II

INTRODUCTION

The reign of Henry II (1154–89) was remarkable for English government and law. It stands out with the reigns of William I and Henry I in this book as one of the three reigns that witnessed great events, change and development in England.

Henry II inherited an ancient kingdom with developed rights and customs, which had adapted and evolved after the Norman Conquest. His grandfather Henry I had revolutionised the royal finances and ensured a period of peace for nearly thirty years. Henry II re-established peace and stability in England, which endured, apart for a brief period in 1173–74, for forty-five years. This peace continued throughout the reign of his son Richard, and was only ended by baronial rebellion under his youngest son John, in 1214.

The Angevin 'empire'

The impact of the Norman Conquest was far reaching. Henry II inherited from Stephen not only England, but also Normandy (conquered by his parents from Stephen) and Anjou, his family home. England was now going to be ruled not even by a Norman, but by a man from the heart of France. Furthermore, in 1152 he had married Eleanor, Duchess of Aquitaine in her own right. Aquitaine was the region stretching from the border of Anjou to the foothills of the Pyrenees. The king of England was going to be lord of half of France.

This transformed the Anglo-Norman realm, which had existed since 1066. The impact on English government, already revolutionised under Henry I, would be immense. The so-called 'Angevin empire' which placed an otherwise obscure count of Anjou, great-grandson of the Conqueror, in command of a vast conglomeration of territories, put England at the centre of Continental affairs. The English wealth and resources at Henry II's disposal were ruthlessly exploited to maintain this 'empire.'

The impact on English kingship and government was considerable. Henry II was absent for long periods of time, more so than any of his predecessors. The reconstruction of government after the dislocation under Stephen led to major reforms and innovatory practices in law and administration. Despite Henry's betrayal by his sons at the end of his life, his empire was handed over to Richard in one piece.

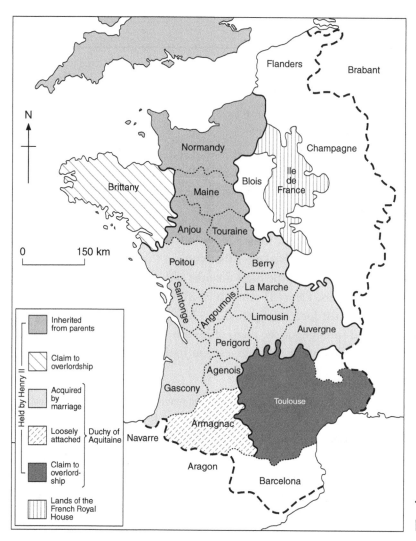

Flanders

Brabant

N

Normandy

Champagne

Brittany

Blois

Ile
de
France

Maine

0   150 km

Anjou Touraine

Poitou

Berry

Saintonge

La Marche

Angoumois

Limousin

Auvergne

Perigord

Agenois

Gascony

Toulouse

Armagnac

Navarre

Aragon

Barcelona

Held by Henry II

Inherited
from parents

Claim to
overlordship

Acquired
by
marriage

Loosely
attached

Duchy of
Aquitaine

Claim to
overlord-
ship

Lands of the
French Royal
House

**The dominions of
Henry II, 1154–89**

HOW DID HENRY II SECURE THE REALM?

Henry of Anjou had three advantages at his disposal when he became king of
England at the end of 1154:

- He was the undisputed heir to the throne. Henry's succession was the first
  smooth succession since Edward the Confessor's in 1042, over a hundred
  years earlier.
- Henry had a year, from the treaty at Winchester when he was recognised
  as Stephen's heir, to the death of Stephen. This gave him time to
  familiarise himself with the kingdom and choose his chief ministers who
  were accepted by all.
- When Henry became king there was a great desire to keep the peace and
  to end the disorder that had prevailed under Stephen in some parts of the
  country.

Immediately after his coronation Henry made several key appointments to his government that were based on his experience in England before Stephen's death. The new king also had to overcome potential baronial opposition and to restore law and order in his new kingdom.

The justiciars

Henry chose two men to be in charge of the royal administration, both styled 'justiciar'. Henry chose Richard de Lucy, a man of great experience who had fought against him. Richard had been sheriff and royal justice in Essex under Stephen and was in charge of the Tower of London and Windsor Castle. He was one of Stephen's most trusted servants and a member of the knightly class. Richard was one of the men who had risen in the service of Henry I and served Stephen faithfully so that he was known as 'the loyal'.

Henry also appointed Robert Beaumont, Earl of Leicester. He was the son of the Robert Beaumont who had fought at the Battle of Hastings and had been made earl of Leicester by William I. Beaumont was the twin brother of the more notorious Waleran, Count of Meulan, but gave his support to Henry in 1153; he was well educated and highly intelligent, judging by contemporary accounts. He was noted for his prudence and discretion in the post until his death in 1168. His wife was the daughter of the earl of East Anglia and his cousins were earls of Warwick; after the death of Ranulf Earl of Chester in 1153 he was the most powerful English earl.

The chancellor

The chancellor was the master of the royal chapel and head of the royal secretariat. He was the man who made the royal will possible through the creation of charters, letters and writs. Again, Henry may have been expected to appoint someone from his own chapel, but he consulted the archbishop of Canterbury, Theobald, who recommended his favourite clerk, Thomas Becket, Archdeacon of Canterbury. Henry's choice not only won him the confidence of the archbishop and therefore the support of the English Church, but the fact that Becket had served as clerk and accountant to the sheriffs of London, gave Henry some affinity with the Londoners who had played such a large part in excluding his mother the Empress from the throne of England.

Dealing with the barons

The new king still had the task of dealing with the overmighty barons who had flourished under Stephen. Although the civil war had effectively ended on the death of Robert of Gloucester and the departure of Matilda in 1147, much of the country remained in a state of disorder. The royal writ did not run in parts of the country and finances paid into the Exchequer were far from consistent. Sheriffs and royal justices were hindered by local disturbances and the stranglehold of the rival magnates. The treaty between Henry and Stephen was not going to put an end to this quickly.

Henry achieved peace and stability within a year in the following ways:

- By expelling the Flemish mercenaries.
- By demolishing the illegal castles that had sprung up during Stephen's rule.

These were the two obvious points of continuing uncertainty in the kingdom. The departure of the Flemish mercenaries weakened the king's military base, but the positive effect on public opinion was remembered a generation later.

The demand for the barons to give up their castles to royal control and/or demolition was an attack on the heart of baronial power in the provinces. Henry relied upon the rivalries between the barons and was helped by the fact that he was the undisputed king of England. However, he did face opposition from several quarters, including the earl of York, William le Gros, the earl of Hereford, Roger, and Hugh Mortimer, Lord of Wigmore. Henry marched against William within a month of his coronation (December 1154) and the earl was forced to surrender his castles. Roger followed suit but Hugh held out and Henry had to lay siege to his castles at Cleobury and Wigmore and the royal castle at Bridgenorth. The king took the castles and Hugh submitted in July, before an assembly of archbishops, bishops, earls and barons.

Other earls shied away from confrontation but the greatest success for Henry was the self-imposed exile of Henry of Blois, Bishop of Winchester, brother of the late King Stephen. The Bishop virtually ruled Hampshire and in his absence his castles were demolished.

Law and property

Justice had been a major casualty during the reign of Stephen. The first year of the new king's reign was spent largely in hearing grievances regarding rights and lands. This was not easy after twenty years of confusion and conflict. The starting point for 'lawful possession' was the death of Henry I but the lack of established hereditary practices, interference from the Crown and gifts and grants made by Stephen and Matilda to win support, made Henry's task a balance of justice, equity and political expediency. This he seems to have managed with a great degree of success, so much so that he was named 'Henry the Peacemaker' by one chronicler.

WAS THE NATURE OF KINGSHIP CHANGING?

Kings in the later twelfth century were still the protectors and military leaders of their people. The king was the chief instrument in the divine scheme for the ordering of the world; Henry II was very much 'King by the grace of God' as he stated on his charters and coins. And, after the Norman

Conquest, the king was the feudal overlord, disposer of land and recipient of homage from his tenants-in-chief and fealty from his subjects.

Writers of the later twelfth century were very aware of the nature of kingship. John of Salisbury distinguished between the true king who had respect for law and the liberties of his people and the tyrant who reduced law to his will, though he admitted that a tyrant might be an instrument of God's will. Other writers saw respect for the law as essential, though again it was agreed that subjects had no right to question the actions of kings.

The reality of kingship was not what the academics and chroniclers wished or pretended it to be, but rather what historical development, circumstance and personalities determined. Kingship was a living, constantly adaptable thing; kingship was what a king made of it and what his subjects would accept. Henry II was well aware of his rights and prerogatives and used them effectively to wield power over his feudal subjects.

Itinerant kingship

Historical development in reality meant that Henry ruled over an ancient kingdom with established rights and practices. These rights had indeed been disturbed by the reign of Stephen, but Henry managed to effectively restore peace very quickly.

The circumstances of Henry II as duke of Normandy, count of Anjou and ruler of Aquitaine in his wife's name inevitably led to change in the government of England. The king, unlike Stephen, would be absent from the kingdom whilst ruling his continental lands, and these lands extended much further than those of Henry I, William II and William I. In the period 1154–73 Henry II spent only a third of his time in England and was twice abroad for more than four years.

The king was continually on the move. In the thirty-four years of his reign Henry II spent Christmas at twenty-four different places; he crossed the English Channel at least twenty-eight times and the Irish Sea twice. Sea travel was not easy and could be dangerous. Floods and snow could obstruct land travel; roads were virtually non-existent. But the king was on the move whatever the weather and conditions.

The *curia regis*

With the king travelled his court, the *curia regis*. The king's court was the government; it acted for the king during his unavoidable absences. The king's court constantly dealt with legal cases as well as running government on a daily basis. Wherever the *curia regis* travelled, it absorbed the local law courts. If there were important barons present, then the council merged into the court; if such powerful men as the justiciar and the chancellor joined the king in his hunting lodge at Clarendon, then they could settle a legal dispute on the spot. For more momentous business, the 'great council' could be summoned, but this was still the *curia regis* on a more formal footing.

The king did not act without the advice of his court and his council. The council was the inner group of barons who were duty bound to give the king advice when he asked for it and to pass judgement. These counsellors were not a formal, fixed group, and consisted of men of aristocratic and low birth who might in time be rewarded with heiressess, archdeaconries or bishoprics in return for loyal service. Some of them held a specific office in the chancery (*ministeriales*); some were simply the king's friends (*amici*). Whatever their function or rank, they all formed part of the king's intimate circle, or *familia*.

The personality of the king

At the centre of all the hustle and bustle, hundreds of servants, soldiers and clerks, was the man himself. Henry II was arguably the most energetic, dynamic and intelligent person ever to sit on the throne of England. He was an extraordinary man. He ruled over land stretching from Hadrian's Wall to the foothills of the Pyrenees. His subjects spoke a dozen languages and lived by as many cultures and customs.

Henry II was from the heart of France, and yet bestrode the Welsh mountains, Cotswold Hills and streets of London as easily as his childhood forests of Anjou. His physical energy was such that people thought he could fly, so quickly did he move from place to place. When not pursuing the business of government he hunted obsessively; in between he could not sit still for a moment, standing and eating and doing business all at once. He was a man of wit and intellect, courage and audacity and ruthlessness. He was multi-lingual and, very unusually, literate. He was consistent with his friends (and his enemies), never forgot a face or a kind remark or honourable deed. He was patient, but when angry he raged with more ferocity than his grandfather had ever done, screaming and rolling on the floor.

REFORM AND RECONSTRUCTION

Once Henry II had established his authority in England his next task was to ensure the smooth running of the government. The extent of the dislocation of government under Stephen is not easy to assess. Certainly government was weakened during that time. The creation of a centralised bureaucracy under Henry I was a great achievement, but much of it was based upon fear of the king and the mighty powers invested in Roger of Salisbury. With Roger's removal in 1139 the government had lost its most experienced administrator. Stephen's character had been such that his threats were empty. Sessions of the Exchequer had not been thorough; sheriffdoms had passed back into baronial hands and the local lords had abused local law.

KEY EVIDENCE

From a judgement made by the court at Clarendon (1187) 'This is the final concord made in the court of the lord king at Clarendon … before the lord king and John his son, and Ranulf de Glanvill, and Hubert dean of York, and Ralph archdeacon of Hereford, and Robert of Inglesham archdeacon of Gloucester…'

KEY EVIDENCE

From William of Newburgh 'The History of England' (c. 1196) 'Indeed, so many miseries had sprung up in the previous reign that after their unhappy experiences the people hoped for better things from the new monarch … In the early days he paid due regard to public order and was at great pains to revive the vigour of the laws in England, which seemed under Stephen to be dead and buried.'

From Gerald of Wales, 'Concerning the Instruction of a Prince' (c. 1184)
'Henry II, king of England, was a man of reddish, freckled complexion with a large round head, grey eyes which glowed fiercely and grew bloodshot in anger, a fiery countenance and a harsh, cracked voice … He was a man easy of access and condescending, pliant and witty, second to none in politeness, whatever thoughts he might conceal within himself; a prince so remarkable for charity that as often he overcame by force of arms, he was himself vanquished through showing too great compassion.'

The relief at having a peaceful succession and a strong monarch in the country after 1154 was obvious, even though Henry was only in England twice for about a year in the first eight years of his reign.

The royal finances

Restoring the country to the order of the last days of Henry I was not a quick process. Henry II had to govern and defend Normandy, Anjou, Brittany and Aquitaine. To do this he needed vast amounts of money. Thus reconstruction of the government in England went hand in hand with reform and innovation in order to adapt to the circumstances of 1154, which were very different from those of 1135. The driving force behind these reforms and innovations was the need for money and an efficient bureaucracy to account for the cash.

Henry II reformed and reconstructed the Crown revenue in the following ways:

- He revived the ancient tax of the danegeld.
- He set about seizing lost royal estates.
- Senior ministers of the Crown, such as Richard de Lucy and Thomas Becket, personally held sheriffdoms so that the revenues could be properly assessed.
- A major reform of the coinage was set underway in 1158 and revised more successfully in 1180.

The Exchequer

All of these reforms were dependent on an efficient accounting system. The Exchequer had continued to function under Stephen, but its expertise had almost vanished. To reconstruct the system Henry II turned to the past, and requested his grandfather's treasurer, Bishop Nigel of Ely, nephew of Roger of Salisbury, to come out of retirement. By the time of Bishop Nigel's death in 1169 the Exchequer was working to the full efficiency of the days of Henry I.

Aid A one-off payment to the Crown, usually to pay for a special occasion such as the knighting of the king's son.

Richard fitzNigel and the *Dialogue of the Exchequer*

Henry II appointed Bishop Nigel's son, Richard, treasurer some time before 1160. In 1189 he became bishop of London and remained treasurer until his death in 1198. This meant that three generations of the same family served at the heart of royal administration for most of the twelfth century. During the 1170s Richard wrote a guide to Exchequer practice in the form of a conversation between master and student (disciple), explaining the workings of the Exchequer. This document is the first attempt anywhere in medieval Europe to explain administrative practices. From it we know that twice a year treasury officials met with senior officials from the chancery, the chamber and the constable's department, along with members of the king's inner council. These meetings were chaired by the justiciar and occurred alongside the twice-yearly rendering of sheriff's accounts that had been established by Henry I. In this way the royal will could be discharged efficiently and without confusion between departments and regions.

The audits of the sheriff's accounts were written up on the pipe rolls with intense detail. Taxes, **aids**, debts, fines and rental income were all accounted for. Debts could be paid in instalments. One debtor, Bertram of Bulmer, owed just over £14 in 1159; when he died he still owed over £9. The rolls record this debt year after year until in 1175 it was noted that Geoffrey de Neville had married Bertram's daughter and should therefore pay the debt, which he did within two years. Bertram's debt had been on the rolls for nineteen years.

The royal demesne and the *Cartae Baronum* (1166)

During the reign of William I the **royal demesne** amounted to around a quarter of England; by the time of Henry II this had shrunk by half. Returns at the start of Henry's reign were only £8000. Henry set about restoring royal lands by recovering property that had been encroached upon by landholders during the wars of Stephen (*purprestures*), by updating the rents of existing properties and by recovering land that should have reverted to the king as overlord but had not (*escheats*).

In the first decade of his reign Henry II systematically investigated and improved upon his rights and income from the royal estate. By 1165 there were 70 new items of account. Royal justices were appointed thereafter to track down fresh losses from the royal estate.

Although gains were made in recovering and increasing revenue from the royal estates, Henry II could not run his government by these alone. He needed to know more about the feudal rights owing to him from his fiefs. These rights included military service or money in lieu (scutage), the right to ask for aids, the wardship of minors and the marriage of daughters and widows. Domesday Book was an invaluable reference, but it had become dated. Instead, the first major attempt was made to revise the Exchequer's records in 1166. The tenants-in-chief were commanded to send in sealed returns listing the sub-tenancies on their lands, the amount of knight-service owed by them and the names of the tenants in 1166 and in the time of King Henry I (i.e. before 1135).

These returns are known as the *Cartae Baronum*, the barons' returns. They related not only to the barons, but also to the feudal tenancies of the many thousands of small fiefs that were held from the Crown. This was important; the king of England wanted the allegiance of all his landlords, great and small. In this, Henry II was continuing the practice started by his great-

KEY EVIDENCE

From the *Dialogue of the Exchequer* by Richard fitzNigel (c.1175)

Disciple: Is it then the treasurer who receives the account, although there are many others present who are of higher rank?

Master: That the treasurer shall receive the said account is required from him whenever it shall please the king: for what he had not received could hardly be demanded of him. Nevertheless, there are some who say that the treasurer and the chamberlains are only answerable for what is entered in the rolls as being 'In the Treasury' and for this alone an account may be demanded of them.

KEY TERM

Royal demesne All land in the realm that had not been put into private hands, from which the Crown took rents.

From the *Cartae Baronum* (in the *Red Book of the Exchequer*) (1166) 'To Henry, king of the English, his most revered lord, William son of Siward sends greeting. Your order, promulgated throughout England, has come to me, as to others, through the sheriff of Northumberland, that we should inform you about our fiefs and the holding of them, which we hold from you. And so I am letting you know by this letter that I hold from you a certain village, Gosford by name, and the half of another which is called Milton, for the fee and service of one knight, which I faithfully perform to you, as my ancestors have done to your ancestors; and I have enfeoffed no one but hold as my demesne.'

grandfather, William I, at the Salisbury Oath of 1086. This was especially important in 1166, since the king was planning an overseas expedition which would take him away from England for four years.

The *Cartae Baronum* asked four main questions of the tenants-in-chief:

- How many knights were enfeoffed on your estates at the time of Henry I?
- How many have been enfeoffed since since 1135?
- How many knights are on your demesne in addition to those enfeoffed for knight-service?
- What are the names of your knights?

In this way the king could assess who his landholders were and also use the *Cartae* for financial assessments for his government, which he did in 1168 when he required financial aid for the marriage of his daughter Matilda to Duke Henry of Saxony. The king also wanted to know if there were more knights enfeoffed on his barons' estates than were necessary for the quotas.

The *Cartae Baronum* was in effect a record of the *servitium debitum* that had in the majority of cases been fixed in the reign of William the Conqueror. The document is essential for the study of Anglo-Norman feudalism.

The financial demands made in the *Cartae Baronum* were not new, however. Henry I demanded payments on the number of knights' fees created instead of actual service (scutage), as the 1130 pipe roll from his reign shows. Henry II was reviving and updating his grandfather's practice.

The *Cartae Baronum* was therefore very useful to the Exchequer; so much so that it was copied out twice in the thirteenth century. It enabled the king to fully exploit his rights over lands granted out as fiefs.

The Inquest of the Sheriffs (1170)

The key personnel at the heart of Henry II's financial and administrative reforms were the sheriffs. These were the men who represented the king in the provinces. There is no doubt that by the mid-twelfth century the sheriffs of England had become too powerful. Barons had acquired sheriffdoms as part of their personal estates before the reign of Stephen, and the civil wars only served to encourage this movement.

Henry II returned to England briefly in the spring of 1170 after a four-year absence and set up a special commission to enquire into malpractices into local government. Such inefficiency had been an issue since the start of Henry's reign, but the administration of the royal demesne, the *Cartae Baronum,* the aid for the marriage of the king's daughter in 1168 and royal justice had thrown up all sorts of concerns. Not only did the king's justices enquire into the activities of the sheriffs, but they also investigated financial payments made to archbishops, bishops, abbots, earls, barons, knights, citizens, merchants, stewards and servants. It was, in the words of one chronicler, a 'miraculous inquest'. The king wanted to ascertain the financial exploitation of the country in the four years of his absence since 1166 and the *Cartae Baronum*.

The fragments that survive of the returns of the inquest reveal the astonishing detail and tenacity of the enquiries made. The 'Inquest' reflects the authority of the English Crown in carrying out such an investigation; any such event in France or Germany would have been unthinkable.

As a result of the inquiry, almost all of the sheriffs were replaced, as the pipe roll of 1170 shows. Of the six who continued in office, four were members of the king's household. Until 1170, sheriffs had generally been local barons; after 1170, sheriffs were civil servants, members of the bureaucratic class and agents of the king who owed everything to royal service.

ROYAL JUSTICE AND THE DEVELOPMENT OF ENGLISH COMMON LAW

Henry II took old English laws and customs and applied his bureaucratic reforms and Angevin investigative powers to reform, reshape and fundamentally alter the law of the land, creating a framework for English common law. In doing so he standardised legal practices, created a judiciary and rationalised judgements by common use of the jury.

One of the causes of the Inquest of Sheriffs was the administrative reform to English law begun in 1166 by Henry II. The **Assizes** of Clarendon and Northampton made great changes to government administration and subsequently transformed English justice by standardising customary law.

English common law also owed much to the use of Roman Civil Law and the itinerant justices who travelled around in circuits (**eyres**), dispensing justice. Judgements, penalties and the use of the jury (not in itself new) were standardised across England. Furthermore, these law courts dealt not only with criminal cases but also with the multitude of property disputes and questions of land ownership amongst the growing knightly class.

English laws and law courts

English law and custom were diverse. There were courts of law of the vill (for village by-laws) and the manor (for the landlord's private estate), hundred courts (for petty crimes of lowly types), shire courts and borough courts (for more serious crimes and debts), honorial, feudal courts (for dealing with inheritances, dowers, vassals' obligations), courts of the bishops and archbishops (for the care of souls and the discipline of the clergy), and the court of the king – the highest court in the land, where the king's rights were enforced, and which also functioned as the final court of appeal from the lesser courts. The divisions between these courts were not often clear and it depended on the nature of the offence and the status of the accused as to which court dealt with the case.

Most criminals were dealt with locally and according to procedures of Anglo-Saxon law. Anyone caught red-handed was hanged on the spot or condemned to death at a court hearing.

The question of proof

Once public accusations had been made by a jury of twelve men sworn in, or by a formal complaint, proof had to be supplied; this was another problem that had no simple solution. Oath and ordeal were the two main methods used. Proof by oath involved one or both parties recruiting a number of **oath-helpers**. Proof by **ordeal** involved water or iron, but the Normans introduced trial by battle.

By 1215 the Church had withdrawn its support for forms of trial by ordeal. By this time, however, judgement reached by the testimony of the sworn jury had become far more common and it was this that became the cornerstone of the royal courts of Henry II's reign.

In ordeal by iron, the accused carried a hot metal bar until his hand blistered; proof was demonstrated by rapid healing of the blister.

The Assizes of Clarendon (1166) and Northampton (1176)

Royal justice in the first decade of Henry II's reign was no different from the early years of Henry I's reign. But when the king and his barons met at Clarendon in 1166 they made substantial modifications to the customary law. The sheriff and county justices were ordered to make inquiries into those suspected of the crimes of murder, robbery or theft. This was to be done through juries. Such juries were not new. They consisted of representatives of the hundreds and village communities, who all testified under oath to all the crimes committed in their neighbourhood.

What was new?

- The Assize insisted that testifying under oath should become standard procedure everywhere and that juries should also testify about crimes committed since Henry II became king.
- Those indicted of serious crimes were to be put on trial not by the shire court but by the ordeal of trial by water.
- The sheriffs were to hunt down suspects and bring them to trial, regardless of the rights of holders of **franchises**. This meant that the sheriffs could for the first time pursue justice on land and property from which they had previously been excluded.

KEY TERM

Oath-helper A man who swore a solemn oath to the truth of his declarations supporting the oath of another. They could lie, of course, but would be damned to eternal hell if they did so.

KEY TERM

Ordeal (Old English *ordel* 'judgement') in the ordeal by water, the accused was bound with a rope which had a knot above his head. If he sank down as far as the knot he was pulled up and saved. If he floated he was judged to be guilty.

KEY TERM

Franchise A privilege or right, usually legal, granted by the king.

- Once the criminal was convicted, his lands passed back to his lord, but his chattels (home and belongings) were sold off by the sheriff and the money sent to the treasury.

The Assize of Clarendon was to remain in force as long as it pleased the king and, ten years later, at the Assize of Northampton, it was re-enacted and the procedures were gradually accepted as normal administration.

Itinerant justices in 'eyre'

Soon after the Assize of Clarendon, Richard de Lucy, one of the justiciars, and Geoffrey de Mandeville, Earl of Essex, set off on a 'general eyre' of the country. They had covered half of England by October, when Earl Geoffrey fell sick and died. It was not the first time in the reign of Henry II that royal justices had been out to the shires, but it was the first 'general eyre' attempted probably since 1135. The difference between those counties visited and those not was obvious. The pipe rolls recorded thirty-one felons in Essex and Hertfordshire, thirty-nine in Lincolnshire and one hundred and one in Norfolk and Suffolk, all visited by the justices. By contrast, the sheriffs of Gloucestershire, Hampshire, and Wiltshire reported eight, four and three: these counties had not been visited. Such a great discrepancy prompted the king to set up the Inquest of the Sheriffs in 1170s to ensure that the sheriffs were pursuing criminals efficiently.

Soon after this first 'general eyre' a new plan was devised. Several groups of justices visited every shire in the country over the next three years, sometimes twice. As a result the administration of royal justice was taken away from the sheriffs and county justices and placed in the hands of the itinerant justices.

The court of King's Bench at Westminster

Ranulf de Glanvill was justiciar of England from 1180 to 1189 and probably wrote the lawbook entitled *The Treatise on the Laws and Customs of England*, which described the workings of the royal courts at the end of Henry II's reign. By this time a chief court had been established at Westminster, a court that travelled around the country with the itinerant royal justices, and the king's court that travelled with the king. The first two types of court worked systematically, hearing pleas brought by the plaintiff who had applied to the chancery for a writ. Writs were then sent to the sheriff, instructing him to empanel a jury and prepare the evidence for the impending arrival of the justices.

The court at Westminster was the headquarters of the itinerant justices. Here justices could seek advice from colleagues, finish cases from the shires and receive plaintiffs who could afford to bring their case without waiting for the justices to come to the shire. It became the nerve-centre of the new judicial administration that was revolutionising English justice. It was here that rolls

---

KEY EVIDENCE

From the Assize of Northampton (1176) 'If anyone has been accused before the justices of the lord king of murder or theft or robbery or of harbouring men who do such things, or of forgery or of arson by the oath of twelve knights of the hundred, or, if knights be not present, by the oath of twelve free and lawful men and by the oath of four men from each vill of the hundred, let him go to the ordeal of water, and if he fail, let him lose one foot.'

KEY EVIDENCE

From the Chronicles of Roger of Howden (c. 1200) 'And when a robber or murderer of thief or receiver of them has been arrested … if the justices are not about to come soon enough to the county where they have been taken, let the sheriffs send word to the nearest justice by some well-informed person that they have arrested such men, and the justices shall send back word to the sheriffs informing them where they desire the men to be brought before them.'

of the judgements were kept (plea rolls have survived since 1194) so that lawyers could refer to previous cases.

Much of English common law was judge-made law. The justices were appointed by and supervised by the king. They were professionals, experienced and intelligent. In short, they were the new judiciary.

Novel disseisin

The king wanted not only to ensure that criminals were convicted and punished by his courts but also to ensure that his judges dealt with disputes over property. The massive land-grab by the Normans after 1066 and the subsequent creation of hereditary estates amongst the Anglo-Norman landholding class resulted in continuous disputes over property. Some time around 1176 Henry II issued his assize of *Novel disseisin*, by which all freemen could sue in the royal court to recover seisin (feudal possession) of land that they claimed had been rightfully theirs. Once the plaintiff had purchased a writ from the chancery, a date was set for a trial, either before the king's justices at Westminster or the justices in eyre. The plaintiff, the defendant (or his bailiff) and a jury of twelve neighbours had to be present, without delay or excuse.

Mort d'ancestor

<table>
<tr><td>

KEY EVIDENCE

From Ranulf de Glanvill, *The Treatise on the Laws and Customs of England* (c. 1185) 'The king to the sheriff greeting. Summon by good summoners those twelve knights (naming each) that they attend on such a day before me or my justices at such a place, prepared on their oaths to declare whether R or N has the greater right to one hide of land (or in the subject matter of dispute) which the aforesaid R claims against the aforesaid N…'

</td><td>

This legal action may have settled the right to property but did not settle better right for all time. In 1176 the king devised the assize of *Mort d'ancestor*, by which the plaintiff was given seisin of his father's lands if the jury recognised that his father had died in possession and that the plaintiff was his father's heir.

Often the litigants came to a private agreement, offering money to withdraw from court. The final agreement was drawn up in duplicate under the supervision of the justices; these 'fines' survive from 1163 and were used as title deeds to property. From 1195, the court kept a third copy, the 'foot of the fine'.

These legal actions were very popular amongst the landed class and changed the way property disputes were dealt with. They also introduced into English law the key concepts of possession and ownership.

The 'grand' assize

If the litigants came to court and the defendant did not offer convincing evidence or a compromise, then the dispute was tested by a duel. After 1179 however, an alternative was offered; trial by 'grand' assize, which was a jury of twelve knights of the shire, as opposed to the 'petty' assizes of the jury of freemen. The grand assizes could only take place in the royal courts and was a serious affair. The knights were carefully selected and sent to view the property.

</td></tr>
</table>

WALES, SCOTLAND AND IRELAND
Wales

Henry II's success in re-establishing strong royal government in England was
not reflected in his efforts towards the Welsh. Two great Welsh leaders of the
later twelfth century were Owain of Gwynedd and Rhys ap Gruffudd. These
leaders enjoyed greater powers than any Welsh leaders in the time of Henry
I. Henry II's expeditions into Wales in 1157, 1163 and 1165 had mixed
results. After Owain's death in 1170, Henry recognised the lords of
Gwynedd and Deheubarth as subordinate kings; Rhys was appointed
'justiciar of all Deheubarth' and supported Henry II in the rebellion of
1173–74.

Scotland

Henry's successes against the Scottish were great. In 1157 he regained
Northumbria and Cumbria, returning the border to that of 1136. The king,
young Malcolm IV, recognised Henry's military might, and was able to
retain the earldom of Northamptonshire. Malcolm's brother, William the
Lion, joined in the rebellion against Henry II in 1173 but was captured at
Alnwick in 1174. Now Henry was in a stronger position than ever before.
William was forced to become Henry's 'liege man' for Scotland; the bishops,
abbots, earls and barons of Scotland were all forced to swear fealty to Henry
and his heirs.

Ireland

During the eleventh century Ireland was a centre of trading (slaves and furs),
a country of hostile raiders and an ancient Christian community. During the
later twelfth century Ireland became a place of conquest and colonisation
under the Anglo-Norman aristocracy. This started when the exiled king of
Leinster, Dermot MacMurrough, sought Norman soldiers from Henry II.
Given the king's permission to do so, he found many Anglo-Norman lords
from south Wales, in particular Richard of Clare, Lord of Chepstow. These
lords landed near Waterford and Wexford in 1169 and 1170 and assisted
Dermot in capturing Waterford and Dublin. But when Dermot died in
1171, Henry II recalled those lords under pain of severe punishment, as he
was preparing a royal expedition to Ireland. He could not afford any
independent alliances between his chief tenants and other Irish kings.

Henry II's invasion of Ireland in 1171–72 created an Anglo-Irish lordship.
The Anglo-Norman lords and the Irish kings recognised the authority of the
English Crown. There followed within the space of a generation an English-
Irish pattern of government, with counties, sheriffs and coroners, central
courts and an Exchequer, all modelled on English government. The great
feudal fiefs of Leinster and Meath were subdivided into baronies and knights'
fees. This submission of Ireland and subsequent expansion into the rest of the
country introduced an entirely new political structure to Britain.

WHY WERE HENRY II'S RELATIONS WITH HIS FAMILY SUCH A FAILURE?

Henry's sons

Henry's problems lay with his sons. He had four healthy sons in 1173; the eldest was eighteen, the youngest four. The sons were Henry, Richard, Geoffrey and John. Henry had been recognised as Henry II's heir to England in 1155; in 1158 he did homage to Louis VII of France for Normandy. The other lands would not all pass to Henry, however. Richard was regarded as his mother's heir to Aquitaine from early on, and Geoffrey was the future duke of Brittany. The problem was that Henry outlived two of his sons and denied them all power in his lifetime so that they grew bitter and treacherous.

Marriage alliances

Henry made arrangements early on to secure his dynasty so that his kingdom would not suffer the same fate that had followed the death of his grandfather,

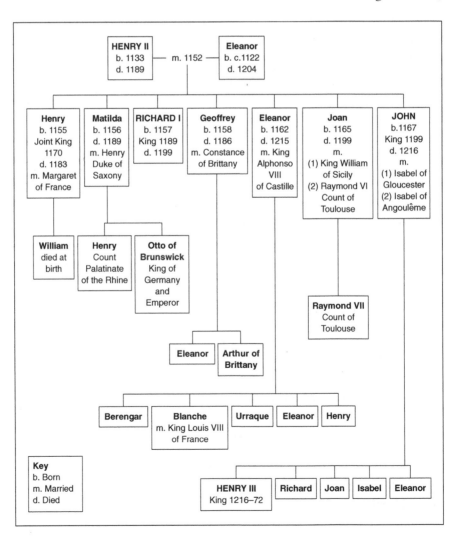

The Angevin genealogy

Henry I. Henry sealed his sons' inheritances by marriages; Prince Henry married Margaret, the third daughter of Louis, in 1160, and Richard was betrothed to Louis's fourth daughter, Alice. Geoffrey was betrothed to Constance, daughter and heiress of Conan, Duke of Brittany, and received the homage of the Breton barons in 1169. To secure young Henry's inheritance, the prince was crowned king of England at Westminster in 1170. This was not normal in England, but Henry II cited continental custom and hoped that it would guarantee a smooth succession. Richard was invested with the duchy of Aquitaine in 1172. John, the youngest, aged four in 1173, was betrothed to the daughter and heiress of Count Humbert of Maurienne and Savoy, though he had no inheritance.

The 'Great War', 1173–74

In the spring of 1173 Henry's empire was engulfed in rebellion. Henry's sons, denied power by their father, made war on him with the assistance of the king of France and the encouragement of their mother, Eleanor.

As part of the marriage treaty between the infant John and Humbert's daughter Alice, Henry II gave John three major castles in Anjou. Young Henry, now crowned king of England and recognised as duke of Normandy but without any real power or castles, protested and demanded to be able to govern part of his inheritance. Henry II refused his first-born any say in government, at which young Henry escaped from his father's court to Paris in March, followed by Richard and Geoffrey, equally denied any power by their father. At the heart of this remarkable family rebellion was the boys' mother, Queen Eleanor, who was captured in November and imprisoned in England.

In Paris, young Henry made promises he could not keep and denounced his father's government to anyone who would listen. His father-in-law, King Louis VII of France, the counts of Flanders, Blois and Boulogne, supported him; local revolts occurred across the Angevin lands on the Continent and the earls of Chester, Leicester and Norfolk rebelled in England. The king of Scots, William the Lion, invaded the northern borders.

The king did not panic. In the autumn he captured the earls of Chester and Leicester, chased the invaders out of Normandy and crushed the Angevin revolt. In July, 1174, the king of Scots was captured at Alnwick and in September Henry forced Louis into accepting a truce. Richard, the young duke of Aquitaine, was attempting to raise revolt against his father in southern France, but was outmanoeuvred by his father.

Henry II's triumph was complete. Rebel castles were demolished and rebels fined. Henry was stronger than ever in England. The captured Scottish king received Scotland back as a fief and paid homage for it. The Welsh princes agreed to a settlement and the king of Connaught became Henry's vassal in Ireland. In this mood, Henry returned to England in 1175 and inaugurated a second wave of legal and administrative reforms in his government there.

In 1181 Geoffrey married Constance and ruled Brittany in her name. Richard spent more time in Aquitaine, ruling the local barons. Only the young Henry, with an allowance of £15,000 and just two Norman castles, had nothing to do. When Henry II demanded that Richard and Geoffrey should do homage to their elder brother, Richard refused. Young Henry and Geoffrey then turned on Richard and made efforts to drive him out of Aquitaine. In the summer of 1183 young Henry contracted dysentery and died.

Philip II of France

Richard was now the heir-general to the Angevin empire. There was no effort to crown him king of England however, as his brother had been. That was not the only thing to change since the great rebellion. In 1180 Louis VII died, to be succeeded by his young son, Philip. This king of France was to prove the greatest enemy of the Angevins, first to Richard and then to John. He spent his life plotting and conspiring to bring down the Angevin empire and finally succeeded in 1204.

Betrayal, desertion and death (1189)

Henry II wanted nothing but peace in his approaching old age. However, in 1186 Geoffrey was killed in a tournament. In 1187 Philip of France invaded Anjou and Henry was forced to give up territory, the first time he had done so in his reign. When Richard savagely put down a rebellion in Aquitaine, Philip appealed to Henry to control his son, but Henry was unable to do so. Philip then mercilessly invaded the western Angevin counties of Berry, Auvergne and Touraine. Henry was again forced to sue for peace late in 1188

Chinon Castle, Anjou, France

but refused to allow Richard to take possession of Touraine, Maine and Anjou. Richard, already distrustful of his father and jealous of his brother, joined Philip – which he had planned on doing anyway – and in the summer of 1189 they invaded Maine and Anjou, the heartland of the Angevin empire.

In July Henry II was forced into unconditional surrender. Philip of France had cynically and ruthlessly exploited Henry's poor relations with his sons and the inflexibility of the king had left him in an impossible position. So ill with fever that he had to be propped up on his horse, Henry surrendered lands, castles and payments for Philip's expenses. 'May the Lord spare me until I have taken vengeance on you,' the king whispered into his son's ear as they exchanged the kiss of peace.

Henry then asked to see the list of traitors who had sided with Richard and Philip. At the top of the list was John, his youngest and his favourite son. When he saw this, he lost the will to live. On 6 July 1189, Henry II died in his great fortress at Chinon, deserted by his sons, his wife imprisoned, his ancestral lands in tatters.

CASE STUDY 4

ELEANOR OF AQUITAINE: A STUDY IN MEDIEVAL QUEENSHIP

No twelfth-century woman captures the imagination as much as Eleanor of Aquitaine, queen first of France and then of England. Eleanor outlived Henry II and three of their sons, to die in 1204 aged eighty-two, venerated and loved by her subjects. Although an heiress and queen twice over, her power was limited and expressed largely through her husband and sons.

Marriage to Louis VII of France

Eleanor was born in 1122 and was fifteen when she married Louis VII of France. She was a headstrong, black-eyed beauty and Louis was no match for her. Educated as a monk, he was famously dull. Eleanor was the only daughter and heiress of Duke William X of Aquitaine. Aquitaine was in southern France and Duke William's court at Poitiers played host to a very different culture of courtly love and **troubadours** singing the *chansons* of love. Eleanor inherited Aquitaine in 1137, the year she married Louis. After fourteen years of marriage they produced only two daughters – a serious concern for the French Crown (Eleanor later produced five sons for Henry). In 1152, Louis obtained a divorce based on their close blood-ties, but within eight weeks Eleanor, aged thirty, was married secretly to Henry, who was nineteen.

Marriage to Henry II

The moment Eleanor was divorced she was in a perilous position. Louis had not only given up his wife but also Aquitaine, as it was Eleanor's in her own

From 'Concerning the Instruction of a Prince', by Gerald of Wales (c.1192) 'His groans ever increasing, he spake these words as from a full heart and wrung from the remnant of his thought by the violence of his malady and the gravity of his grief and indignation, "Shame, shame on a conquered king!" and so he laboured in his death-agony. At length, uttering words of dire calamity, he passed away and went to his resting-place, overwhelmed and oppressed with grief rather than succumbing to a natural death.'

Troubadours

These were singer-songwriters who were especially popular in southern France. Eleanor's grandfather, Duke William IX, was a troubadour as well as a ruler. The songs of the troubadours told of war, politics and women. They developed a cult of platonic love, when the lady was unattainable, usually married and of great nobility. Women in the south were in this way idealised and this contributed to their improving status. Eleanor grew up in this environment, which was different from the north, where women were seen chiefly as child-bearers.

right. Any man who married her would thus be in command of the duchy in her name, even if it meant abduction – a not infrequent event. Eleanor managed to ride from Paris to Poitiers, avoiding an ambush by Henry's younger brother Geoffrey, and also the count of Blois who had designs on the now free heiress. Louis made a grave error, not in divorcing Eleanor – as it was clear that she was not going to give him a son – but in failing to prevent the marriage, as it enabled Henry to gain half of France to add to an inheritance that would certainly include Anjou and Normandy and, a year later, the kingdom of England when Stephen met Henry at the Treaty of Winchester.

Political eclipse

Eleanor was often formally involved in government, issuing writs in her own name down to 1163, and also acted as regent if she did not accompany Henry abroad. However, it was a marriage of equals but in an unequal world. The years of travel and childbearing were a sharp contrast to life in Louis's court and she was totally overshadowed by her second husband. The reasons for this were first that Henry had an even more dominant personality than his wife, second that she was kept busy producing sons and heirs for him, and the third factor here was that Henry and Eleanor grew apart.

Six sons and three daughters were born in the period 1153 to 1167 (Henry, Matilda, Richard, Geoffrey, Eleanor, Joan and John, her last child, all survived to adulthood). If we include probable miscarriages and unrecorded infant deaths, Eleanor must have been in a constant state of pregnancy and recovery – the usual lot of medieval woman, whatever her class and status.

Rebellion

In 1173, Eleanor reappeared in the political world. Now aged fifty-three, she was past childbearing age. Her husband was in his prime, at forty-one. Henry had secured his boundaries, instigated financial and administrative reform in England and crowned his eldest son king. Eleanor had appeared very briefly as his regent, but such was the energy of her husband that by 1173 it was clear to Eleanor that she was never going to exercise any political power in her own right. When her favourite son Richard was invested as duke of Aquitaine in 1170, Eleanor expected to govern the region with him, but Henry maintained a tight control of the reins.

In 1173 the sons rebelled against their father, demanding more power. The eldest, Henry, was eighteen; Henry II had been given Normandy at sixteen but refused to grant his son any real power. At night, from the great fortress of Chinon, three sons slipped away, to the court of Louis VII. Eleanor attempted to follow them, disguised as a man, but was captured by her husband's soldiers, and imprisoned for the next sixteen years. Why did Eleanor encourage her sons to rebel against their father? Presumably because she herself had no power under Henry and now that her sons were growing up, she wanted to find influence through them. Possibly she was jealous of Henry II's adulterous affairs, especially with Rosamund Clifford, the love of his life.

Years of imprisonment

Any pretence Eleanor and Henry might have had of marital happiness ended in 1173. Henry lived openly with Rosamund after 1173 until her death in 1176. Eleanor was not kept in a prison cell, but was under close watch and virtual confinement until 1189. After 1183 she was sometimes allowed to appear publicly with the king, but she was never his companion. Evidence from the Exchequer shows that she was kept at Winchester, guarded by Ralph FitzStephen, one of Henry II's most trusted officers of the chamber, for twelve years. She did appear at the Christmas court at Windsor in 1184 and travelled with the king in France from 1185–86, and she was allowed contact with her children.

Widowhood and power

The last fifteen years of Eleanor's long and eventful life illustrate that she was capable, when permitted, of wielding political power to great effect. She was instrumental in securing power for both her remaining sons, Richard and John. One of Richard's first orders as king of England was to release his mother from captivity. This was due of course to filial duty, but also because his mother could tour England proclaiming her son's title as king. The royal succession, as we have seen in 1066, 1087, 1100 and 1135, was not something to be taken for granted. Eleanor was given wide-ranging powers, which were not merely ceremonial. She attended courtly functions and councils, but it was in the absence of Richard that Eleanor stepped into the limelight.

Richard set off on what became the Third Crusade in 1190 and did not return until 1194. During his absence his younger brother John schemed to take power in England but their mother, Eleanor, played a large part in ensuring that the barons remained loyal to Richard and, on Richard's return, Eleanor mediated between the two brothers. Eleanor travelled abroad for Richard, accompanying his bride-to-be Berengaria to Sicily in 1191 on what was an important diplomatic mission and going on to meet the Pope in Rome. In 1194, at Richard's request, she travelled to Germany to meet the Emperor to negotiate her son's release from captivity. During Richard's imprisonment Eleanor helped to organise the ransom for his release.

After Richard's return home, Eleanor retired to the monastery at Fontevrault in the heart of Anjou. She was now seventy-two. But on Richard's sudden and unexpected death in 1199 she came out of retirement and played a part in assisting John to establish power. In July 1199 she did homage to Philip

II for her duchy of Aquitaine. This was no mere ceremony: Eleanor reaffirmed her role as duchess of her own inheritance in the name of her son John. This meant that Philip could not exploit John's rival for the lands of Aquitaine, his nephew Arthur. Alongside this homage, Eleanor and John issued documents stating that John was Eleanor's rightful heir to the duchy. This was a deliberate move to prevent Philip from intervening in Aquitaine. He would have to summon Eleanor, not John, to account for any activities in the region.

Ingenious though these schemes were, Philip's plans paid little attention to legal niceties. The opportunities of Richard's sudden death and the appearance of a rival to John, already seen as weak leader, were too good for Philip to miss. The disappearance of Arthur in 1202 and the death of Eleanor in 1204 opened the floodgates and the Angevin 'empire' was simply swept away.

The remarkable life and career of Eleanor of Aquitaine, twice queen, mother of two kings, duchess, regent and prisoner, illustrates the power and the limits of power of high-born women. As heiress to Aquitaine she was of major importance politically, but as a woman she was eclipsed by a more dominant husband who needed her to produce his heirs. But also as a woman she was mother to those heirs and wielded great influence after his death. It was her personality that was a vital factor in Eleanor's place in politics, but the opportunities had to be there also. Eleanor's career shows that ultimately her power was expressed through men and was therefore dependent upon their requirements, needs and weaknesses. As if to underline this, Eleanor

The effigies of Eleanor of Aquitaine, Henry II and Richard I at Fontevrault Abbey

was buried at Fontevrault and lies between the two men in her life – her husband Henry and her favourite son, Richard.

CONCLUSION: A LEAP FORWARD?

Many of the great legal and administrative reforms of Henry II's reign were instigated during his time in England in 1166, 1170 and from 1175 to 1180. So much bore the stamp of the king's personality. Henry of Bracton, a thirteenth-century lawyer, recorded a tradition that the king and his lawyers spent sleepless nights devising the writ of *novel disseisin*; Walter Map, a contemporary writer, said that Henry II was a 'subtle deviser of novel judicial processes'.

Historians differ in their views on Henry II's legal reforms. Some see his reforms as a genius producing a more rational law in place of the less rational feudal justice. Others see the king and his advisors simply reworking the old customs but in doing so producing a common law. It is probable that Henry had no overall policy for English law but that his reforms went beyond simply making the old system work better. He was no visionary and no genius. There was no leap forward. The reforms in royal administration made before 1135 were very important. The systems were in place. The language of law was in place in 1135. Government under Stephen had indeed been disrupted and damaged, but the systems were not destroyed or replaced. The changes brought about by Henry II after 1166 were indeed fundamental, but were essentially an acceleration of administrative change following the restoration of peace.

Future difficulties

Henry's vast dominions lasted as a political unity for fifteen years after his death. Brought together by a series of accidents, they were pulled apart very quickly by the weakness of Henry's youngest son John, the death of Eleanor and the ruthless skill of Philip of France. Successful though Henry was at securing peace in England, his intrusive measures in extorting his royal rights and his relentless taxation of England – continued by his son Richard – may well have sown the seeds for the baronial revolts against the Angevin government that engulfed England in 1215 and which triggered a fundamental revolution in kingship and government: Magna Carta.

SECTION 4

Good King Richard, bad King John?

INTRODUCTION

Outside the Houses of Parliament in London there is a statue of Richard I.
He is on horseback, holding a sword aloft. One might well wonder why it is
that a medieval Frenchman who spent only six months of his ten-year reign
in England, who died in central France and is buried in France, is
commemorated in such a way. Perhaps because Richard was Richard 'the
Lionheart', the Crusader, the brilliant general and chivalric hero who fought
off the king of France to keep the Angevin empire intact. There are no such
statues to John. John 'Lackland', John 'Softsword', the spoilt favourite of his
father, the treacherous, duplicitous child-murderer and child-kidnapper, and
loser of the family lands to Philip. But Richard, as we shall see, was not
'good' for the traditional reason of crusading chivalry and John, arguably, was
not 'bad' for the traditional reasons of evil and greed.

The key issues concerning Richard are:

- whether he bankrupted England and his Angevin lands with the result
  that John could not afford to hold out against Philip in 1204.
- whether Richard's absence had any damaging effect on English
  government.

Where John is concerned, the key issues are:

- whether his loss of the Angevin empire was due to circumstances outside
  his control or to his incompetence.
- what impact the baronial rebellion in 1214–15 had on English
  government and kingship.

THE SUCCESSION OF RICHARD

Soon after Henry's death at Chinon on 6 July 1189, Richard viewed his
father's body at Fontevrault. Not trusting the reports that his father was
dying, he did not come to his deathbed but arrived at the monastery at
nightfall, knelt, said a prayer, and departed to take possession of his kingdom
without a word. One legend has it that blood flowed from the nostrils of the
corpse in indignation when Richard knelt.

From Fontevrault Richard set off for Rouen, where he was girded with the
ducal sword and received the oaths of fealty from the Normans. He was in no
rush to get to England. The country had been at peace since the brief war of
1174. Richard was the first son to inherit the kingdom of England from his

father peacefully for centuries. He arrived at Portsmouth in August and was crowned at Westminster in September.

The Third Crusade

Richard had only one ambition to fulfil: to make the arduous journey to the Holy Land on the armed pilgrimage, known today as the **crusade**. This was to be Richard's driving force for the next five years. He left England in December 1189 and did not return until March 1194. Richard has been much criticised for being absent: why, one might ask, would a ruler desert his people? That is not the issue, however. In 1187, a Muslim army captured the city of Jerusalem. The Pope died of shock when he heard. All the major rulers of the West took vows to go to the Holy Land, including Henry II, Philip and Richard. Spiritual imperatives of the age may baffle us today, but to contemporaries they were all-consuming.

DID RICHARD BANKRUPT ENGLAND?

Crusade-fever swept across Europe. Religious fervour was all very well, however, but a lot of cash was needed to run a crusade. The Third Crusade, as it is now known, was the first crusade that involved English troops in large numbers, and Richard saw it very much as his crusade. Indeed, the German Emperor, Frederick, drowned on the way; Philip of France returned early, and Richard was left to deal with Saladin.

How did Richard raise the money?

- He made a peace treaty with William 'the Lion', king of the Scots in December 1189, whereby he formally acknowledged the independence of Scotland from England. This, known as the 'Quit-claim of Canterbury', put £6000 into Richard's treasury.
- He sold earldoms, lordships, sheriffdoms, castles, towns and lands to the highest bidders he could find. The Bishop of Winchester paid £3000 for two manors in Hampshire. Richard boasted that he would 'sell London if I could find a buyer'.
- He seized estates and fined incompetent and corrupt officers. When the Bishop of Ely died intestate (without a will) Richard was entitled to take the £2000-worth of coin, gold and silver plate belonging to him. Robert Marmion, Sheriff of Worcestershire, was removed from office and fined £1000. Of the twenty-seven men who were sheriffs in 1189, only five remained in office under Richard.

These measures worked. The Exchequer audited £31,089 in 1190 – twice as much as the previous year. Richard spent the money on equipping his men and £5000 on ships, as he intended to go by sea, via the Mediterranean.

The Crusades

The Crusades began in 1095 when Pope Urban II preached for the salvation of the Holy Churches in the East. His appeal was met with an astonishing response: tens of thousands of men, women and children set off for Jerusalem. Many thousands perished on the way, but the military crusade reached the Holy City in 1099 and, after a brief siege, captured it and slaughtered all the defenders. The Christians then established a kingdom with castles. The Second Crusade of 1144–47 failed to halt the growing unity of the Muslim armies and declining Christian numbers and poor leadership led to the catastrophic defeat of the Christian army by Saladin and the recapture of Jerusalem in 1187. Unlike 1099, however, there was no similar massacre, and Christian pilgrims were allowed to visit. The reaction in the West, however, was one of horror and fury.

Was Richard reckless and negligent?

No:

- Contemporaries saw the Crusade as Richard's highest duty.
- The Quit-claim secured peace with Scotland until 1215.
- There was nothing unusual in selling offices and titles. The men who took the posts were men of experience and not strangers to the realm. What was unusual was the short space of time in which this was accomplished.
- Richard treated his brother John with care, granting him vast estates in England, including six counties, numerous lordships and castles. John's marriage to Isabella of Gloucester brought him Bristol, Glamorgan and Newport. John was thus a great power in England and as the brother of the king would have been expected to maintain the peace.
- Richard had also placed four 'co-justiciars' in assistance to his chancellor William Longchamp, including William Marshal, Earl of Pembroke, Geoffrey fitzPeter, who had control of the lands of the earldom of Essex, William Briwerre and Hugh Bardolf. The first three of these co-justiciars came from families who had spent more than one generation in royal service.

England without Richard

In July 1190, Richard and Philip met with their armies and began the journey to the Holy Land. They were not to arrive in the Holy Land until the summer of 1191; *en route* Richard settled a succession dispute in Sicily and conquered Cyprus, turning it into a crusader base for the next century. On arriving in the Holy Land, Richard immediately captured the vital port of Acre, which had been under siege for two years, and set about re-establishing crusader castles and bases at Tyre, Ascalon and Jaffa. He defeated the legendary Saladin in battle at Arsuf but was unable to recapture Jerusalem. His peace treaty with Saladin did, however, preserve the crusader kingdom for another hundred years.

Richard departed from Jaffa in October 1192. The Angevin 'empire' that he had inherited from his father was still intact. Although there had been reports of disputes between Richard's chancellor, William Longchamp, and Prince John, Walter of Coutances, Richard's nominee, replaced Longchamp. It was not Richard's absence on the crusade that caused uncertainty in England, but his capture and imprisonment on the way home.

The imprisonment of Richard

Richard had many enemies. Philip of France, never a trustworthy or genuine crusader, had returned to France by Christmas 1191, openly boasting that he was going to destroy the king of England's lands. Richard's other enemies included the Count of Toulouse, the German Emperor Henry VI, and the

Duke of Austria, Leopold. This meant that a large part of the western Mediterranean coast was unsafe for Richard to set foot on. Richard headed instead for the Adriatic, but was shipwrecked near Venice, tracked down and seized by the Duke of Austria's men. Leopold had reason to hate Richard: Richard had torn down Leopold's flag at Acre because he was not equal to Richard or Philip; Richard had deposed Leopold's relative, Isaac, from Cyprus in 1191 and Richard was also wrongly blamed by Leopold for the murder of Conrad of Montferrat, Leopold's cousin. Leopold's lord and master was the Emperor Henry VI of the Hohenstaufen dynasty, systematically opposed by both Richard and his father in favour of Henry the Lion, Duke of Saxony and Richard's brother-in-law. For over a year Richard was kept in prison while kings and princes bartered over the cost of his freedom.

The treachery of John

To Philip of France, the imprisonment of Richard was heaven-sent. In 1189 Philip had only really succeeded in humiliating a sick old man; he had made no great gains from Henry II's demise. In Richard he faced a far greater military rival than he ever had in Henry. With Richard indefinitely detained he set about his lifelong ambition to bring down the Angevin hegemony by doing what he was best at: creating dissent between the Angevin brothers. Early in 1192 he offered John all the Angevin lands in France. At this point, Eleanor, fearing for her favourite son's possessions, crossed to England with Walter of Coutances and persuaded John to remain in England. But after Richard's imprisonment became known, John went to Paris in 1193 and did homage to Philip for Normandy and all Richard's other lands. John then returned to England to stir up rebellion, but failed utterly. The Quit-claim with the Scots ensured their loyalty; his mother Eleanor and Walter of Coutances mustered loyal troops and John was left with a few Welsh and Flemish mercenaries in Windsor Castle. Even so, John and Philip, who had caputed Gisors, one of Richard's great fortresses on the Normandy border, played upon the possibility that Richard might never be freed, reminding people of Duke Robert of Normandy, captured at Tinchebray and imprisoned for life by his brother Henry I of England.

A king's ransom

Having had a fortune extorted from it to pay for the crusade, England now had to contribute another fortune to pay for the ransom that had been set by the Emperor Henry VI at £60,000. Richard's trusted mother and justiciars set about raising England's share of the ransom, but John and Philip approached the Emperor with a new deal: they would pay Henry £1000 for every month he kept Richard, or £100,000 to hand him over to them or keep him for another year. Henry was tempted, but instead made Richard hand England over to him as a fief and promise to pay a further £5000 a year (this was kept quiet in England).

How did England contribute?

- Eleanor and the justiciars levied a 25 per cent tax on income and moveable property.
- A year's wool crop was taken from the Cistercian monasteries.
- Gold and silver plate was taken from churches.
- The earls and barons were encouraged to contribute as much as they could in the knowledge that the king would thank them.

HOW EFFECTIVE WAS RICHARD'S GOVERNMENT?

The financial cost to England and the Angevin lands was great, but government continued to work well in Richard's absence. The system of itinerant justices continued until John's rebellion in 1193. When Richard was away on the crusade, people continued as if he were returning, but with Philip home and Richard imprisoned, loyalties were stretched to breaking point.

Richard was finally set free in February 1194, after a year, six weeks and three days in prison. Once news was out that Richard was released ('Look to yourself; the Devil is loose', Philip wrote to John), any rebels in England knew that their time was up. The castellan of St Michael's Mount in Cornwall died of fright; the council of the realm declared John's estates forfeit and the bishops excommunicated him.

Revenge and recovery

John threw himself on the mercy of his brother, which he received. He had done nothing to damage the empire, which he would inherit five years later – except prove to the world how treacherous he was. Richard apparently received his tearful younger brother with good-humoured contempt, saying to him: 'You are a child. You have had bad companions'. John remained loyal to Richard, helping him regain much of the lost lands Philip had seized (with John's help) during Richard's imprisonment.

For Philip there was to be no mercy. From May 1194 until July Richard hounded Philip and his French allies, defeating him twice and regaining security in Aquitaine. The Norman-French border was more problematic, however, and when the two sides agreed to a truce, Philip had control of a large part of eastern Normandy.

This truce did not last long. For the next four years intermittent warfare went on along the Angevin-Norman-French border, Philip constantly raiding, besieging and attempting to cause revolt in the Angevin lands, Richard countersieging and counter-attacking. In 1196 Richard began building a great castle above the Seine on the Isle of the Andelys, called Château-Gaillard ('Saucy Castle'). It was a brilliant piece of engineering and architecture; Richard claimed that he would hold it even if its walls were

made of butter. Remarkably, it
was finished within two years
and cost £12,000, a staggering
amount (Richard spent £7000
on all the English castles in the
whole of his reign). Château-
Gaillard was to be the forward-
base for the reconquest of
Richard's Norman inheritance,
dominating the Seine and
hammering Philip's castles.
Unfortunately, it turned out to
play a defensive role in the
shambolic collapse of
Normandy under John.

Château-Gaillard, Normandy, France

Diplomatic triumphs

Richard secured his frontiers not just by making war on Philip but by a
series of intelligent diplomatic alliances:

- In 1196 he arranged an alliance with Count Raymond VI of Toulouse, the
  enemy of the Angevins since 1159. The Count agreed to marry Richard's
  sister Joan; this secured the southern borders of the Angevin empire.
- In 1197, Richard scored another major diplomatic victory, making a
  treaty with the Count of Flanders; this ensured that some of the major
  coastal ports facing England were no longer hostile.
- In 1198 Richard's preferred candidate to the German throne, Otto of
  Brunswick, an Angevin friend and count of Poitou since 1196, was
  elected and crowned king.

Seeing which way the wind was blowing, many border barons went over to
Richard. It was, as one chronicler said, because Richard was 'a good deal
richer in lands and in money, than the king of France'. Richard's diplomatic
warfare was winning, backed up with victories in the field. Philip had spent
all his money; French choniclers despaired, the English knew they were
winning.

Hubert Walter and the governance of England

During this time the government of England was entrusted into the hands of
one remarkable man, Hubert Walter, Archbishop of Canterbury and nephew
of Ranulf de Glanville, Henry II's justiciar. Hubert, as Bishop of Salisbury,
had accompanied Richard on the crusade and won his absolute confidence. In
May 1193 he was elected archbishop of Canterbury and at Christmas Richard
made him chief justiciar; in 1195 he was also made papal legate. In the
words of historian John Gillingham, Hubert Walter was 'one of the most

outstanding government ministers in English history'.

That said, the government of England was very much the king's business. During the crusade and Richard's imprisonment, no new assizes were issued; but on his return, there were instructions to the judges in 1194, a royal edict of 1195, concerning keeping the peace, a revised Forest Assize and the Assize of Weights and Measures in 1197. On Richard's charters the final words were *teste me ipso* 'myself as witness'. To fund his wars against Philip, Richard took great care over finances and logistics, as he had done over preparing for the crusade. Portsmouth became a naval base with a royal palace and a royal charter; Richard introduced a royal customs system, levied at a rate of one tenth on overseas trade. Anyone who resisted the command of the justiciar was sent to the king, who was now increasingly in Normandy.

Death of the Lionheart

When Richard left England in May 1194 he was never to return. He spent most of his time in Normandy after 1196, dealing with Philip. In the spring of 1199 he headed towards the southern borders of his lands, into the Limousin. The Viscount of Limoges and the Count of Angoulême had been Richard's enemies since 1176; Richard laid siege to the Viscount's castle at Chalus-Chabrol, south of Limoges. After three days the castle was on the verge of surrender, but on the evening of 26 March 1199, a crossbow bolt hit Richard in the shoulder. He was not wearing a mail coat as the only threat was a single crossbowman who was using a frying pan as a shield. Richard applauded the well-aimed bolt but ducked behind his own shield too late. Retiring to his tent without a fuss, Richard broke off the shaft, but the iron barb was wedged deep into his shoulder. A surgeon dug it out but it was a mess. Infection spread and Richard sent for his mother; he died on the evening of 6 April.

Richard's death, when the news was out, caused a tremendous shock. He was the first king of England since Harold Godwinsson to die of wounds sustained in action; he was the last until Richard III in 1485. Furthermore, he left behind no son, though he designated John his heir as he lay dying.

Richard had managed to maintain control of his father's empire. More than that; he had done so while absent on crusade and imprisoned, in the face of opposition from the king of France, the emperor of Germany, the duke of Austria and his own brother. After his return he regained much of the territories Philip had taken. He showed that he could run England while in Normandy from 1194 to 1199. True, Richard spent vast amounts of money on the crusade, his ransom and making war on Philip, but he had vast resources at his disposal. His father's administrative reforms ensured the smooth running of government in his absence. Five years after Richard's death it was all lost.

WHY WAS THE REIGN OF KING JOHN SUCH A DISASTER?

The youngest son of Henry II ruled England from 1199 to 1216. During the course of his reign he lost almost all of his family lands in Normandy, Anjou and Aquitaine. Whilst on campaign in England, John died, aged forty-nine, leaving a nine-year-old son and half the kingdom occupied by a French army. Ironically though, John spent more time in England than either his brother or his father and was buried in England, at Worcester.

Although a disaster for John, his reign is of monumental importance to English constitutional history. It witnessed the decisive separation of England and Normandy after 138 years and the inauguration of a new monarchy confined with legal limits. What is also fascinating is that the personality of the king played a major part in these events; the loss of Normandy and the Magna Carta were by no means inevitable. Just as the wisdom, energy and political skills of Henry II and Richard held together the Angevin empire, the flaws of John lost it all.

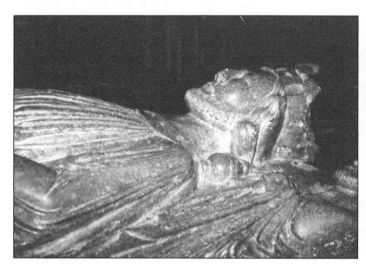

King John's effigy, Worcester Cathedral, England

The reasons for John's disastrous reign include:

- His nephew, Arthur, disputed the succession to the throne.
- John's marriage to a girl who was already betrothed caused great upset.
- There was already mutual distrust between John and the barons in France and England because of John's behaviour during Richard's absence.
- Philip of France had resources as great as John's by 1200.
- John lacked the generalship of Richard and the diplomatic skills of his father, Henry II. He favoured a small group of men who gained too much power.
- John's murder of his nephew caused widespread disgust amongst the barons and lost him support.
- John spent the remainder of his reign attempting to regain his lost lands and this contributed to baronial rebellion in England.

The succession of John: younger brother or nephew?

Unlike his father Henry II, who took almost two months from the death of Stephen to his coronation (the longest interval for over a century) and his brother Richard, who was absent from his kingdom for over four years, John faced a rival to his throne. Whilst some form of hereditary custom had been established since the Norman Conquest, the *coups d'état* of Henry I and Stephen showed that this had not been refined. The problem facing John was that although Richard declared him his heir as he lay dying in the tent at Chalus-Chabrol, he had a nephew, Arthur, who was the son of John's elder brother, Geoffrey. By strict succession, therefore, Arthur should inherit. But Arthur was a child, heavily influenced by his Breton mother, Constance.

The *History of William Marshal,* a biographical poem written in 1226, tells vividly of the dilemma facing the barons at the unexpected and premature death of Richard. William Marshal was the husband of the Countess of Pembroke and a major baron and loyal servant to the Angevin dynasty. Late at night, the earl, who had just got out of bed, supported John, quoting Norman custom that 'The son is nearer the land of his father than the nephew is'. The Archbishop predicted that he would be sorry for his decision but backed down. William Marshal and the Archbishop headed for England and secured from the barons an oath of loyalty to John. Several nobles had grievances from the reigns of Henry II and Richard, which John promised to address if they swore fealty to him; at his coronation in May the new king issued a charter promising good government and the abolition of Richard's 'evil customs'.

Securing the Angevin inheritance

When news of Richard's death spread, the nobles of Brittany, Anjou, Maine and Touraine recognised the twelve-year-old Arthur as his heir. Arthur was in the custody of Philip of France, who was all too willing to assist the boy. One of the factors that did not help John was that Richard had initially declared Arthur his heir in 1189, but had then made John so powerful that Arthur's succession was bound to be massively contested by John. However, it was the septuagenarian Eleanor who took action on her son's behalf. Eleanor went to Poitou to receive the homage of her subjects and did homage herself to Philip for the duchy. She then ceded Aquitaine to John, who returned it to his mother to rule in her lifetime. This guaranteed John's authority over south-western France and denied Philip any excuse to intervene – at least until the death of Eleanor in 1204.

Peace with Philip

This left Anjou, Maine and Touraine – the Angevin heartland – and Brittany. After intermittent warfare with Philip, John occupied Le Mans in September 1199 and in the spring of 1200 Philip accepted that John was Richard's legal heir. In return John accepted that he was Philip's vassal and that Arthur would hold Brittany and Anjou from him. This was significant: what had been a general expression of homage under Henry II and Richard was now a legally binding agreement under French jurisdiction. However, John had secured his inheritance and bought time to consolidate his hold over his continental possessions.

WHY DID JOHN LOSE NORMANDY?

In 1199 it would seem that John's character was that of a powerful Angevin prince guilty of little more than the family vice of rebellion born of insecurity with his own inheritance. Since Richard's return in 1194 he had led a useless but blameless existence. In 1199 he acted decisively, securing Normandy and England and winning recognition of his Angevin inheritance over Arthur. Why, then, in the space of four years, did he lose his continental possessions?

The answer lies in John's marriage to Isabelle of Angoulême, his murder of Arthur, Philip's skill in exploiting the barons' distrust of John and John's inability to manage his resources.

The abduction of Isabelle of Angoulême

Soon after the treaty with Philip, John married Isabelle, daughter and heiress of Count Ademar of Angoulême. John's first marriage, to Isabelle of Gloucester, had produced no children; as they were cousins an annulment was no problem (John also kept her lands). Marrying Isabelle of Angoulême was a strategic gain for John because the Angoulême territory connected Poitou and Gascony and the Angevin passage to Bordeaux. This southernmost part of the Angevin 'empire' was least controlled by the duchy of Aquitaine and was an area of potential weakness to the Angevin empire. It was, after all, the region where Richard had died besieging a rebel castle.

John's marriage to Isabelle was a further advantage to him because she was already betrothed to Hugh, Lord of Lusignan, who hoped to acquire Angoulême; Hugh had also won control of the lordship of La Marche. Once married to Isabelle, he would be lord of three powerful regions in Aquitaine and would alter the power balance in the south. By taking Isabelle from him, John hoped to emulate his father Henry II when he married Eleanor and gained the duchy of Aquitaine.

Although the advantages of marriage to Isabelle were great – she was also of French royal descent – John's mishandling of subsequent events proved fatal. Hugh of Lusignan was outraged, not just because he had lost territory in losing Isabelle, but because by law he was already married to her, having exchanged marriage vows. The only thing he had not done was consummate the marriage, because Isabelle was at the most twelve years old, perhaps as young as eight or nine, to John's thirty-three. Her first child with John was not born until 1207, which supports this view of her pre-pubescent age in 1200. If Isabelle was legally married to Hugh, then it made John's marriage to her extremely irregular.

Whatever the advantages of marriage to Isabelle, John's plans backfired drastically, leading ultimately to the loss of Normandy. This was not necessarily due to the marriage with Isabelle, but to John's handling of the (understandably) disgruntled Hugh. John made no attempt to compensate Hugh, who eventually appealed to King Philip as the ultimate overlord. Philip summoned John to his court but John refused, saying that as duke of Normandy he was only obliged to come to the borders of the duchy; Philip replied saying that John was summoned not as duke of Normandy but as count of Poitou. The French court then condemned John to be deprived of the lands he held from the French Crown, because of his refusal to offer the obedience of a vassal. Philip was now able to launch war on John and to accept Arthur's homage for John's lands. This was a direct consequence of the agreement John had made with Philip in 1200.

The murder of Arthur

The alliances with the Count of Flanders set up by Richard in 1197 and dropped by John in 1200, would have forced Philip to fight on more than one front. John's difficulties were added to when the Count of Toulouse changed sides, another alliance that Richard had established. Even so, the two kings attacked and counter-attacked across the Angevin frontiers without a breakthrough until the summer of 1202, when John learned that his mother was under siege from Arthur and the Lusignans at Mirebeau castle, just north of Poitiers.

John took action that was to prove the most brilliant of his military career. He rode south from Le Mans to Mirebeau, covering the 80 miles in 48 hours, surprising the besiegers before breakfast and defeating them. He captured Hugh of Lusignan and Arthur and a great number of prisoners, forcing Philip to give up his attack on the Normandy frontiers. But flushed with success, John did not use mercy. Twenty-two prisoners died under harsh conditions and John's seneschal of Anjou, William des Roches, defected to Philip. This was followed by other betrayals and when rumours of Arthur's death spread, many more rebelled, so that John was faced with attack from all sides in the spring of 1204.

Arthur was out of sight for about a year but John had made the decision to kill him by Easter 1203. Initially, John had intended to castrate or blind him – the common punishment meted out to political prisoners to render them powerless – but the gaoler, Hubert de Burgh, refused to carry out the command. John himself, or a hired thug, killed him, stabbing him to death and tying a stone to his body before throwing it in the river Seine. Arthur was a traitor to his lord, so a lawful execution would have been acceptable; Pope Innocent III did not condemn lawful acts. However, murder was not lawful execution; in an age where family bonds were close, the murder of a nephew made every baron shiver. From that moment on, John lost moral authority.

The fall of Château-Gaillard and the death of Eleanor

In the autumn of 1203 John made efforts to invade Brittany in order to draw Philip from his siege on the great castle at Château-Gaillard, Richard's 'saucy castle'. This campaign failed, and so did an attempt to relieve the siege on the castle. John retired to England for the winter but had by no means given up the defence of the duchy, which was still holding out for him. But on 6 March 1204, Richard's monumental castle was eventually captured by Philip, apparently because a French squire squeezed through a window in an extension built by John and opened a side-gate for the main force to storm through. The defenders, already starving, were defeated easily. Following that, Philip was able to overrun the duchy, encircling Rouen, which surrendered in June. The news of the capture of Château-Gaillard arrived in England just as John was preparing to return to France.

A double blow was delivered to John when his mother Eleanor died on 1 April. This meant that Philip was no longer obliged to stay out of Aquitaine, so his troops overran the duchy during the summer. Only two fortresses,

Anjou and Normandy, scene of the fighting in 1203–04

Chinon and Loches, held out until the spring of 1205. John was faced with treachery everywhere he turned.

Why did the nobility support Philip?

Although Philip had very cleverly exploited the niceties of feudal law over the Lusignan affair and the claims of Arthur, and John had made a bad situation far worse, the defections of the barons across the Angevin dominions finished off John's hopes. John became locked in a cycle of suspicion and fear; the murder of Arthur created distrust, and the promises of goodwill from Philip tempted Norman barons, who had already moved away from an 'Anglo-Norman' unity and who saw English barons as quite distinct from themselves. The centralising zeal of Henry II, when his justices interfered in local business, and the exhausting fundraising of Richard were well remembered. Philip was prepared to grant away castles; he also promised independence for the Norman Church, whose bishops did nothing to support John. They looked to Paris rather than Canterbury for leadership. As part of Capetian propaganda, Philip played very upon the idea of a 'greater France', stating that the Angevin possessions were only temporary and really belonged to Paris. Regaining those territories had always been Philip's ambition and now he was able to realise it.

The problem worsened when John used foreign mercenaries. He used them because he did not trust his own men, but their brutal behaviour made John's reputation far worse; some contemporaries thought for many years that John lost Normandy because of his use of mercenaries. The cost of the mercenaries made John extort even more money from his subjects, thereby causing greater dislike and hatred.

By the autumn of 1203 relations were so bad that William Marshal said to him: 'Sire, you have not enough friends. You have not been careful to avoid irritating people. If you had, it would have been better for us all'. John wasted a good deal of energy riding from one place to another, raising support and persuading barons to remain with him, rather than actually combating Philip. Some chroniclers believed he had been bewitched or at least infatuated by his child-bride and was unable to get out of her bed to deal with his collapsing empire; others saw him as lazy and indecisive. In the end, he believed that the barons were planning to capture him and take him to Paris.

Was John bankrupt?

A factor that played a part in the loss of Normandy and Aquitaine beyond personalities, circumstances and events was the underlying issue of finance. Conflict along the borders of the Angevin empire with France had almost become constant since Philip's accession in 1180, and the costs of warfare were huge. To cope with this, Richard and John effectively developed a 'war economy'.

Richard had proved that a large supply of cash made warfare successful in late twelfth-century Europe. It was no longer a matter of a few hundred men on horseback riding at breakneck speed to seize small timber castles or ambush unwary enemies. Warfare was now an expensive business: castles were built in stone and could hold out for many months; siege machinery needed to be the latest equipment. Troops more often than not were hired professionals formed around a core of aristocratic knights in the lord's or king's household. Richard was nothing if not a genius of logistics in his organisation for the Third Crusade and the defence of Normandy after his imprisonment.

But had Richard's vast spending and the increasing interference of Angevin officials under Henry II, Richard and John exhausted Angevin reserves so that Philip had more money than John in 1204?

Yes:
- Richard's crusade and ransom had cost vast amounts. Richard's castle-building (Château-Gaillard alone cost £12,000) and defence of his lands from 1194 to 1199 continued to crush the Angevin taxpayer.
- John had less money from Normandy than Richard did. His revenue for the years 1199–1202 were 45 per cent of Richard's in the year 1198. Richard's vast expenditure on his ransom and fortifications in Normandy had left John with insufficient cash to garrison and maintain those fortresses.
- The costs of maintaining the royal court in the lavish style expected of a period witnessing a renaissance of culture, arts and patronage had spiralled.
- Philip had put in place financial innovations and reforms which maintained his reserves more successfully than the Angevins. Philip could afford to hire a permanent force of mercenaries against Richard and John. Sir James Holt has suggested that by 1203, John may have had no more than 74 per cent or even as little as 41 per cent of Philip's funds. Holt argued that the royal income from England was only £34,500.

No:
- The wealth of the Angevins was legendary, second only to their greed. 'The lord king thirsts for money like a dropsical man for water,' wrote one contemporary of Richard. John, at the Christmas court of 1205, spent £700 on robes, and this was the year after he lost Normandy (the average annual income of a knight was £20).
- The historian John Gillingham argues that Holt's estimate of £34,500 for the English royal income is too low and that French estimates are inflated by borrowed funds and reserves. Adding up income from Normandy, England and Ireland, Gillingham estimated £63,000–£77,000 for John and £51,000–£72,000 for Philip. N. Barratt has also recently estimated

that between 1207 and 1212, John's revenues in England stood at £49,000 on average, double the figures for Richard I and Henry II.

- Gillingham also argued that John would have had income from Anjou and Aquitaine, which were rich. He argued that John's problems were not because he had inherited financial problems, but because he did not know how to rule.

Due to the lack of evidence and the way in which the incomplete evidence is interpreted, there is no solution to the problem of the relative finances of Philip and John. The French audit for the year 1202/3 is the only record for Philip's reign and so may not be a true reflection of his income. No records survive from the Anjou and Aquitaine areas of John's empire, so the record of John's income is not complete. The Normandy records for the year 1202/3 are incomplete and no figure for the extraordinary taxation in England for the year 1203 survives.

That said, the vast expenditure accrued by Richard certainly left John saddled with debt and with a smaller income from Normandy. Philip had certainly reformed and improved his financial system so that he was able to take on the Angevin dominions in 1203 to great effect; and once Philip had conquered those dominions he immediately benefited from the income those lands brought in. John also suffered the consequences of inflation (see page 193).

WALES, SCOTLAND AND IRELAND
Wales
The network of allegiances Henry II had established between himself and Rhys ap Gruffudd fell apart after Rhys's death in 1197. Llewelyn ap Iorwerth emerged as the principal leader of Gwynedd and expanded his powers into Carmarthen and Cardigan during the baronial rebellions against John in 1215–17. In 1218 he secured his dominance with a treaty with the English government and reigned until 1240, never losing that dominance.

Scotland
In Scotland, King William was able to free himself from the humiliating terms of the 1174 treaty with Henry II on the king's death in 1189. Richard I was so eager for cash for the crusade that he released William from those agreements in return for William's oath of loyalty and, more importantly, over £6500. Under John, William failed to regain Northumbria and was forced to hand over a large amount of money and two of his daughters to be married. William's son, Alexander II, exacted revenge during John's crisis years of 1215–17, marching to Carlisle and as far south as Dover to link up with the French prince who had invaded England. In 1217 he did homage to Henry III and peace was secured for decades after.

Ireland

Henry II had plans for his youngest son. He intended to make him king of Ireland and in 1185, at the age of seventeen, John led an expedition to the new Anglo-Norman colony. It was a disaster: soldiers were unpaid, the native Irish were deeply offended by the Anglo-Norman behaviour (apparently, John's men pulled their beards) and John never became king. Instead, on his accession in 1189, he became 'King of England and Lord of Ireland' which remained the standard title until Henry VIII took the title 'King of Ireland' in the sixteenth century.

In 1210, John led an army into Ireland on a far more successful expedition. He rooted out treacherous barons and secured the submission of many native Irish kings.

WHY WAS THERE A BARONIAL REBELLION IN 1215?

Cash flow, treachery, indecision and personality all played their part in the loss of Normandy, Anjou and Aquitaine in 1204. These themes continued to dominate John's reign because the king never saw the loss of these territories as permanent. He remained fixated with regaining those lands and in doing so, bullied and harassed the English baronage for military service and money to pay for his foreign campaigns, which were increasingly irrelevant to the English. Also, and for the first time since Stephen, the king of England was almost permanently resident in England. This resulted in a far closer involvement in the daily government of the realm. It meant that royal officials resented the interference of the king and, worse still, that the king could now be personally blamed for perceived injustices and cruelties. Thus, nine years after the loss of his continental possessions and after several failed attempts to regain them, John was faced with the most serious baronial rebellion any of his family had ever experienced.

The government of England

In 1204, however, rebellion in England was a long way off. Several highly capable men who had served under Henry II and Richard headed John's government. These men had also persuaded the barons to accept John over his nephew Arthur. They included: William Marshal, Hubert Walter, Archbishop of Canterbury, Geoffrey fitzPeter, justiciar, William of Ely, treasurer and Hugh de Neville, chief forester. After his coronation, John created William Earl of Pembroke and Geoffrey Earl of Essex; both held their titles in the name of their wives. Hubert Walter, Richard's brilliant justiciar, was made chancellor. All except Hubert Walter, who died in 1205, remained in office and at John's side until the last years of his reign.

Many of Richard's barons and clerks remained in office under John. They served as barons of the Exchequer, justiciars and bishops. The greatest of them was Peter des Roches, a Poitevin who became Bishop of Winchester in 1205 and justiciar in 1214. Continuity from Richard's reign was a key element in John's administration. Most of these men would serve John loyally. Many of them were either new men who had risen through their service to the Angevins or who came from families with a tradition of service with the Angevins.

The problem for John was, however, that these men would serve him so loyally as to enrich themselves and their families and to exclude the barons of England from the business of government, thereby increasing baronial discontent.

Efforts to regain the Angevin inheritance (i): Poitou (1206)

John remained obsessed with recovering his lost lands from Philip. His son, Henry III (1216–72) inherited this desire. It was only in 1259 that the Crown of England formally recognised the status of French ownership over the lost Angevin empire. The rest of John's reign was determined by the consequences of the events of 1204.

John's plan was to secure a land base south of the Loire so that he could launch an invasion into Anjou and Normandy. In the winter of 1204/5 invasion from France was feared. For the first time since 1066, the south coast of England had become a hostile boundary with France. The invasion never happened and in the summer of 1205 John planned a naval invasion on Normandy and a land attack from Poitou. Although a large fleet was assembled at Portsmouth, the barons refused to serve overseas and complained at John's extortionate taxation. John was forced to abandon this invasion and instead sailed to La Rochelle in 1206. Employing Poitevin mercenaries and barons, he managed to occupy Gascony and raid deep into Anjou. In October he concluded a two-year truce with Philip, resulting in his command from Poitou to the Pyrenees.

Efforts to regain the Angevin inheritance (ii): foreign alliances and the defeat at Bouvines (1214)

Retaking Aquitaine encouraged John into thinking that Anjou and Normandy were within his grasp. He devised a highly ambitious plan that took years to develop. John aimed to attack Philip on two fronts. The counts of Boulogne and Flanders feared Philip's growing power; John made an alliance in 1207 with his nephew, Otto of Brunswick, a contender for the imperial crown of Germany, and other German princes. The grand plan to attack Philip from Poitou and from the Low Countries was foiled in 1212 by English baronial opposition to fighting in Poitou and in 1213 by an attempted French invasion of England by Philip's son Louis. John's navy smashed the French fleet in the harbour of Damme.

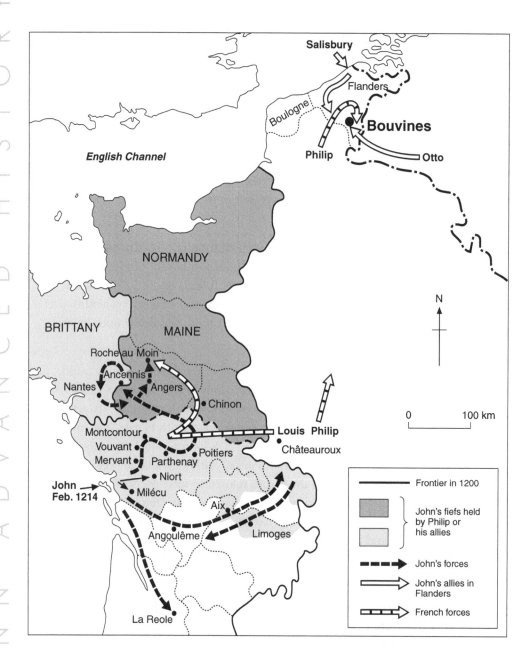

In February 1214 John eventually landed at La Rochelle and reasserted his authority over Aquitaine. The Viscount of the Limousin and the Lusignan brothers swore homage to him. By the summer of 1214 John had crossed the Loire to Nantes and Angers, his ancestral capital. But the arrival of Louis with a large French force and the refusal of the Poitevins to fight forced John to fall back to La Rochelle.

Meanwhile, the counts of Boulogne and Flanders and the earl of Salisbury, John's illegitimate brother, awaited the arrival of Otto of Brunswick and the German princes from the Rhineland. Philip, now that John had retreated,

King John's campaign of 1214 and Bouvines

and while the Flemish counts waited for Otto, was able to point all his resources in one direction without John at his rear. The allies met Philip's army at Bouvines, where a pitched battle occurred (rare in medieval warfare) and Philip's army won a decisive victory.

Bouvines crushed John's hopes. He had to offer Philip a truce. Never again could he raise the troops and arrange such elaborate alliances. If Philip had lost Bouvines then John might well have regained all his ancestral lands and permanently confined Philip to the lands he had occupied in 1180. But John's Poitevin barons refused to fight Louis; the Flemish counts had to wait for Otto and Philip was able to pick off one enemy army at a time. Philip took the considerable risk and won. For John, a decade's energy and hopes went for nothing.

The king and his barons

The methods used to gain the resources for the grand plan and the failure of the campaign of 1214 to recover the Angevin possessions contributed to rebellion at home in 1215. The loss of Normandy and the character of the king put immense pressure on the relationship between the king and his barons:

- John's almost continuous presence in England after 1204 weakened the role of the chief justiciar and by 1209 the independent law courts at Westminster had been closed because most cases were heard at the king's court. John had been a student of Ranulf de Glanvill, the brilliant justiciar under Henry II, and he knew his law. But this reduced access and placed greater personal responsibility (and, therefore, blame) on the king's actions.
- To recover Normandy, John had placed huge financial demands on the barons. Most of the northern barons in the rebellion were deeply in debt to the king or to the Jews. Sir James Holt said that the rebellion was 'a rebellion of the king's debtors'.
- John aggressively pursued his feudal rights over the barons, including scutage (many barons refused to fight in Poitou so John taxed them instead), inheritance tax (reliefs), rights over wards (minors) and the property of widows.
- John exploited royal justice, extracting huge fines and selling offices. He removed boroughs and farms from the control of sheriffs and sold them. Barons were encouraged to bid for offices with money they did not have. Justice was seen to have been removed from the traditional officials and debts spiralled in the competition to buy favours and offices.
- John's suspicious character led him to fall out with some of his most trusted barons, including William Marshal. He often took barons and

their sons as hostages for surety of their good behaviour, but his persecution of the Braose family was extraordinary. William de Braose, once a trusted ally, defaulted on an unrealistically huge fine; John hounded him out of England and starved his wife and eldest son to death. Braose died in exile in Paris in 1211 and his other sons were not released until 1218.

- John was also accused of seducing or at least coercing barons' wives into sexual relations. These accusations may have been exaggerated to justify the rebellion.

There were also long-term factors, accrued over a period of thirty years, that led to baronial revolt and that were outside John's immediate control:

- The already intrusive administrative innovations and financial exactions started by Henry II's government were unreasonably abused by Richard's crusade and ransom demands and John's war efforts. As the historian Sir James Holt said: 'John consummated what Henry II had begun'. These exactions and abuses have been termed the 'Angevin despotism'.
- The English baronage (about 165 men) were by the early thirteenth century a body with collective rights who opposed John on principles.
- The centralising practice of Angevin kingship reduced the role of the baronage in local justice and castle-holding.
- Feudal barons were replaced by 'court' barons, appointed by the king to oversee justice, finance and castle-guard in the provinces. Since the reign of Henry I, specialist clerks and soldiers found service in the household and were promoted. Itinerant Angevin kingship depended on the loyalty of these 'new men'.
- The Angevin kings built upon and extended the ancient rights that placed the king above the law; Henry II added the term 'by the Grace of God' on his charters and John claimed almost imperial status on his, as well as reintroducing crown-wearing and spending lavish amounts on regalia. The other school of thought, however, saw the laws of England made on the advice of the magnates. Both contradictory views were presented in Glanvill, so even contemporary writers did not have a solution.

But this baronial rebellion was not inevitable and the barons did not present a united front against King John.

Who were the rebel barons?

The evolution of a baronage increasingly aware of its rights in a developing legalistic age, and the centralisation of government over the twelfth century, coupled with the loss of Normandy, the defeat at Bouvines and John's character, had created a baronial opposition party by 1214.

KEY TERM

Angevin despotism The term sometimes used by historians, for example, Professor Frank Barlow, to describe the methods employed by Henry II, Richard and John to raise heavy taxes and pass harsh laws on their subjects without consent. Henry II is sometimes called 'tyrannical' in his methods.

By the spring of 1215, this included 39 (out of 165 in the kingdom) of baronial rank and some 1400 knights (out of 6500). The core of rebels were embittered personal enemies of the king, including Robert fitz Walter, Eustace de Vesci, Roger Bigod Earl of Norfolk, Geoffrey de Mandeville, Earl of Gloucester and Essex, Henry de Bohun, Earl of Hereford and Giles de Braose, Bishop of Hereford (related to William de Braose, whose family John had so cruelly persecuted). The rebellion was concentrated in three regions: the north of England, the west and East Anglia. Although the barons from the east of England emerged as the leaders, the northern barons hated John; they shared a common refusal of overseas service and the payment of scutage in 1213–14 and many families were bound also by ties of kinship and friendship.

The northern barons had conspired with Philip of France as early as 1209. In 1212 there were rumours of a plot to kill the king and John had to abandon his planned invasion of north Wales. As a result, the king modified his harsh financial policies and in 1213 made promises to restore the ancient liberties to the northern barons; but equally, the king demanded hostages, charters of fealty and more cash to pay for his continental campaign.

John's problems with the papacy and his archbishop, Stephen Langton, caused him political problems, too. (See below, pages 224–6 for the Church.) John reached a peace settlement with Pope Innocent III in 1213, which allowed some rebels to return to England and with them, the Archbishop, who immediately informed the barons about their lawful rights.

The course of the rebellion

John returned from the disastrous Bouvines campaign of 1214 in October, bankrupt and discredited. Hostile barons gathered at Bury St Edmunds demanding reform in November and in January 1215, John summoned a council to London. Here he delayed answering the barons' demands, saying that he would not answer to force; the barons said that the king refused to recognise their ancient and customary liberties. John prepared for war. His loyal earl, William Marshal, and Stephen Langton met the rebels at Oxford in February; John met some of them also at Oxford in April, but no agreement was reached. John had made concessions, promising to abolish evil customs, but he had also taken up crusader's vows, which placed him under the Church's special protection – a stroke of diplomatic genius. The barons gathered troops and marched to Brackley in Northamptonshire to meet the king in late April. They made non-negotiable demands and sent them to John at Wallingford. At the end of April, John received letters of papal support and refused to make any concessions that would threaten the Crown's traditional rights.

On 5 May, the rebels formally renounced their fealty and chose the East Anglian baron, Robert fitz Walter, as their leader. Fitz Walter was something of an extremist who had displayed little respect for the law before 1215 and stood in the way of a peaceful settlement after 1215. He had been implicated in the plots of 1212 and had returned to England under papal protection in 1213.

John played the diplomatic game cleverly. He had already secured papal support. He did not rise to the forceful demands of the rebels. He proposed concessions for a peaceful solution in May and offered the rebels the proper procedure of law and judgement by their peers in the royal court. But after May the rebels were in no mood to negotiate and put their trust in the law. Rebellion began with the attempt to take Northampton Castle, which failed, followed by the successful occupation of London. This was aided by Robert fitz Walter's lordship over Baynard's Castle, London's second fortress after the Tower of London. This was a blow to John: many who had previously been uncertain now joined the rebels and John missed his chance to crush the rebellion early.

The 'Articles of the barons'

At the end of May John came to terms with the rebels in order to buy time. It is unlikely that he ever had any intention of giving up his monarchical powers. Negotiations between John's agents and rebel agents got underway at Runnymede near Windsor in June 1215, with Archbishop Stephen Langton acting as mediator. The provisional 'articles of the barons' was the draft for the final, great charter, or Magna Carta. This was drafted by experienced statesmen such as Stephen Langton, Henry Archbishop of Dublin and Peter des Roches Bishop of Winchester, four royalist earls and several royal officials – but no great rebel barons. As the historian Sir Maurice Powicke argued, the Charter reflected the views of the moderate barons, the bishops and the administrators. Final agreement was reached by 19 June when the rebels exchanged the kiss of peace with the king and renewed their homage to him. Chancery clerks then drafted copies of the Charter with the king's seal; four copies survive today.

HOW SIGNIFICANT WAS MAGNA CARTA?

Two schools of historical thought exist over the making of Magna Carta:

- The barons or Stephen Langton and churchmen were formulating a visionary document protecting the people's liberties. The Victorian historian Bishop Stubbs wrote: 'The barons maintain and secure the rights of the whole people as against themselves as well as against their master'.
- The Charter was a feudal document aimed at protecting the barons' own positions. As the historian Frank Barlow wrote, 'The charter of 1215 was

a response to complaints against John's authoritarian, arbitrary, and capricious government'.

The significance of Magna Carta was far more than a list of baronial grievances, however the rebels may have felt about John's kingship. Those who stood to benefit from the Charter included the bishops and clergy, the knights, the lesser free landholders, the merchants and the liberties of cities, towns, boroughs and ports. The Charter certainly had its precedent in the royal coronation charters of liberties of Henry I, Stephen and Henry II, and the barons wanted a return to the good old days of laws and customs which, as always with the 'good old days', never actually existed. But while the basics of Magna Carta were conservative and feudal, some of these areas contained ideas that could be expanded in the future.

The 1215 Magna Carta consisted of 63 chapters covering five main areas:

- The protection of the rights of the Church (which was not new).
- The feudal concerns of the barons (limiting the king's demands on aids and scutage, his control over wards and widows).
- The administration of justice (with particular concern as to access of the common-law courts).
- The guarantee that John would carry out his promises (a committee of twenty-five barons sharing power with the king, which would prove impossible).
- The protection of the freemen of England: the right to the lawful judgement of one's peers (which the barons called government *per judicium*), and the right to advise the king (which the barons called government *per consilium*).

How had kingship changed?

Magna Carta was, therefore, more than a list of baronial grievances; it was a far-reaching document that affected many types of people. This was because kingship had developed since the early twelfth century. Government had changed; a bureaucracy had emerged. Expectations had changed also: barons, knights, merchants and freemen saw the role of the king and his government in a different light.

Two broad views of kingship prevailed in the early thirteenth century:

- John believed that his royal power was above enacted law. This had its roots in **St Augustine's** *De Civitate Dei* (*The City of God*) and was echoed in the *Dialogue of the Exchequer*, which stated that kings' subjects 'have no right to question or condemn their actions'.
- The other theory of kingship stressed the king's subjection to the law. The Laws of Edward the Confessor, a twelfth-century collection of laws and customs, stated: 'Law is always made by right; but will and violence

KEY AUTHOR

St Augustine
A fourth-century bishop and theologian. He wrote 113 books, including *The City of God*, which emphasised the powers of spirituality above the material, ordinary world.

and force are not right'. Some saw John as a tyrant, because he ruled by will and not in accordance with the law.

These two views of kingship (which may be summarised as 'law' and 'will'), with a king who was both above and below the law, caused an insoluble problem and were the result partly of the growth of legal consciousness among the landholding classes during the later twelfth century.

To these two established views of kingship and government may added a third, reflected in the barons' demands in Magna Carta:

- 'Contractual kingship' – implicit in the Magna Carta is the tie between the king (the lord) and his barons (his vassals). The barons saw Magna Carta as a means of stating John's contractual obligations to them. This extended the feudal relation between lord and vassal to a larger ruler–subject relationship.

The growth in laws and rights: government *per judicium*

The establishment of a common law during the reign of Henry II led to more and more landholders bringing suits involving many people of little power and small amounts of land. This litigious landholding society grew aware of its rights and the fear expressed in Magna Carta was that the king was threatening the lawful rights of the landholder (these rights were encouraged by the very machinery of justice Henry II had set up). Complaints had been made under Henry II and Richard, but John's presence in England after 1204 and his keen interest in the law linked the complaints to the person of the king himself. The barons in 1215 therefore demanded government *per judicium* or through the processes of the law, which to them was a feudal principle with its roots in the past. As the Victorian legal historian F.W. Maitland wrote, 'the charter contains little that is absolutely new. It is restorative. John in these last years has been breaking the law; therefore the law must be defined and set in writing'.

The concern with the law of the land and legal processes were not just for the barons or knights but also for the free man. Most of England consisted of unfree peasants who lacked security, but as the free class in society increased during the later Middle Ages so this clause became crucially significant. It did not, however, entitle free men to trial by jury, but it did protect them from illegal treatment by the king and his agents, allowing them access to the common-law courts, trial by combat and the ordeal.

The common counsel of the realm: government *per consilium*

The principle of government *per consilium* was also of great significance in Magna Carta. This too, had its origins in past feudal practice. The barons were the tenants-in-chief of the king and his immediate vassals, and expected the king to seek their advice. The growth of a bureaucracy within government in the chancery and the Exchequer had perhaps distanced the

Magna Carta, from Chapters 12 & 14 'No scutage or aid is to be levied in our realm except by the common counsel of our realm.'

king from his great landholding barons. Certainly it was a very different relationship from the original feudal settlement begun by William the Conqueror when the new Norman earls were his half-brothers and cousins. If government was no longer a family business, then the barons in 1215 wished to act for a community of a different sort, a community of the realm. This, as American historian R.V. Turner writes, was a 'radical trend of thought'. Phrases in Chapters 12 and 14 of Magna Carta, such as the *communa tocius terre* and *communa consilium regni* reveal that the barons saw the kingdom as a commune of free men that could set limits to royal power.

Magna Carta, 1225. The version issued by Henry III which entered the statute book. This authorised copy has the young king's seal attached

Radical though the concept of the kingdom as a commune was, there is no reference to consent or general taxes paid by the whole population – only feudal payments by the king's tenants. What was new, however, was that the king sought counsel before imposing a scutage.

WHY DID THE WAR RESTART?

In 1215 Magna Carta was a failure. As a law code it was unrealistic and ineffective. The problem was that Magna Carta was a compromise that was never going to work. One of its clauses was that a baronial committee would be elected to share power with the king; the representatives the barons chose for this committee were rebels rather than moderate men. The barons continued to hold London and in August John persuaded Pope Innocent III to annul the charter. Magna Carta was therefore in force for just two months. The Pope also described the charter as 'illegal and unjust', and published a letter excommunicating disturbers of the kingdom.

John had powerful support from the great Marcher barons William Marshal and Ranulf of Chester, the earls of Sussex, Surrey and Salisbury, and from the bishops and the Pope. The only rebel bishop was Giles de Braose.

John campaigned very successfully against the rebels in the autumn of 1215, isolating the rebels in London. Although the rebels occupied Rochester Castle, John brilliantly took it after a seven-week siege; this encouraged other rebel castles to surrender. By Christmas 1215, John was in Nottingham and the northern castles began to surrender to him; in January he was in Northumberland and in March he was in East Anglia. John now had control over the north, the east, and the south and west of England. Only London remained in rebel hands.

The invasion of Prince Louis and the death of John

The situation was radically reversed when Louis, son of Philip of France, invaded England in 1216. The support of Louis meant that the rebels could not now claim to represent the 'community of the realm', as they had done at Runnymede. Louis made a totally ridiculous claim to John's throne, which was privately, but not publicly, supported by his father. John's kingship was once again threatened by the long arm of Philip 'Augustus' (the Great) who was not content to stop at taking the Angevin lands in France, but who now seemed to want the very shirt from John's back.

John had his navy waiting off Dover, but a storm dispersed the fleet in May and Louis landed unopposed weeks later. John withdrew to Corfe Castle and Louis took Rochester and Winchester. Four earls left John for Louis, including the Earl of Salisbury, John's half-brother. John's situation was further threatened by the presence of Alexander II, king of the Scots (always ready to exploit the king of England's difficulties) who met Louis at Dover in September. John, who was ill, had spent the summer in the West Country, and now struck into Lincolnshire. In a final disaster he lost his baggage-train, including his regalia, in the Wash. John was so ill that he halted at Newark, where he died in October, aged forty-nine, leaving a nine-year-old son, Henry III, his heir.

'BAD' KING JOHN?

King John has gone down in history as one of the least successful kings of England. He contrasts unfavourably in so many ways to the brilliant administrative successes of his father and the military glory of his brother. He was defeated at home and abroad; he was betrayed by the closest of his barons and councillors; he resorted to murder and terror in his own kingdom; he lost his own crown jewels and left a boy as his heir in a war-torn land half-occupied by a foreign prince.

It could have been very different. John's treatment of the Lusignan brothers and murder of Arthur showed poor political judgement; Philip exploited this. But the death of Eleanor and the reduced finances at John's disposal were outside his control. The reluctance of the English baronial class to serve in Poitou foiled John's ambitious plans in 1206 and 1214. The defeat at Bouvines – which could have gone either way – ended his chances of recovering his inheritance. Had Otto triumphed at Bouvines,

John might well have regained all the lands he lost in 1204 and become the master of western France with his nephew as emperor of Germany. Instead, Otto fell to his Hohenstaufen rival Frederick, who became Emperor Frederick II and Philip became the greatest ruler of France since Charlemagne.

Even after 1214, John exercised great political skill in dealing with the rebels, and his military campaigns of 1214–16 showed him to be the master of castle-breaking and forced marches. The invasion of Louis tipped the balance and, like his father, John died alone and betrayed. Had he lived longer – forty-nine was no great age even in the early thirteenth century – he might have defeated Louis and the rebels and Magna Carta would not have become a permanent tool of English politics.

John also died as a vassal of the Pope and had taken crusader vows. He had exploited, ruthlessly at times, the administrative and financial framework established by his father and Henry I, but he had rarely strayed over the limits of what was conventionally expected of a monarch. He was generous to the poor, liberal to churches and rewarded loyal servants; he employed brilliant men in his household and skilfully deployed his traditional rights with the rebels who in the end did not represent the 'community of the realm'. He was personally courageous and a skilled military strategist who carried off some astounding feats.

However, the judgements of his contemporaries, and of historians, have been harsh. John was nicknamed 'Lackland' and 'Softsword' in his own time, well before 1215 (probably by 1200). He was unfortunate enough to reign in a period when the golden age of medieval English historiography had come to an end. The authors Ralph Diceto and Roger of Howden were not monks and wrote with support for the royal government, but they died early in John's reign. The two authors who most vilified John were Roger of Wendover and Mathew Paris, monks of St Albans; they wrote with an extraordinary anti-royalist bias. Roger was not writing about John until 1216; Mathew Paris took over as late as 1235. By contrast, French histories written by the monks of St Denis glorified Philip's reign.

Modern English historians took up the theme of the moral condemnation of John, particularly those writing in the late nineteenth and early twentieth centuries. Kate Norgate referred to John's 'superhuman wickedness' (1902) and Sir James Ramsay called John 'a selfish cruel tyrant of the worst type' (1903). But in 1945, Professor V.H. Galbraith called for a reassessment based not on the biased chronicles but on the systematic use of documentary evidence. The historians Warren (1978), Holt (1985) and Turner (1994) took up this theme and it is now accepted that while John's reign was a failure, the loss of Normandy and his immense financial problems were not his fault.

For all the apologies and reassessments, John's reign was still a monumental failure by the standards of his own day. His starvation of prisoners and hostages was outside the rules of war of the time. His abduction of and marriage to a girl possibly as young as nine contributed to gossip about John as a sexual predator. The hero of the *History of William Marshal*, the Earl of Pembroke, stuck by John through thick and thin, but even he fell out with the king and left sons hostage in the royal court. The continuous vein of treachery and suspicion running through John's life, from the betrayal of his father in 1189 to his own ignominious death at Newark in 1216, leave us with a picture of a man whose kingship was, personally as well as financially, bankrupt.

THE SUCCESSION AND MINORITY OF HENRY III, 1216–28

On King John's death his nine-year-old son Henry was crowned hastily, at Gloucester. In the words of the *History of William Marshal*, 'he was a fine little knight'. John on his deathbed he had left the defence of his son's inheritance to the care of a council of thirteen executors. After the coronation, William Marshal was elected rector *Regis et regni* (Regent of England).

How was peace secured?

The balance between royalist and rebel parties hardly moved during the winter of 1217. In the spring, several prominent rebels joined the royalists, including two of William Marshal's sons. When Earl Ranulf of Chester attacked Mountsorrel, whence his grandfather had been ousted in Stephen's reign, royalist troops pursued the rebels to Lincoln. With the septuagenarian Marshal at its head, the small royalist army entered the gates of the town and surprised the rebels. After a short street fight, during which the Count of Perche was killed, many rebels were killed and prominent leaders, including the earls of Winchester, Hereford and Lincoln, were captured.

The events at Lincoln were not quite enough to send Louis packing. He remained in London and when his wife sent reinforcements, William Marshal sent a fleet, which defeated the French off Sandwich. The regent and the young king watched from the clifftops; Hubert de Burgh and Richard of Chilham (John's illegitimate son) were the commanders. Seeing that God was not on his side, Louis took the hint and left England.

The Regency to 1228

The men at the heart of government included all the great loyalist barons of John's reign: William Marshal, Earl of Pembroke and regent (who died in

1219), Ranulf, Earl of Chester, William de Warenne, Earl of Surrey, and William, Earl of Salisbury. The justiciar was Hubert de Burgh, a longstanding agent of John (and the gaoler who had refused to murder the boy Arthur).

Much of the government was not concerned with constitutional issues, but rather with the settlement of claims and the distribution of lands and offices. Because of the minority, government was in the hands of a small group, which had to meet and agree before taking any action. Rebellion was always a possibility, and there were several minor risings in the 1220s.

The re-issues of Magna Carta: 1216, 1217 and 1225

John's premature death ensured that Magna Carta developed from a fledging set of promises to a permanent addition to English medieval kingship and government. It was re-issued after John's death in 1216 and 1217 and again, definitively, in 1225.

The council ruling in Henry's name re-issued the charter in November 1216 with few revisions. This had the support of the new pope, Honorius III. The charters of 1216 and 1217 were issued under the seals of the papal legate Guala and the Earl of Pembroke, William Marshal. These re-issues were very much made to deal with the civil war and to seek peace. They were made by loyalist barons who carefully retained much of the Angevin systems of government. They asked for charters of fealty and for hostages from the rebels, permitted lords to levy aids and pursued royal debtors. Hostages were demanded; aids were levied on as many occasions as before 1215. As Professor James Holt says, 'the administration of the minority of Henry III was not kid-gloved'. Many clauses from the original 1215 charter were removed in the 1217 edition. The most damaging clauses to kingship and royal government were removed, especially the council of the twenty-five barons, not needed now that John was dead. Liberties and free customs among the higher ranks of the Church and nobility were protected; the king was to be informed of any changes to local administration.

The charter was reissued in 1225. Nine of the twenty-five barons originally on the council of 1215 had died. Nine of the survivors witnessed the new charter with the great loyalist magnates, including Ranulf of Chester, William of Salisbury and Hubert de Burgh. In the words of Professor Holt: 'This was the final moment of reconciliation'.

In 1237 Henry III confirmed Magna Carta in a binding form. After 1225 it was increasingly recognised as law. Stephen Langton pronounced excommunication against violators in 1225. The reissues of 1217 and 1225 were statements of law.

CONCLUSION: A NEW KINGSHIP?

The twelfth century had seen several major rebellions against the Crown, including a damaging civil war. But the reigns of Henry I and Henry II were characterised by long periods of peace and tremendous reform in government. The rebellions before 1215 were feudal in nature, in that they were concerned with the acknowledgement of the king and struggles for territory. The rebellion of 1215 was different. It had, for the first time, a written programme. Magna Carta set in writing the nature of government, which formed a precedent for future reform. Various kings before John had made vague promises of good government, abolishing the evil customs of their predecessors and maintaining the laws of England. Some of these promises were written in the form of charters, but Magna Carta was the law, the earliest statute on the English Statute book.

Kingship was now going to be restricted and confined within the limits of this new law. At the heart of charismatic kingship lay the strength of personality of the monarch; Magna Carta represented the triumph of bureaucratic kingship. Thereafter, the activities and ambitions of the king, whilst still requiring a great character, were defined by what his government would allow. This was the consequence of the developing government throughout the twelfth century.

The rise and fall of the Angevin 'empire' had occurred alongside increasing English dominance over the British Isles. South Wales was colonised, but lordship over the north was to be based upon homage rather than direct lordship. Not until the reign of John's grandson, Edward I (1272–1307), was north Wales conquered. In Scotland, John undid Henry II's successes and although English superiority was recognised, lordship was not direct. John had greater success in Ireland but the policy was the same: native kings and princes were not removed as long as they recognised English superiority.

English kingship at the beginning of the thirteenth century was still based primarily on rulership and ownership. It was still a feudal monarchy. Great changes had occurred but the distinction between private and public customs remained slight. The king was still anointed by God to rule, as nobody else was. It was his task to guard his subjects and the Church and to maintain peace in his realm. That said, the world the kings of England lived in had changed. Language, literature, art and architecture had diversified and expanded. England, joined firstly to Normandy after 1066, had then been linked to large parts of France after 1154. The world was a smaller place in 1228 than in 1100. The Pope in Rome had established greater powers over the rulers of Europe. These factors of change made the world of King John a very different place to that of his great-grandfather, Henry I. And it is to these factors that we turn in the final sections of the book.

SECTION 5

How did English society develop in the twelfth century?

INTRODUCTION

No great technological, economic or social revolutions occurred in the period 1100–1228. The mass of people remained peasants, tied to the villages where they were born, conditioned by limited food production and lack of education. The understanding that they were born to a certain station in life and would remain there, ruled by their noble master, did not change.

The period did witness many social changes, however. The population doubled; England was at peace for most of the twelfth century; learning and literature flourished and towns expanded. A new aristocracy emerged, ready to flex its muscles at the beginning of the thirteenth century; urban society developed a political consciousness and the country as a whole prospered under the Angevin kings.

THE EXPANDING RURAL ECONOMY

The period 1100–1228 witnessed greater exploitation of the physical resources of an already rich and diverse geographical land mass. The population of England doubled; woodland was cut back and villages began to use three fields to grow their crops. But medieval farmers lived close to the edge: the system of cultivation was communal, and production in arable farming was low. There was no provision for the large-scale storage of food. Thus the success of the annual harvest was critical to the survival of the elderly, the young and the sick. Linked to famine was disease. It was a pre-industrial society and life was precarious.

Population changes

The population of Domesday England (1086) is understood to have been 2,250,000; by 1228 it was considerably more, perhaps as much as 5,760,000. This rise in the population was not, however, a 'boom': it was the continuation of the long-term trend that had begun in the Anglo-Saxon period.

The most densely populated part of England was East Anglia. Cornwall, the northern counties and the midland counties of Cheshire, Staffordshire and Derbyshire were the most sparsely populated.

Changes in land use

Change in population was accompanied by changes in land use over the period. This occurred in three main ways:

- Peasant holdings were subdivided, either by partible inheritance (that is, each son acquired an equal share on the father's death) or by sale of land.
- Smallholdings were also formed out of the original demesne land of the lord during the twelfth century; these lands could be rented out to peasants in parcels of an acre or so.
- New land was cleared and cultivated. Much of this came from woodland. It is estimated that around 15 per cent of England was woodland in 1086; this had fallen to around 10 per cent by the mid-fourteenth century. The newly cleared land was called an 'assart' and the word occurs often in the sources.

In these three ways, new peasant holdings appeared. One study suggests that the number of peasant holdings on English manors increased by 256 per cent in the period 1086–1230.

Farming techniques and food production

No great change occurred in farming techniques up to the early thirteenth century. The chief crops in England at this time were cereals (wheat, rye, barley and oats). Arable land was cultivated in long strips so that the plough-teams did not have to be turned round too often. These strips, called 'furlongs' (one furrow length) measured about 220 yards (200 metres).

The arable land was divided into three fields; to avoid exhausting the soil, land was left fallow (uncropped) one year in three. The fallow field was used for grazing animals, whose droppings fertilised the field in preparation for the next year's crop. This was known as the 'open-field' system. Not all villages used this system, but there is plenty of evidence that it existed in the middle of the twelfth century.

Due to the low productivity of arable farming, other means of food production were important. Much food was produced in the cottage garden and suburban market gardens. Livestock included pigs, sheep, goats, hens, geese, ducks, pheasants and pigeons.

Sheep were indispensable. Cheese was made from their milk, parchment from their skins and wool was the raw material for the cloth industry. In 1086 the Abbey of Ely had 13,400 sheep on its manors in six counties. Wool was the main cash crop in England and developed massively during the twelfth century: English wool was prized as far afield as Florence.

Fish were another vital natural resource. Meat was in short supply, for most people, and fasting was obligatory for all. Rivers and the fens produced salmon and eels in large quantities.

The manorial economy

The pattern of life for most people was determined by the relationship between the peasant tenants and their aristocratic landlords. The peasants had to pay rent for their holdings, in cash, labour or produce; estate servants, the tenants of hired labour, worked the land of the lord, the demesne. This system of land management was known as the manorial system and had been developing since the tenth century. The lord of the manor owned the estate and controlled the judicial as well as the agricultural rights of his tenants. Tenants had to pay their lord for permission for their daughters to marry (the merchet) and on inheriting land, had to pay the lord a heriot. But the role of the lord was primarily economic, not social: he was interested in the production of food for his estate and his family.

The manorial economy varied from region to region. A manor might include three or four villages, or just one; the definition of the manor was a legal one, which defined the lord's rights in the area, not necessarily the geographical boundaries of the settlement. Settlements in eastern England continued their rent-paying holdings (known as 'socage') whereas the Midlands continued payment in labour and goods.

Estate surveys, records and accounts at the end of the twelfth century show that many more rent-paying tenancies were created from demesne lands and assarts from land clearances. Rights and obligations were not fixed and varied from region to region, manor to manor and year to year. Free peasants could by charter dispose of their land as they wished.

HOW DID RURAL SOCIETY CHANGE?

England in the period 1100–1228 remained a peasant society. Many of the peasants were villeins, and were unfree. Freedom, however, meant little without land to cultivate. Land was in the form of smallholdings; the amount of land a peasant possessed determined his wealth and his status, free or not. A substantial peasant holding, called a 'virgate' in the twelfth century, was around 30 acres, which was a quarter of a hide.

The free and the unfree

The emerging English Common Law of the twelfth century excluded villeins (who were mostly peasants). The Common Law protected freehold and the law of the freemen but not the unfree. Therefore the need to draw the line became important. The unfree could be treated like cattle, tied to the land on which they worked, even sold along with land and chattels; if they escaped, they could be placed in chains. The free had the right to bear arms and to leave the village and did not work on the lord's land. Many cases of freedom had to be proved in court in the presence of a jury. The payment of merchet and heriot became a legal test for villeinage.

KEY EVIDENCE

From a survey of manors belonging to the Abbey of Peterborough (1125–28) 'In Thorpe Achurch [Northamptonshire] are 2 hides and 1 virgate for the king's geld. And there are 12 full villeins and each one of them holds 11 acres and works for the lord 3 days each week … And all of these make a customary payment of 10 shillings … And all these men plough 16½ acres for the lord's work … In the court of the demesne [lord] there are 2 ploughs with 16 oxen, and 3 cows and 8 beasts for food and 1 draught horse and 8 pigs.'

KEY EVIDENCE

From a charter of Ketel Dumping in favour of Lincoln Cathedral (1176) 'Know all of you that I have given to God and St Mary 5 acres of my free land, and that I have offered them with my son, Odo, at the altar of St Mary in pure and perpetual alms. And the said Odo will hold the aforesaid 5 acres from God and from St Mary by hereditary right by paying 12 pence a year on Whit-Tuesday to the canons of St Mary.'

In reality, everyone had obligations and limitations on their freedom at every level. Society was complex; customs and conditions varied.

Slaves and 'freedom'

The early twelfth century did see the end of slavery. 10 per cent of the Domesday population had been slaves. Every summer, Irish pirates raided the coast of north Devon and carried off anyone they could find to sell into slavery. This was condemned by contemporaries and finally stopped by Archbishop Lanfranc. The slave population in England had been declining before 1066, after which slaves gained their freedom by the process of 'manumission' (from the Latin *manumittere* 'to send forth from the hand'). By 1120 slaves had disappeared in legal language, but many people who had been slaves might now be known as something else, such as an ox-man or a household servant. Although people were no longer carried off and sold overseas at random, the lords could still sell the unfree, so the concept of freed slaves was a relative one.

The role of women

In an age when it was legal to chain or sell an unfree tenant, when living conditions and health were at the mercy of the weather, and when survival often depended on physical strength, life for women was not rosy. According to the Bible, God had created Adam first and Eve from Adam; therefore women were inferior to men. Their role was domestic; they had children, brought them up, ran the house, cooked for their husbands. In an age of limited contraception – abstinence was a virtue preached by the Church – pregnancies were frequent, though malnutrition and poor health meant that women were less fertile than today. Childbirth was dangerous: blood-loss, infection, shock and heart failure were not easily dealt with. In a spiritual age lacking in medical understanding, survival was attributed to the will of God.

In law, women are rarely mentioned, as a woman was the property of either her father or her husband. A woman was allowed to bring two criminal charges on her own behalf: the murder of her husband and rape. In the case of rape, the victim had to take evidence of the assault to the 'responsible men' of the nearest village, bring her complaint before the hundred-reeve and make a public accusation at the next meeting of the county court. Of the hundred recorded private prosecutions in the period 1194–1230, not one resulted in conviction. The usual punishment was to pay a fine to her master, or marry the woman.

Once married, a woman was the property of her husband, and could not even make a will without his consent.

The Norman Conquest had little effect on women; there was no mass migration and therefore few mixed marriages. Most womens' horizons were

KEY EVIDENCE

From a survey of the manor of Elton (Huntingdonshire) for the Abbot of Ramsey, in the reign of Henry II (1154–89) (note how the working year is measured by Christian festivals) 'And this is the work and the service of the holder of 1 virgate: From Michaelmas to the beginning of August he works for 2 days in each week and ploughs for a third, except at Christmas and Easter and Pentecost. And from the Nativity of St Mary [8 September] until Michaelmas works every day except Saturday. In winter he ploughs half an acre, and sows it with his own seed; and he harrows and reaps this, and also another half-acre in August ... He makes payments for rights on the common ... He pays also 4 pence at Michaelmas, and 1 halfpenny for wool...'

limited to the house, children and the animals, and very little is known of ordinary women – as indeed, little is known of ordinary men.

HOW DID URBAN SOCIETY CHANGE?
Towns and ports

Towns all across Europe grew in the eleventh and twelfth centuries, and England was no exception. Domesday Book listed 112 towns in 1086; by the 1220s a further 125 towns had appeared in England. The chief towns in England in the twelfth century were all based on rivers, and included London, Winchester, Lincoln, York, Norwich, Canterbury, Colchester, Oxford, Gloucester, Worcester, Leicester and Wallingford – all ancient towns by 1066 and most of them Roman in origin.

During the twelfth century these old and new towns increased in size and developed their own laws and self-governing rights outside the rural economy.

Urban society

At the top of the urban hierarchy were the royal officials, priests and clerks who represented the Crown in London or Winchester, or the Bishop in a cathedral town, such as Lincoln, York or Canterbury. Below them came the craftsmen, the goldsmiths, tailors, dyers, weavers and fullers; then the tradesmen, the butchers, bakers and brewers.

These townspeople, or 'burgesses', had different rights and laws from those living in the countryside. They had to pay for each urban plot of land (a 'burgage'), guard the town and repair the town-ditch. They had their own town court. Freedom was the essential concept of urban society: a villein who lived in the town for a year and day was free. The burgage was freely held and could be sold; burgesses did not pay heriot or merchet. Towns began to develop their own laws and customs and when a town acquired its own charter it might model itself on the laws of another town.

The Guilds

The various craftsmen were organised into 'guilds' and had been since the Anglo-Saxon period. The most powerful guild was the guild merchant, the town's merchants and chief burgesses who governed the town. These emerged in the twelfth century and defined the new legal and economic identities of the developing cities. From the guild merchant the aldermen, bailiffs, coroners and beadles were elected; they formed the town government.

TRADE

Trading became increasingly important during the twelfth century. England was a supplier of food and raw materials for northern Europe's most urbanised region, the Low Countries. Commercial venues such as weekly markets and annual fairs multiplied greatly. The fairs at Boston, Stamford and Winchester were international and attracted merchants from Scandinavia, Flanders, France and Germany. England exported metal and the Forest of Dean (Gloucestershire) dominated English iron production. Tin from Cornwall and Devon was the greatest metal export and rose dramatically under the Angevins.

Textiles

The textile industry was the main industry in England. Cash from the cities of Ghent, Bruges, Arras and Antwerp flowed into England to purchase the finest wool in Europe. The process of the industry required people of skill and places of manufacture. Women spun the wool; men then wove it on the looms. Then the fullers beat it; during the twelfth century, fulling mills were using water power to beat the wool with hammers. Finally, the wool was dyed. All these processes required skills, specialised labour, different venues and capital at various levels.

COINAGE

England in the twelfth century, as in the eleventh, was not a monetary society. Cash was not common. But during the twelfth century the number of coins in circulation increased dramatically. Society did become more monetised and commercial.

The kings of England strictly controlled coins; they were a source of profit and a symbol of royal power. Therefore the moneyers only struck coins from centrally issued dies and every two to three years the coins were reissued. The silver content of English coins was high. Fines and harsh punishments were inflicted on those who tampered with the silver content and who issued old coins.

Currency and minting

The currency was in pounds, shillings and pence (£ s.d.). This had been the system since the early ninth century and continued until 1971. There were 240 pence to a pound, twelve pence to a shilling. The mark was also used an accounting unit (13s. 4d.). The penny was the only coin. The weight of the penny, which was silver, was maintained at a standard weight (1.45 g.). Gold coins were not minted in England but came in from the Mediterranean region.

Royal control over the minting of coins tightened across the period. In 1086 there were 65 mints in England; by the 1170s there were twelve, and by 1220 there were six mints. These were at London, Canterbury, Durham, Bury, York and Winchester. But the production of coins increased hugely in the later twelfth century. There were about 9 million pennies in circulation

KEY EVIDENCE

From a charter of Henry II in favour of Nottingham (1157) 'And if anyone from elsewhere lives for a year and a day in the borough of Nottingham, in time of peace, and without dispute, then no one afterwards except the king shall have rights over him. And any burgess who buys the land of his neighbours and possesses it for a year and a day without any claim by the relatives of the seller, the same relatives being in England, shall afterwards possess it in quiet. And let everyone living in the borough, no matter to whose fee he belongs, join in paying the tallages and the fortfeitures of the borough.'

at the time of Domesday Book. In the years after 1158 about 500,000–750,000 pennies were minted each year; by 1220, London and Canterbury – the most active mints – were producing around 4 million coins each year. The estimated number of coins in circulation in early thirteenth-century England was about 60 million.

Price rises and inflation

In the early thirteenth century prices rose sharply. The price of oxen increased by 125 per cent in the period 1190–1220, from 3s. to just under 8s. Wheat sold at 2s. a quarter in the 1160s but rose to 6s. after 1200. The prices of wheat and oxen fell back but remained well above the pre-1200 prices.

Reasons for inflation include the volume of silver that was flooding the market, and demand exceeding supply in the following ways:

* Business was conducted more through cash than services or payment in goods.
* Peasants were paying rent in cash, buying and selling smallholdings in cash.
* The war economy created by Richard and John to defend and then reconquer their continental possessions drove the need for cash.
* Professional soldiers wanted payment in cash, not land; landholders at home paid cash to avoid military service; siege machines, arms and armour required cash.
* The population had expanded but the means of production had not advanced.
* More coins were minted but the number of horses and oxen used to plough the fields remained the same – there was more money to spend, but food production had not increased.

Whether the inflation of the later twelfth century was as steep as was once supposed has been questioned. Economic prosperity was a long-term event across the century, and apart from a few years under Stephen in certain parts of the country, it was uninterrupted. There was no 'boom' at the end of the century that led to sudden inflation. Professor J.L. Bolton suggests that the flow of silver into England was perhaps not as great as was once thought, given the wars between Richard, John and Philip that disrupted trade with Flanders. John's strategy for reconquering his overseas lands after the failure of the 1206 expedition led him to store vast amounts – millions – of coins in his castles, in preparation for the 1213/14 campaign. These factors would have had a deflationary impact.

The sharp rise in prices in the first few years of John's reign is accepted by historians and the economic consequences for John, at the very time he was dealing with the greatest crisis to engulf any Angevin king, would have been severe.

THE JEWS

The Jews in England were unique. They were the only non-Christian group legally tolerated in the kingdom. They did not fit into the feudal and communal structures of English society. They were only allowed to live in England, as in France and Germany, under the protection of the ruler. The royal charter of 1201 confirmed their rights. Their inheritance rights, chattels and debts were guaranteed and Jews were free from tolls and customs.

This came at a price. The Jews were more than simply under royal protection; they were the king's property and as such could be taxed whenever he chose. Richard I and John exacted vast amounts from the Jews of England. After 1194, all loans from the Jews were registered and recorded so that the Crown could collect the debts if the lender died intestate.

The presence of Jews in England increased after 1150. Until the 1140s the evidence suggests that only London had a Jewish population. In the second half of the century some twenty towns had a Jewish population. After London, the cities of York, Lincoln, Canterbury, Northampton, Winchester and Norwich were the main Jewish settlements. The total Jewish population in England was only around 5000 in 1200.

Moneylending and taxation

Moneylending was the chief business in which Jews were engaged. They were debarred from many occupations and as non-Christians were able to lend money at interest. The earliest record, the pipe roll of 1130, shows that the Earl of Chester was in debt to the Jews of London. One of the wealthiest moneylenders was Aaron of Lincoln, who died in 1186. The amount of money owed to him was so great that a separate Exchequer, the 'Exchequer of Aaron', had to be created to deal with the debts and was not concluded until 1194. Only a fragment survives, but it reveals how deep the culture of debt had become in the late twelfth century. Money owed to Aaron ranged from £115 to 6s. 8d.; interest varied between 22 per cent, 44 per cent and 66 per cent (one, two, or three pence per pound per week).

Why were the Jews persecuted?

Law never prohibited the Jewish religion. Jews were banned from the civil service and the legal profession, but the Church decreed that there should be no violence, no forced labour, no desecration of their dead and that Jews should be allowed to observe their holy days. The medieval popes advocated tolerance but worked for the conversion of the Jews.

The reality was different. A small group of people specialising in moneylending with the protection of the Crown was bound to cause resentment. The Jews were seen as bloodsuckers of Christian purses. The first accusation of ritual murder came from Norwich in 1144, when an apprentice called William was supposed to have been tortured and murdered. This charge of ritual murder became standard in England and Europe as the level of **anti-Semitism** increased in the twelfth and thirteenth centuries.

Large-scale attacks, or pogroms, began after the First Crusade (1095). A religious reason was now added to economic envy. The Jews were the people who had condemned Christ to die on the Cross. Northern France and the Rhineland saw massacres and forced conversions during the First and Second Crusades (1146).

England was not much involved in the first two crusades, but the coronation of Richard was marred by killings of the Jews, who Richard of Devizes described as 'bloodsuckers', 'worms' and 'diseased matter'. Violence and killings occurred in Norwich, Lynn, Lincoln, Stamford and Bury St Edmunds. The slaughter at York, however, was the most notorious. As at Stamford and Lincoln, the Jews sought refuge in the royal castle but found themselves besieged by a large force of noblemen – who were deeply in debt to the Jews – and crusaders, apprentices, peasants and clerics, who stirred up the attackers into a frenzy. Facing certain defeat, some of the Jews committed suicide, killing their wives and children first. Others surrendered, promising to convert, but were all slaughtered on leaving the castle. The crusaders and clerics saw this as 'godly work', while those in debt to the Jews saw it as a convenient means of getting rid of their debt.

The government was furious at this slaughter, which was seen as an attack on Crown property. The sheriff and castellan were dismissed and those who had led the slaughter were fined and imprisoned. The Jews returned to York and quickly established one of the richest communities in England.

LANGUAGE AND CULTURE

There were three languages spoken and written in England after the Norman Conquest: French, English and Latin. Latin was for the literate classes, the educated community of monks and churchmen; French was the mother tongue of the Norman ruling élite of England and English was spoken by the mass of the population, the conquered English. There were many in Norman and Angevin England who were fluent, or could get by, in two or more languages, including Henry II.

French was the first language of the Conqueror and his sons; Stephen and Henry II were French aristocrats before becoming kings of England. Richard I spent only six months of his reign in England. Outside the court circle, the use of French varied; to some of the nobility it remained important, others allowed it to die out. The French spoken by those who grew up in twelfth-century England and never visited France was different from the French spoken in Paris. The aristocracy with lands and connections in France developed the habit of sending their young sons abroad to be educated in French language and culture.

The vast majority of people spoke English. The language had evolved from the early Middle Ages (the seventh and eighth centuries) and by the twelfth century was made up of many dialects, with a marked difference between the north and the south. English was seen as 'barbaric' by monks and was still not known by the royal family: Eleanor of Aquitaine needed a translator in 1192. Also by the twelfth century, there was a distinction between Old English and Early Middle English. Word order was standardised; genders, adjectives and verbs were simplified so that English would become the least Germanic of the Germanic languages. Early Middle English would develop continuously into Middle and then Modern English.

English remained the language of the nation; French place-names were not common, as Scandinavian names had been when the Vikings settled in the ninth and tenth centuries. The French words adopted in the English language reflect the upper-class usage: the English peasants tended the cows and pigs while their Norman lords ate the beef (*boeuf*) and pork (*porc*).

Literature

Written English suffered a decline after 1066. All the writs and charters were now produced in Latin; poetry and religious works in English also came to an end – some monasteries such as Canterbury, Rochester and Worcester copied old texts, but by the early thirteenth century this was a rarity.

French literature was far more common, due to the patronage of the Norman-French ruling class. Poems, histories, romances and saints' lives (hagiography) were all popular in French.

Latin was by far the most common written language. Government and ecclesiastical writs, laws, letters and charters were all in Latin; literary texts such as histories and romances were also in Latin. From the beginning of the twelfth century in England there was massive expansion in written texts as governments formulated chanceries and bureaucratic systems to record and refer to laws and land grants. The Church, too, needed systems to facilitate the flow of letters and directives from Rome and within the kingdom. Sermons, works on law, theology and science were written in Latin.

Universities and learning

Knowledge of spoken and written Latin created access to a basic education (for boys). Elementary school education was in existence in every region of England in the twelfth century; these were parish schools, run by the priests. Other schools of a larger sort were the song-schools or grammar schools attached to the cathedrals.

KEY EVIDENCE

From Walter Map, *Of Courtiers' Trifles* (1181–93)
'In physical capacity he [Henry II] was second to none, incapable of no activity which another could perform, lacking no courtesy, well read to a degree both seemly and profitable, having a knowledge of all tongues spoken from the coasts of France to the river Jordan, but making use of Latin and French.'

The real change in twelfth-century learning came in the expansion of higher education in the form of universities that created a class of graduates ('Masters') who sought employment in the Church and in the households of the king. By the beginning of the thirteenth century the bureaucracies of Church and State were dominated by the graduates. Two universities emerged in twelfth-century England: Oxford and Cambridge. The Chancellor of Oxford was first mentioned in 1214, the Chancellor of Cambridge in 1225. The University of Oxford developed out of schools that had been there since the mid-twelfth century. Cambridge was formed from teachers and students who left Oxford in 1209 in protest at the hanging of the roommates of a student who had fled after murdering a woman.

Durham Cathedral combines Romanesque architecture with the beginnings of the new Gothic style

English students had contributed great numbers to the European schools at Bologna (which offered the best training in Roman and canon law), but mainly in northern France, in Paris and Laon, because England used customary law rather than Roman law. Roger of Salisbury sent his nephews Nigel and Alexander to study in Laon; Nigel became royal treasurer and bishop of Ely. By the 1130s, Paris was the intellectual centre of north-west Europe.

Art and architecture

The twelfth century witnessed an explosion not only in the production of literature but in buildings and artefacts. The growth of monasteries and the new Norman cathedrals (see above, page 88) illustrated the magnificent architectural styles of the Romanesque period. During the twelfth century a new style emerged: Gothic. This style originated in France, possibly at St Denis, in Paris, then Sens, and then Sainte-Chapelle. From France, Gothic spread across Europe. The style was distinguished by pointed arches – which differed from the Norman rounded arches – soaring vaulted ceilings, slender windows and flying buttresses (external stone supports). In 1174 Canterbury Cathedral burned down and the French architect, William of Sens, rebuilt it in the new 'Gothic' style. In 1185, when an earthquake struck Lincoln, all but the west front was destroyed. In 1192 Hugh of Avalon rebuilt it in the Gothic style, completed in the early thirteenth century. Dark, polished

How did English society develop in the twelfth century?   197

Purbeck marble shafts with decorative mouldings that set the tone for the following two centuries, offset the soft gold limestone.

The cathedrals, monasteries and parish churches that were built in the Romanesque and Gothic styles in the twelfth century housed great works of medieval English art. Wall paintings, or 'frescoes' decorated the interiors of these buildings in a blaze of colour, such as the

Doorway of Kilpeck Church, Herefordshire

painting of St Paul in the Anselm chapel in Canterbury. Sculptures on the fonts and on the walls also existed. The so-called 'Hereford School of Sculptors' left their mark at Kilpeck and Brinsop churches in Herefordshire with intricate carvings of animals and mythical beasts on the doorways and chancel arches.

Cathedrals, abbeys and churches were not the only architectural advances in this period. Castle-building represented secular development. Richard I's new castle at Château-Gaillard has already been mentioned, and many new fortresses sprang up all over England. Rather than the square Norman towers, round towers and elaborate gateways ('barbicans') were built, often around the stone keep. Crusaders returning from the Middle East brought back new ideas on architecture, as well as science, medicine and the visual arts.

The twelfth century was a time of flourishing decorative and book illustration. The great illuminated manuscripts were produced at St Albans, Canterbury, Durham, Bury St Edmunds and Winchester. The style changed from Anglo-Saxon to English Romanesque and the artists were increasingly becoming professionals, rather than the abbots and bishops themselves doing the painting as in the Anglo-Saxon period.

ARISTOCRATIC SOCIETY

The class of people who financed the arts, inhabited the new buildings and benefited from education at home and abroad were the aristocrats. 'Aristocracy' is a term used to describe the land-holding classes. Land meant wealth; birth and pedigree meant power. When William the Conqueror invaded and settled England there occurred a revolution in land-holding. By 1086, the date of Domesday Book, all the major landlords, secular and ecclesiastical, were either Norman or French. The greatest lords in William I's England were less than ten in number, were related to the king and were well established in Normandy. They included William I's half-brothers, Robert Count of Mortain and Odo, Bishop of Bayeux and Earl of Kent and his cousin William fitzOsbern, Earl of Hereford and Lord of the Isle of Wight. These men at the highest end were the earls, only seven of them and the only formal honorific title of the time. The next group of lords included fewer than 200 baronial families, a group that included a wide range of incomes. Below the barons came the knights, who numbered some 5000 by 1228.

By 1228 the character of the aristocracy had changed greatly from that of 1086. True, the great estates were still held by a handful of families and intermarriage between the baronial families resulted in an extraordinary exclusiveness. But if the relationship between king and aristocracy had been one of common enterprise when William sailed to Pevensey in 1066, then that had broken down entirely by the reign of John. The Anglo-Norman aristocrats had sunk their roots in England and considered themselves 'English'; what happened abroad did not concern them – as John was to discover to his cost.

The first century of English feudalism

By the reign of Stephen (1135–54) it was accepted that land held by military service should descend to the tenant's heirs and that the amount of the service should be definite. The 1166 *Cartae Baronum* list 7525 knight's fees, almost all of which had been created before 1135. But this system was neither uniform nor universal in the reign of William the Conqueror. The three private enfeoffments discussed above (pages 74–7) reveal the differences in the conditions of service. As Professor Sir Frank Stenton, one of the great early twentieth-century historians put it, 'there could hardly be a clearer illustration of the danger of assuming that the conception of military tenure which prevailed under Henry II had existed ever since the introduction of this form of tenure into England after the Norman Conquest'.

When, then, did these feudal conceptions gain clarification? Stenton argued that it was during the reign of Henry I. During this time, many feudal arrangements were written up into standard charters of enfeoffments wherein the land in question is held in fee and inheritance is to be held of the grantor and his heirs. The crucial difference from the late eleventh century was that the fee was to be passed on to his heir and this was the eldest son in the system of primogeniture. This custom became universal during the twelfth century and ensured that the family estate remained intact. Only in the case of daughters was the estate split up.

The custom of lineal descent (a single heir) over collateral descent (partible inheritance, or equal inheritance amongst the children) was established in Normandy before the Conquest and brought to England. Primogeniture, the inheritance of the eldest surviving son, was a Norman custom and took a generation or two to establish. A distinction was made in the first generation of Norman settlers between the inheritance and the acquisition. The inheritance had to go to the eldest son but any acquisitions could be distributed at will. William fitzOzbern's eldest son, William, inherited Breteuil, the Norman family lands; the second son, Roger, inherited the earldom of Hereford. The most obvious case of this was the sons of William I: his eldest inherited Normandy but the kingdom of England, an acquisition, went to William Rufus, the second son.

Very soon after the establishment of the feudal holdings as seen in Domesday Book came the creation of 'subtenancies' whereby the original grant from the king or earl was subdivided by the lesser landlords, often more than was needed for the overlord's quota to the king. Knight's fees were thus split into fractions, so that knights might hold various fractions, which in total might equal their service to the king. Not all holders of fractional fees did knight service; those who were eligible often offered to pay scutage rather than serve abroad or fork out the cost of arms, armour and horses.

The result was that feudal society was composed of ever-increasingly complex webs of tenancies and overlords with a variety of services and loyalties, which did not form a single hierarchy. The literary explosion under Henry I may have seen a great many charters of enfeoffment but the civil wars of Stephen highlighted the need for household knights, armed escorts and castle garrisons either for or against the king. In that way the intricate networks of family and local connections found a rather different purpose. The *Cartae Baronum,* however, illustrate that there was a great deal of continuity in the fees before and after the reign of Stephen.

Who were the nobility?

The earls and barons composed the nobility, the upper end of the aristocracy. During the twelfth century this group of landlords grew apart from the monarchy and began to assert their legal rights over matters of land and politics. Although this was not a straightforward process of conflict with the Crown, some of the great Norman earls lost their titles within a generation of the Conquest. Roger of Breteuil, son of the loyal William fitzOsbern, lost Hereford in 1075, along with Ralph, Earl of East Anglia; the Montgomery family, earls of Shrewsbury, rebelled in 1088 and 1095 and were eventually destroyed by Henry I. At the start of Stephen's reign there were still only seven earldoms, but both Stephen and Matilda created new earldoms to gain favour; Henry II did not suppress these new titles and the number of earldoms remained at around twenty into the thirteenth century.

From a charter of Anselm, Abbot of Bury St Edmunds (1121–48) 'I bid you to know that I, with the consent of the whole chapter, have granted to Adam of Cockfield and to his heirs that he should now hold in heredity and by the service of 1 knight the land in Cockfield and in Lindsey with all that pertains to it, to wit, the land which his father held...'

Charter of Stephen creating Geoffrey de Mandeville Earl of Essex (1140)
'Know that I have made Geoffrey de Mandeville earl of the county of Essex in heredity. Wherefore I will and grant and firmly order that he and his heirs after him shall hold by hereditary right from me and my heirs well and in peace, and quietly and honourably ... with all dignities and liberties and customs with which the other earls aforesaid worthily and freely hold.'

Those possessed of comital rank (i.e. with an earldom) needed the wealth to support such a title. All those with more than 100 knights' fees on their estates in the *Cartae Baronum* of 1166 were earls, with incomes of at least £800 a year. The creation of more earls after 1135 does not necessarily indicate that the nobility were suddenly becoming wealthier; rather that those already wealthy, and of old families, were acquiring the titles that Stephen was more ready to give out. It remained very difficult to join the ranks of the earls without land and the right pedigree. The earls took their titles from the shire town, for example Leicester, Chester, Hertford, Pembroke. By the end of the twelfth century the new earl would be girded with the ceremonial sword. From the county they also received a third of the profits from the county court and the royal boroughs.

In 1166 there were 134 tenants-in-chief whose estates had ten or more knights' fees. These were the barons. The size of the baronial class was around 150–200 with an average income of £200. There was much change within the class, due to the failure (lack) of male heirs; this was when the estate, or honour, escheated (returned) to the overlord – usually the king, in the case of a baron. The king could control the marriage of the heiress. Of 189 baronies in 1166, 54 descended through the female line – a not insignificant 29 per cent. The death rate was high, but collateral heirs, such as grandchildren, nephews and cousins, could normally be found. Forfeiture after rebellion was another means of failure for the barony, but this was rare after 1115, and sometimes brothers or cousins were allowed to succeed, so that the barony remained in the same family.

Inheritance through females and forfeitures in the baronial class opened the way for new men entering baronial society. Henry I is famous for promoting 'men raised from the dust' as the monk Orderic Vitalis called them. However, these men who were promoted by their royal services as sheriffs or lawyers were in existence before Henry I and never rose to the highest levels of the baronage. If they did succeed in acquiring preference then it took three or four generations.

The new knighthood

The Domesday *miles* or 'knight' changed too. From being a member of a rather general and ill-defined class of minor landholders and household soldiers, the knight was by 1228 defined by a code of social conduct which included military and spiritual values. The earlier half of the twelfth century saw the crystallisation of inheritance customs and the conditions of service, but knighthood was transformed in the later twelfth century. The increasing logistical complexities and rising costs of warfare, coupled with inflation in the last decades of the twelfth century, determined that those who became warriors came from a narrower social group. The remaining lesser landholders, in effect, became farmers whose right to bear arms was rarely realised.

There were around 4500 knights at the start of the thirteenth century. Knights, unlike earls and barons, could exist without land. They found service in the household of a great lord or the king himself, hoping to receive a grant of land or an heiress. Those who were enfeoffed with land became increasingly active in local government, attending the county court, serving as coroners, tax collectors or stewards for a baron's estate. The development of the Common Law under Henry II placed an emphasis on the role of the knights. Only those who were knights could sit on the jury in the Grand Assize; only knights could transfer the county records to Westminster and serve as county coroners. If a defendant failed to appear at the court on the third summons from the sheriff, then four knights were sent to his house to see whether he had a lawful excuse (*essoin*). The knights who appear in the legal records, which date mostly from the 1190s, are drawn from estates of varying sizes; all had a claim in the region in which they lived. They could only serve in administrative and legal capacities if they had land in the relevant county.

Knighthood was a widely shared status. Contemporaries realised that there were differences between land-holding, office-holding knights, household knights and those with very small amounts of land. There was also a major distinction between those who fought and those who did not. The numbers of fighting knights decreased in the later twelfth century. Scutage was levied increasingly by Henry II and by John; John's barons refused to serve in Poitou to assist the king in reclaiming his lost territories. The king could still draw upon his household knights, though. In 1227 Henry III had 127 household knights, each with his own retinue. Furthermore, the king paid for mercenaries, often from Flanders. Knight-service in its purest form – before it was commuted to money payments – involved garrisoning the royal castles, but after the civil wars of Stephen, England was at peace from 1154 to 1215 apart from the abortive rebellion of 1173–74.

Henry II attempted to increase the size of his feudal levies in the military reforms of 1181 in the Assize of Arms. This illustrates the status of the knights and of free men who were expected to bear arms. Every year these men had to swear allegiance to the king. Juries would be formed to swear to the number of those eligible for service; those who did not were liable to arrest.

The shortage of knights and soldiers was not easily solved. The Assize of Arms was reissued in 1230, but before that Henry III's government had taken steps to force those with a knight's fee to take up knighthood. This was called 'distraint' of knighthood. Military service, increasing unpaid

KEY EVIDENCE

Writ of Henry I concerning service of castle-guard from the tenants of Abingdon Abbey at Windsor castle (1100) 'Henry, king of the English, to all the barons of the abbey of Abingdon, greeting. I will and I firmly order you to perform my guard of Windsor...'

From the Assize of Arms (1181)

'Let every holder of a knight's fee have a hauberk [coat of chain mail], a helmet, a shield and a lance. And let every knight have as many hauberks, helmets, shields and lances, as he has knight's fees in his demesne. Also, let every free layman, who holds chattels or rent to the value of 16 marks [£10] have a hauberk, a helmet, a shield and a lance.'

administrative duties and cost of arms and armour led to many individuals not formally assuming the role of being a knight. The first distraint was issued in 1224, in preparation for an expedition to Gascony. The income of a knight was set at £20 a year from his lands.

Cost was the key factor in the declining number of knights at the beginning of the thirteenth century. Advances in armour-making came with the introduction of the face-concealing great helm, cloth trappings for horses and surcoats worn over the hauberk. The great warhorse was the most expensive; this was the 'destrier' (from the Latin *dexter* because it was led from the right) and was bred for war. A knight only rode this horse into battle, however; he required a palfrey to ride on normal duties, a packhorse to carry his equipment, and a mounted squire to assist him.

The rising prices and inflation discussed above would have squeezed out the lesser landholders from affording full knighthood. However, it was the increasing consumption by the upper aristocracy and greater knights that contributed to such inflation. For those who could afford it, therefore, knighthood was becoming a mark of the social élite.

What was chivalry?

The new social élite that emerged in the later twelfth century spent its money on the trappings of status. The word 'chivalry' comes from the French *chevalier*, 'knight', and literally means a body of armed horsemen, a group of *chevaliers*. It meant more than that, however; the sources speak of it as a social class, an 'order' and a code of values. The Church, the knighting ceremony, tournaments and literature all played a role in transforming knighthood in the later twelfth century:

- The Church had attempted to channel warrior energies from the eleventh century. Following the success of the First Crusade in 1099, knights were needed to garrison the castles of the Holy Land. Military orders, the Hospitallers and Templars, half-monk, half-knight, were set up; they were the *milites Christi* – the 'soldiers of Christ'. Theologians and political writers compared the violent, greedy knights of old to the new, godly warriors who protected the weak. Knighthood was becoming a worthy profession requiring honest, obedient and devout members. When the English became heavily involved in the Third Crusade, the aristocracy dominated crusading. The leaders of the Fifth Crusade (1218–21) included the earls of Chester, Derby, Arundel, Winchester and Cornwall, as well as many leading barons.
- The ceremony of knighting was the entry point into the profession and became increasingly elaborate in the later twelfth century. It normally took place in a man's late teens. Henry I was knighted by his father in 1086 when he was seventeen; Henry II was knighted in 1149, aged

sixteen and he knighted his son, John, in 1185 when John was seventeen. At the heart of the ceremony was the 'dubbing' of the new knight. This involved the formal delivery of arms, which signified the joining of the warrior class but also the feudal bond between lord and man. In the Bayeux Tapestry, William gave Harold arms and armour and Harold, in Norman eyes, became William's 'man'. The giving of weapons was a simple act but by the late twelfth century the ceremony had become a sophisticated business charged with symbolism and mystique. The candidate was bathed, dressed in sumptuous clothing, belted with his weapon and given his armour. Feasting and tournaments followed.

- Tournaments became very much a part of chivalric life. Mounted troops at Hastings used lances couched under the arm; a trained cavalry charge could deliver a heavy blow to the enemy. This tactic also led to the development of single combat between mounted soldiers. Young horsemen were trained in this art and sought one another out in battle. The first references to tournaments, which were staged training grounds for warfare, come in the early twelfth century, but were banned in England by Henry I and Henry II. Tournaments flourished in northern France, where the highest nobility were involved. Richard I allowed them in England after 1194. By that time only those wealthy enough to have horses, arms and armour could participate; if a knight or any of his equipment were captured, it would cost a small fortune in ransom money. It was an opportunity for landless knights to make some quick cash. Tournaments in England, however, were always viewed with suspicion by the government, as any gathering of armed soldiers could disguise a more sinister purpose – rebellion.

- Romantic literature illustrates how exclusive the new knighthood had become by the end of the century. Chrétien de Troyes was the best-known author of romances and described chivalry as an order. The knights were sent on missions, which had moral, religious and political meanings. Women were worshipped from afar; adultery was the ultimate temptation. English literature had its own, home grown hero: the legendary King Arthur. Geoffrey of Monmouth relaunched the legend in the first half of the twelfth century and the Norman poet Wace first mentioned the Round Table, in 1155. Names, events, and rituals in life and in art were imitated by the new knighthood so much that Arthur was thought to be real and even, in some circles, still alive.

CASE STUDY 5

THE CAREER OF WILLIAM MARSHAL, EARL OF PEMBROKE, REGENT OF ENGLAND (1147–1219)

The greatest exponent of the chivalrous life was the remarkable William Marshal, who has been mentioned above as a key character in the reigns of

Richard and John. The biography of this man, commissioned by his son in 1226, was written as a Middle French poem of 19,214 lines, known as *The History of William Marshal*. The Marshal's life resembles an epic, and the biography – the first of a non-royal, non-spiritual person to survive – tells the astonishing story of the rise of a penniless, landless younger son of a minor Wiltshire baron to earl of Pembroke, chief counsellor and regent of England. William's life and career were played out in the heart of the Plantagenet dynasty, spanning the reigns of Henry II, Richard, John and the first years of Henry III. He saw service in France, England and Ireland, witnessing the Angevin 'empire' at its height and at its fall. The story of his life was seen originally as the exaggerated boast by his family of a typically illiterate, rather simple warrior who got lucky through devotion and loyalty.

Politics and patronage

Revisionist historians throw a different light on William Marshal's career. Professor David Crouch has used the 67 charters of William Marshal in conjunction with the poem to show that William Marshal was actually a cunning operator who became a political master in the treacherous, devious Plantagenet courts. Marshal was illiterate, which was untypical of the nobility of his age. He was doggedly loyal, first to the young Henry, then to the old King Henry II. His lack of inheritance meant that he had to find security in royal service and when Henry II promised him marriage to Isabel, heiress to the earldom of Pembroke, his fortunes were transformed.

The knight bachelor and the chivalric life

When William was in his early teens he was sent to a relative of his mother's family, William de Tancarville, Chamberlain of Normandy, where he learned hunting, hawking and all the skills of courtly life. He was knighted in a simple ceremony at the age of twenty, whilst on campaign with the Lord of Tancarville.

William's father died in 1165, leaving him nothing. Two brothers were dead, and John, the eldest, inherited everything. William was a free man, a knight with social expectations, but no source of income. On leaving Tancarville's service, William had to sell the new cloak he had received at his knighting to buy a new horse. His poverty reflects the economic hardship that so many of his class and generation faced; he was free to pursue a chivalrous career but he was free also to starve. The tournament saved him. Over the next year or so, in 1167–8, he established a reputation at tournaments and won enough to feed himself.

In 1168 William returned to England and sought out his uncle, his mother's brother, who was the earl of Salisbury. Family connections helped him. The earl was about to embark on a campaign to Poitou and he took William into his household. The earl of Salisbury's task was to guard the queen and deal with the Lusignan rebels, but on one occasion they were ambushed. The queen was taken to safety but the earl was killed; William fought by himself until wounded and was captured for ransom. After a few months he was freed, his ransom paid by Queen Eleanor herself.

This was William's first big break. For the next twenty years of his life he served the Plantagenet royal households, first the queen, then her son Henry, then the old king, Henry II. The prime of William's life was passed in the service of the Prince Henry who was crowned king in 1170 in his father's lifetime. William was to become his *carrissimus*, his closest servant. But his time with the young king witnessed the great rebellion of 1173 (when he joined the rebels) and years of boredom as the old king never gave his son any responsibility. The young king spent his time at tournaments and spending vast amounts of his father's money. Such was William's standing with the young king that he knighted him, a privilege reserved for the king of France by Henry II. In 1183, when rebellion broke out again between Henry II and his sons, the young king died of dysentery, with William at his side. As he died, he gave William his cloak, which had the crusader cross stitched into it. He asked William to fulfil his vows and go to the Holy Land. William then accompanied Henry's body to Le Mans and met King Henry II who, shaken by his son's death (he had thought the fever was a trap so had not visited his dying son, sending a ring instead), promised to take on Marshal on his return from the Holy Land.

William spent two years in the Holy Land. This was now another established act of the chivalrous knight. The pilgrimage had long been a tradition in Western society but William went as a Christian knight to discharge his dead lord's vows. Thirty-six years later, as he himself lay dying, Marshal became a Templar knight and was buried in a Templar church.

When William returned, in Easter 1186, he joined the service of the old King Henry II. No more tournaments are mentioned in the poem. From now on, William was a trusted advisor in government, and when he was granted a royal estate in Cartmel, Lancashire, he at last joined the ranks of the landed knighthood, aged forty. His fortunes were set to rise much higher with the promise of marriage to Isabel, heiress to Pembroke when the old king died at Chinon, Marshal at his side.

Earl and justiciar

Richard I confirmed Marshal's marriage to Isabel (though not as earl of Pembroke). He needed William as a power in England during his absence on the Crusade. William was now a great baron of England, lord of the powerful castles of Chepstow and Usk. Richard also granted him estates in Gloucestershire and soon afterwards, William sealed his rise in the nobility by founding a priory at Cartmel and at the king's coronation, he carried the sceptre. In 1190 Isabel gave birth to a son and heir, William. She went on to produce five sons and five daughters.

In Richard's absence, Marshal became one of the king's co-justiciars, to govern England along with the chancellor William de Longchamp. Now one of the key players in England, Marshal was playing a different game from that of his bachelor tournament days. Even so, the diplomatic skills he had learned paid off in dealing with Longchamp and John, the heir apparent. Marshal trod carefully with John, not moving against him until it was clear that Richard was returning home after his imprisonment in Germany.

Marshal's ambiguity towards John reaped rewards when Richard died suddenly in 1199. Marshal played a part in persuading the reluctant Archbishop of Canterbury to back John, rather than the boy Arthur. Marshal's prominent support got him the earldom of Pembroke, used on his charters from June 1199 for the rest of his life.

Out of favour
Marshal had remained in France with Richard for most of the period 1194–99 and he remained equally high in favour with John through the disasters of 1204. However, it was after the loss of Normandy that he began to lose favour. For once Marshal was outmanoeuvred by changing circumstances. Like many of the aristocracy, he had lands in Normandy, and faced the prospect of having to chose between two overlords. His solution was to urge John to make peace with Philip and whilst on an embassy to Paris for John in 1204 he came to a private agreement with Philip over his Norman estate. In 1205 John gave him licence to go to Philip and do him homage, but William swore absolute homage to Philip for his French lands: this meant that he could not fight Philip without losing his lands, and whenever John attempted to retake Normandy, William could not help him without losing his property. In 1205 John summoned William to go with him to Poitou. William refused, citing his deal with Philip.

The barons patched up the quarrel, but William was frozen out of John's court after 1206. He gave up his son to the royal court as a hostage and went to his Irish estates. Here, however, he came into conflict with the king. Royal authority in Ireland was based on semi-independent feudal lords who had carved out their own territories. Marshal clashed with John over the power and authority of the king and Marshal remained in Ireland from 1208 until 1212. Although John initially suspected him of involvement in the assassination plot in 1212, he summoned Marshal to come to Kent in 1213 to defend the coast against the expected French invasion. From then on, William was loyal to John. At sixty-seven William was the most venerated and respected earl and courtier. He negotiated for John after the defeat at Bouvines led to the barons' demands at Runnymede, and he remained at the core of the loyalist barons after Magna Carta. Interestingly, however, his son, William, raised his banner against the king and was named as one of the Twenty-Five in the charter to sit on the council governing England with the king. It may even be possible, as one chronicle suggested, that the old earl hedged his bets by placing his son in the rebel camp.

Regent of England

On John's death in October 1215, William Marshal managed the funeral of the king and met the new boy-king and arranged for his coronation at Gloucester. Although he was only one of thirteen executors listed in John's deathbed testament, William was elected regent, or 'guardian of the realm', which he accepted once the earl of Chester had declined. From 1216 to his death in 1219 the old earl was the government of England. Many writs and charters were in his name; his seal was on the royal letters; payments to the king were often made to Marshal in person, rather than to the Exchequer.

William Marshal fought his last battle at Lincoln, aged seventy, over fifty years after Neufchâtel. Most of his contemporaries from the heady days of the Angevin empire were dead; now the old earl was leading the fight for the survival of England itself. He led the royalist army, took several blows on the helmet and won the day. A decisive sea-battle off Sandwich finished Prince Louis's hopes and England was able to begin its reconstruction.

The pomp and ceremony of medieval death

In January 1219, William Marshal fell fatally ill. In April he handed over the reins of government and prepared for death in his house at Caversham, near Reading. He took his leave of the young king and made his will. Towards the very end, he distributed robes to his knights and was received into the Order of the Knights Templar. At midday on 14 May 1219 he died, with his son at his side, his wife and daughters weeping outside. His body was escorted by many earls and barons to Westminster and buried in the New Temple church where his effigy survives today.

William Marshal's effigy, Temple Church, London

So died a great medieval baron whose life and career

illuminate the chivalric and courtly politics of the Angevin world. Illiterate, cunning, intelligent, lucky and determined, William Marshal made his way through poverty, social envy and treachery to become the most powerful man in England and the first regent. William's life illustrates the career-path of a member of the new knighthood. His education, training, family connections and expectations put flesh on the bare bones of 'feudal society'. Here we see a knight on campaign, making a living. We also see into the dark heart of the Angevin governments; the broken promises, hatred and ambition that lend colour to the charters and writs. William served as courtier, counsellor and justiciar to four kings. The *History of William Marshal* allows us to see more clearly the twelfth-century aristocratic world and the changes wrought within it.

CONCLUSION: A NEW ENGLAND?

English society underwent several key changes during the twelfth century:

- The population doubled.
- Peasant holdings increased and 'open-field' farming became more widely established.
- The legal status of the free and the unfree gained greater definition.
- Over 100 new towns were created.
- The Jews became an important element of the growing cash economy.
- England was an important part of the European academic and architectural scene.
- Feudal concepts gained greater definition.
- Knighthood underwent transformation as a social code and inflation produced a narrower and more culturally aware class.

Not all this change was due to factors occurring in the twelfth century. The population continued to rise, the social levels of the mass of peasants were not altered by the Norman Conquest and England had not been completely cut off from continental academic and artistic ideas, as Edward the Confessor's new abbey at Westminster and the new Norman cathedrals demonstrate. Trade had always been international, and London had always been a major port. Change was cumulative but certainly accelerated during the twelfth century, with the result that England became part of the European scene with its own cosmopolitan rulers, an increasingly legally aware aristocracy and a prosperous working population that would continue to flourish in the thirteenth century.

SECTION 6

Church and Crown

INTRODUCTION

The Church throughout the period 1042–1228 was one of the most powerful and dominant forces in England. The Church owned one-fifth of the land in 1086; its clergy and prelates spoke, dressed and ate differently from the common people. They lived and worshipped in buildings that were beyond the comprehension of the ordinary man living in his wooden shack. The Church had immense wealth and political power. This meant that relations between the kings of England and the chief leaders of the English Church, the archbishops of Canterbury and the bishops, depended upon co-operation but sometimes resulted in conflict. Above the Archbishop of Canterbury stood the Pope, and the papacy played an increasingly important role in English affairs in the period. The 'Church' and the 'state' in modern thinking were not separate in this period: the Church was all-inclusive. Kings of England never questioned the leadership of the papacy: 'Christendom' was a political reality. Therefore any disputes occurred within the understanding that the Church and secular governments had to function in union.

Conflicts did occur however, and centred on two main issues:

- The appointment of the bishops.
- The legal position of the clergy and their land.

Three archbishops of Canterbury personified the conflicts between Crown and Church: Anselm (William II and Henry I), Thomas Becket (Henry II) and Stephen Langton (John). There were no clear winners or losers in these conflicts and they should not be presented as clear-cut cases of the Church against the king. Matters of character, political expediency and events play an important part in determining the causes and the outcomes of these disputes.

THE CHURCH AS A FEUDAL LANDLORD

Explaining the position of the Church as a major landholder within the feudal system shows why the two issues outlined above were at the heart of conflicts between the Church and the Crown. Not only did the Church own 20 per cent of England in 1086 (which was inalienable, that is, not to be granted away), but its bishops and abbots sat in the king's councils and its clerks formed the ranks of the newly forming bureaucracies in the chancery and Exchequers of Henry I and Henry II. The bishops and abbots managed vast estates, employed dozens of clerks and knights in their own households and supplied knights to the king as part of their quota. They were an

KEY EVIDENCE

Charter of Henry I respecting the barony of the Bishop of Ely (1127) 'Know that I wish and grant and order that all those barons and vavasours [vassals who owe allegiance to a lord and have vassals of their own] who hold such lands as my charter of the Treasury of Winchester witnesses to have been sworn to, have belonged, in the time of my father, to the fee of the church of Ely, shall acknowledge them and shall hold them of the aforesaid church and of the bishop of Ely, now and in perpetuity by performing for them to the Church military service in accordance with their tenures…'

integral part of the land-holding and governing classes of Anglo-Norman England; they were, in short, barons of England, much the same as the knights, great lords and earls.

The choice of prelates (leading churchmen) was therefore vital to the king's government, but the local abbeys and bishoprics often had their own interests, which did not always suit those of the Crown. The clergy were also exempt from many of the royal laws and would be tried in ecclesiastical courts under ecclesiastical jurisdiction. When the legal reforms of Henry II came to be introduced, they found increasing opposition from canon law (the Church law used in Rome), and the clergy continued to appeal to Rome for final judgement. Henry II thought he could get round this by appointing his chancellor and friend Thomas Becket, archbishop; this backfired badly when Becket championed canon law (though without the support of most of the bishops) and his murder broke royal authority over the Church.

Elections and appointments of bishops

There were two schools of thought regarding the appointments of bishops in the period: Norman and Angevin kings assumed that they could appoint bishops; others believed in free elections according to canon law. This meant that the local cathedral clergy elected their own bishop who could be a threat to the king, given the political power that bishops had. No king would allow this, and in the event much bribery and intrigue occurred, usually resulting in the king foisting his candidate onto the local clergy, often at great financial cost. During the reign of Stephen, his brother Henry, Bishop of Winchester, was highly influential in appointments, but the king often withdrew from making a choice. On the occasion when Stephen intervened, at York in 1143, his man was deposed by the Pope, re-elected in 1153 and died, possibly of poison, in 1154.

Bishops usually came from one of three types of background: royal clerks, monks or ecclesiastical clerks, and never totalled more than fifteen, plus the two archbishops. Royal clerks formed almost 50 per cent of the bishops in the twelfth century, with the number of monks declining; ecclesiastical clerks increased in Stephen's reign. Henry II, Richard and John preferred clerks from the royal court. Some bishops could remain in post for a long time – Henry of Winchester held his post from 1129 to 1171.

Ecclesiastical property and royal abuse

The Church had been acquiring property since the fourth century, but in the eyes of kings and emperors those lands had been granted by their predecessors and could by right be returned to them. Church lands were called 'benefices', which also meant 'fief'. At the trial of William Saint-Calais in 1088, the Bishop had all his lands confiscated. In the period after the death of a bishop or abbot, royal officials usually administered the estate and sent the revenues to the treasury at Winchester. Most kings of England in the twelfth century were rarely in a hurry to appoint replacements.

Church law

The clergy claimed to be subject not to the king's (Roman) law but to canon law. The Church had its own law courts and procedures, which were codified during the later twelfth century. Clergy became increasingly specialised in Church law and two popes in particular, Alexander III and Innocent III, were experts in canon law. The big dispute between Becket and Henry II centred upon clerical immunity from secular trial and punishment. This was resolved in favour of clerical immunity after Becket's murder. The Church also had jurisdiction over wills and marriages.

Papal reforms and the investiture contest

The eleventh century was the great century of reform for the medieval Church. Reform came from various parts of Europe, most notably from the monastery of Cluny, but the papacy took the lead in 1048 under Leo IX and most famously under Gregory VII, who fought long and hard over the matter of appointments. William I and Archbishop Lanfranc remained aloof from papal intervention in England, packing the episcopacy (bishops) with royalist men who provided knights for their quota and built Norman cathedrals across the land. William II, however, had in Archbishop Anselm a man committed to papal reform and gradually developed support from the clergy. As we have seen above (pages 94–5) Anselm was reluctant to be invested and argued fiercely with William Rufus over the treatment of Church property and ecclesiastical vacancies. The situation had reached stalemate when Rufus died in the New Forest.

WAS HENRY I ANY KINDER TO THE CHURCH THAN WILLIAM RUFUS?

Due partly to the strong character of Anselm and William II's unpopularity with the Church, Henry I was never as secure as his father in maintaining control over appointments and the control of the Church lands. Anselm's exile in Europe from 1097 to 1100 put him in contact with leading reformers and when Henry invited Anselm to return to England in 1100, Anselm refused to do him homage (although he had done homage to Rufus), and left the kingdom again in 1102. Only when Pope Paschal II allowed Anselm to do homage did Anselm return, in 1106; and in 1107 he and Henry came to a compromise. Henry accepted that no bishop or abbot should be appointed by the king or any other layman (non-churchman). Anselm accepted that any man elected to the position of bishop or abbot could do homage to the king and still be consecrated bishop or abbot.

This agreement of 1105, ratified at Bec in 1106 and at Westminster in 1107, was actually not so much a compromise as surrender by Henry I. The king found himself forced to defend the prerogatives of the Crown: he never asked for homage after 1106 and often allowed free elections. Relations between Henry I and Anselm after 1106 were untroubled.

Anselm's disputes with Henry I were therefore very different to the disputes he had had with Rufus. The issues there had been over preserving the prestige and independence of the Church: Rufus had refused to allow reforming councils that had shaped Lanfranc's primacy and treated bishops and abbots in the same manner as he treated his earls and barons, plundering vacant bishoprics when it suited him. Henry I, however, was more subtle and responsive to Anselm's requests. In 1102 Anselm held a council at Winchester, which was more sweeping than all of Lanfranc's reforms, and another two in 1107 and 1108.

Henry I and the abuse of Church lands

William Rufus had a reputation as a despoiler of churches. At the time of his death three bishoprics and eleven abbeys were vacant. These rendered vast amounts of money into the king's pocket. Rufus had sold offices (simony), sold Church lands and fined clergy. Henry I ceased these activities immediately, promising to do so in his coronation charter. Henry I, the historian C. Warren Hollister argued, managed the Church according to accepted rules. He was generous and did not exploit or plunder monasteries or sees. He was diplomatic and sought the practical, middle road. After the compromise with Anselm, more appointments were made. Simony was rare throughout Henry's reign. Two new bishoprics, at Ely and Carlisle, were established and the Cluniac, Cistercian, Benedictine and Augustinan monastic orders flourished. The Welsh sees were subordinate to Canterbury. Henry founded a new abbey at Reading, where he was later buried, and encouraged his barons to be patrons to the abbeys and monasteries. In the eyes of his contemporaries, Henry I was an effective guardian of the Church.

Henry I and the papacy

Henry I exercised the same tact and diplomacy in his dealings with the papacy. The eternal power-struggles between the papacy and the German emperors allowed Henry freedom in England. Papal control was not extended over the Church in England during Henry's reign. When Abbot Hugh of Reading was summoned to Rome in 1128 by Pope Honorius, Henry vehemently opposed his going, threatening to take back all the gifts he had made to Reading and not to appoint a successor to Hugh. Hugh eventually went in 1129 and when he returned, Henry's fears were justified. Hugh had been charged with the collection of Peter's Pence, long overdue. On the death of Honorius in 1129 Henry supported his successor, Innocent

II, against his rival, Anacletus, and negotiated a reduction and delay of Peter's Pence.

STEPHEN AND THE CHURCH

The achievement of Henry I contrasts strongly with the tyranny and plundering of his brother William II and the poor management of his nephew, Stephen. In Professor Frank Barlow's words, 'Stephen's control of the church was as lax as his control of the baronage'. The two great prelates, Henry of Winchester – Stephen's brother – and Theobald, Archbishop of Canterbury, had the greatest influence and power. Stephen withdrew from influencing most elections of his bishops, preferring to encourage an intellectual and pastoral body of men rather than the court favourites Henry I had imposed. However, Stephen had come to power with the help of Bishop Roger and his brother Henry and although Roger fell from power and Henry fell from favour after 1139, very few of the bishops opposed Stephen. Archbishop Theobald supported him to the end, hearing his confession and burying him. Stephen, it is generally agreed, was a devout and pious man, more so than his uncle and than his successor, Henry II.

How did the papacy react to Stephen's usurpation?

Pope Innocent II accepted Stephen's arguments in 1135 that his oath made in 1127 to support Matilda was void because it had been forced, and that Henry I's marriage to Matilda had been illegal because Matilda had been a nun. The Angevins argued that Stephen was a perjured usurper, but Innocent II gave Stephen and Henry of Winchester his support. Innocent's successors Celestine II and Eugenius III, however, favoured the Angevins against Stephen. Because of this, Stephen was never able to crown his son Eustace and the Angevins were recognised as dukes of Normandy and the rightful kings of England.

Henry of Winchester and Theobald of Canterbury

Stephen's brother, Bishop Henry of Winchester, had played a major part in getting him crowned. Henry's ambition was to become archbishop of Canterbury and in 1137 the monks of Canterbury elected him. But the Pope refused to recognise his election, instead making him a legate (a papal representative in England). The Abbot of Bec, Theobald, was elected archbishop in 1138, with the backing of the powerful Clare and Beaumont families and the support of the Pope. It is possible that at this point Henry blamed his brother for not getting him the archbishopric and even opened negotiations with the Angevin party. After the death of Innocent, Henry's legatine position collapsed along with his dreams of making Winchester a third archbishopric. Theobald continued in a highly successful and loyal manner throughout the remainder of Stephen's reign until his death in 1161.

What impact did the fall of Bishop Roger have on Church and government?

It used to be argued by historians, particularly Professor William Stubbs, writing in the late nineteenth century, that Stephen's dismissal of Bishop Roger, Henry I's chief administrator, was the beginning of the end for Stephen. A more modern historian, R.H.C. Davis, followed this, saying that it led to the collapse of government and to anarchy – Stephen had broken the peace and thereafter nobody could trust him. But recent historians suggest that Stephen's government did not fall apart; Stephen was literate and educated in administrative matters and appointed men to replace Bishop Roger and his nephews.

Nevertheless, Stephen was judged morally for his treatment of Bishop Roger. The arrival of Empress Matilda in England soon afterwards was seen as divine chastisement and Stephen's capture at the Battle of Lincoln in 1141 was seen by some as the just judgement of God. Stephen had sacrificed the Church in search of his security, just as he alienated other groups of people in search of a strong, but dangerously narrow, power base. Bishops and abbots previously sympathetic to Stephen were now more wary and distanced from the court.

What did the Church do about the civil wars?

The extent of the civil wars under Stephen from 1139 to 1147 varied from region to region. No cathedrals were destroyed and building continued at Ely, Lincoln and Norwich. Well over a hundred monastic houses were founded during Stephen's reign, many by the great aristocrats. The bishops made several attempts to limit devastation and to punish those who destroyed religious buildings, but with little effect. The inactivity of the bishops towards the civil wars reflects the fact that the impact of warfare was perhaps localised and not the universal 'anarchy' that was once thought, but also the fact that the bishops saw it as the king's job to keep the peace.

Miseries caused by the wars created, or certainly contributed to, religious enthusiasm exceptional to the time. In 1144 the people of Norwich believed the Jews had sacrificed a boy; the preaching of the Second Crusade by St Bernard of Clairvaux recruited people from England for the first time. Some of the great barons, including Waleran of Meulan and Earl William de Warenne, set out for the Holy Land. Men from Norfolk, Suffolk, London and Southampton sailed to Lisbon and captured it from the Muslims in 1147.

WHY DID HENRY II FALL OUT WITH THOMAS BECKET?

The most famous dispute between an English king and his leading churchman was that between Henry II and Thomas Becket. This ended in more than just exile: Thomas Becket was murdered by four of Henry II's knights in the north transept of Canterbury cathedral, in 1170. The disputes ranged from the petty issues of royal taxation to the main principles of Church property and the legal status of clerics. In 1164 Becket was tried on various charges by Henry and fled in disguise to France, where he remained in exile. Very soon after his return in 1170 he was killed in his own cathedral.

The rise of Thomas Becket

The seeds of the fatal dispute were sown when Thomas Becket was chosen as the king's chancellor in 1155. Becket was from exactly the sort of prosperous family that flourished in the mid-twelfth century. His father, Gilbert, was Norman, and a successful merchant and citizen of London. Thomas had a privileged upbringing and was educated by Augustinian monks at one of London's grammar schools and in Paris. He was not necessarily intended for the priesthood, however, and he never gained the title of 'master' whilst in Paris. His education was enough to recommend him to a London banker – a kinsman – whose accounts he did for three years before joining the household of the Archbishop of Canterbury, Theobald, which was again achieved through connections and kinship. Becket's career so far is a typical example of the prosperity and potential social advancement of the burgeoning English urban society of the time.

Becket served the Archbishop well and was a favourite. He spent some time in Bologna learning canon law, but by 1154 he was still only a household clerk. In 1155, however, he was appointed to the archdeaconry of Canterbury. In order to take up this office he had to be consecrated a deacon, which meant that he was not able to marry or bear arms. The job brought him at least £100 a year, making him wealthy.

Becket as chancellor

When Henry II became king of England in 1154, the English Church wanted an Englishman to take up his chancery, rather than a Norman or another foreigner. Becket was their choice, backed by Theobald and Henry of Winchester. This transformed Becket's fortunes; he was the king's chief ecclesiastical servant in the royal household on the largest salary of all household officials (5s a day). He was in charge of the chapel royal and the writing office. The job itself did not make Becket a great man in the realm, but it did bring him into close regular contact with the king, and it was their personal relationship that was to be at the heart of the fight to the death fifteen years later.

By 1156 Becket had distanced himself from Canterbury. He did not form government policy but he was at the centre of it, acting as diplomat, ambassador and advisor. In 1158 Becket went to Paris for the king, with 200 household men plus servants, eight five-horse wagons, great casks of beer, hawks and hounds fit for a king and twenty-four changes of clothes fit for a bishop. The chancellor spent a fortune on fine foods and accommodation in the city; he gave away all his gold plate, clothes, cloaks and furs and horses. The king of France, Louis VII, was hugely impressed and the embassy was a success. In later years, Becket's friendship with Louis was to pay off during his time in exile.

Why was Becket appointed archbishop of Canterbury?

Theobald of Canterbury died in 1161. On 3 June 1162, Thomas Becket was consecrated archbishop, the day after he was ordained a priest. Becket was everything an archbishop of Canterbury should not be: wordly-wise, a wealthy royal clerk and favourite of the king. He had even led an army into battle in France in 1159. No royal clerk had been appointed a bishop since 1120; only one royal clerk had ever become archbishop of Canterbury. Since the mid-tenth century, archbishops of Canterbury had been monks; three (Lanfranc, Anselm and Theobald) had come from Bec.

The procedure for elections was not precise. They usually took place in the king's council. The king, the bishops and the monks of Canterbury all had their say. The monks believed they had the chief say, but it was the king who in reality made the decision, unless the bishops united against him, which was very rare. And contemporaries certainly believed that the king imposed his choice upon the Church, although nobody protested. Gilbert Foliot, Bishop of Hereford, joked that the king had worked a miracle, turning Becket from a layman and a knight into an archbishop.

There were several good reasons why Henry II wanted Becket as his archbishop:

- Gilbert Foliot, Bishop of Hereford, stood out amongst the bishops as exceptional but he was a difficult man to get on with.
- Henry, Bishop of Winchester and veteran of Stephen's reign, was too old.
- Becket had the support of Theobald; he also knew the Canterbury diocese and had been well educated at home and abroad.
- Becket would be well placed to serve the young Prince Henry, heir to the kingdom of England, whom Henry was planning on crowning in his own reign.
- Henry believed that Thomas, as chancellor, would be his man in controlling the growing rights and powers of the Church; Henry wanted to ensure that all his vassals, ecclesiastical and lay, would owe allegiance to him, and not to the Pope.

The last two points were the most important, and both went badly wrong.

The transformation of Becket

After July 1163, Becket and Henry were no longer friends. This estrangement began as soon as Becket became archbishop: he immediately put the archbishopric before the chancellorship. At his court at Woodstock (near Oxford) in July 1163, the king proposed that sheriff's aid – a supplementary payment by landowners to sheriffs – should be paid directly into the royal treasury, reducing the sheriffs' profits and increasing royal revenue. Becket, as chancellor, should have supported this increase in Crown income, but stated that sheriff's aid was not a royal rent and refused to pay it from his estates or Church lands. Becket won the argument and the king was furious. The row at Woodstock reflected the deep-seated rivalry now emerging. The king had given Becket time to settle in at Canterbury; Becket was impelled by his character to find his own power base away from the king and his court so that he was beyond reproach from the bishops.

By the autumn of 1163 the king had three main grievances against Becket:

- The protection of clerics from lay (i.e. royal) punishment.
- Irregular persecution of the laity for moral offences.
- Disregard for ancient customs and conventions between Crown and Church authorities.

These grievances were in the context of Henry II's plans and ambitions to reform and reconstruct the laws and administration of England, as discussed above (pages 140–7), but they were exacerbated by the king's personal indignation at what he saw as Becket's betrayal.

Things went from bad to worse at a council at Westminster in 1163. Following Henry I and William II, the king requested that the 'ancient customs of the realm' be observed. The bishops supported Becket, stating that these customs should be tested by the 'laws of God', i.e. canon law. The day after the council the king removed Prince Henry from Becket's care and took away all the honours Becket had received when he was chancellor.

The Constitutions of Clarendon (1164)

The king summoned a great council to his palace at Clarendon (near Salisbury) in late January 1164. The great majority of higher clergy, nobility and royal clerks were present. Henry II demanded that all the bishops give their assent, unconditionally, to the customs and privileges that his ancestor, Henry I, and his barons had observed. With great threats from the king and the barons, Becket bowed to the royal will, and told the bishops to declare their assent, which they all did, along with Becket. But when the details were drawn up in sixteen clauses, Becket refused to add his seal. The bishops were horrified; they had given their assent on Becket's orders. At this point, members of Becket's household began to leave his service.

The sixteen clauses of the Constitutions of Clarendon were genuine ancient customs of the realm, but they were also a sign of Henry II's determination to subordinate the Church to his control. The clauses included:

- All clerks who held baronies of the king owed the king all the usual feudal services (Clause 11).
- Barons and royal officials were immune from sentences of excommunication without prior royal consent (Clause 7).
- The Crown had the right to the custody of vacant bishoprics and abbeys (Clause 12).
- Any clerk accused of a felony had to appear before a royal court and answer the charges. The royal court would decide where he would stand trial and if he were referred to the bishop's court, then a royal official would also attend on behalf of the king. If found guilty in the bishop's court, then the clerk would no longer be under the protection of the Church. In other words, he would be removed from Holy Orders, rearrested and sent back to the king's court for a secular penalty (Clause 3).

All these clauses were at the centre of royal and feudal control over the Church. The last clause above was at the heart of the 1164 clash between Becket and the king. Henry II's lawyers had authority from Bolognese law texts to abolish clerical immunity from secular law. Becket's objection was based mainly on moral and theological grounds, which did not gain much support in his lifetime. Certainly he was right to hesitate, because what had been custom in the past was now becoming a rule; it was an innovation to force the bishops to swear to observe the customs of the realm.

The trial of Becket (1164)

Clarendon was the point of no return for Henry II and Becket. The king began to attack Becket whenever he could. He was given a golden opportunity when John Marshal, father of the famous William Marshal, brought a suit against the Archbishop over a piece of land. When Marshal appealed to the Archbishop's feudal superior, the king, Becket was summoned to the royal court, but failed to attend or provide an *essoin* (excuse). Becket was then summoned to attend a council of magnates at Northampton in October; he was summoned not as archbishop but as a baron accused of wrongful behaviour. He was found guilty of failing to attend the king's court but defended himself successfully against Marshal's charges. Henry II did not leave it at that. Becket was accused of failure to repay royal loans, keeping royal income while chancellor and contempt for the oath he had taken at Clarendon to observe the ancient customs of the realm.

Becket would be ruined if the judgement went against him. The bishops did not support him, blaming his indulgent previous life as a layman, and urged him to submit for the sake of the Church. In a dramatic climax in Northampton Castle, Becket was accused of perjury and treachery for refuting the Constitutions of Clarendon. Becket left the court to shouts of abuse and rode to Lincoln, then to Boston, fearing for his life. With a few servants, he made his way south and sailed from Sandwich to Flanders, outside Henry II's jurisdiction. The king always claimed that he would not harm Becket.

Becket in exile (1164–70)

Becket did not return to England until the winter of 1170. He lived in exile in the Cistercian abbey of Pontigny. Both Becket and Henry launched propaganda campaigns to win the Pope over to their cause. Becket gained the advantage when he saw Pope Alexander, threw himself at his feet and offered his resignation. But Alexander disapproved of the Constitutions of Clarendon and handed back Becket's archiepiscopal ring, saying, 'Receive anew at our hands the cure [post] of the Episcopal office'. Becket was now secure that he could not be forced to give up the office.

When the king heard about this he vented his rage on Becket's clerks and their families, tyrannically seizing their property. Becket's revenge came in 1166, after he had been made a papal legate. He solemnly excommunicated Henry's justiciar and other leading barons involved in the Constitutions of Clarendon and condemned the Constitutions as 'depravities'.

Time dragged on. Henry's problem was that he wanted his elder son Henry to be crowned king of England, which Becket was supposed to have done, and he wanted to seal an alliance with Louis VII of France, whose daughter Margaret was marrying his son Henry. In January 1169 a peace conference was arranged and Becket met the kings of England and France at Montmirail, on the Anjou-French border. He knelt at Henry's feet and threw himself on the king's mercy – to everyone's delight – but adding 'saving the honour of God' – to the king's horror. The conference broke up in disorder. Becket went off and excommunicated the bishops of London and Salisbury and some of the king's court, threatening the king; Henry II forbade any communication with the Archbishop, threatening imprisonment of people and seizure of their property if they supported Becket. Many of the bishops refused to swear to this; the Pope did not confirm Becket's excommunications. In November 1169, the two men met face to face at Montmartre but the king refused to give Becket the kiss of peace. Neither man wanted to lose face now.

The king lost patience with Becket and the Pope and ordered the Archbishop of York, an enemy of Becket, to crown his son. This was a direct

William fitzStephen: The Council of Northampton (c.1180s) 'But the archbishop could endure no more and said, "What is this which you would do? Have you come to judge me? You have no right to do so. Judgement is a sentence given after trial. This day I have said nothing in the way of pleading. For no suit have I been summoned hither save only at the suit of John [the Marshal] who has not come to prove his charge. With respect to this you cannot give sentence. Such as I am your father; you are magnates of the household, lay powers, secular personages. I will not hear your judgement." '

**From a letter of
Henry II to Louis
VII, King of
France (1164)** 'Be
it known to you
that Thomas, who
was archbishop of
Canterbury, has
been publicly
judged in my court
by full council of
the barons of my
realm as a wicked
and perjured traitor
against me, and
under the manifest
name of traitor has
wrongfully departed
…Wherefore I
earnestly beg you
not to permit a man
guilty of such
infamous crimes
and treasons, or his
men, to remain in
your realm.'

**From Edward
Grim, one of
Becket's
biographers
(c.1170s)** 'What
miserable drones
and traitors have I
nourished and
promoted in my
household, who let
their lord be treated
with such shameful
contempt by a low-
born clerk!'

affront to the rights and privileges of Canterbury and its primacy over York,
which had been established by Lanfranc. Anticipating papal wrath, Henry
offered to make peace with Becket, restore him to Canterbury and allow him
to recrown his son with his wife Margaret. The two men met again on the
Touraine border at Fréteval; Becket did not insist on the kiss of peace. The
Constitutions of Clarendon were not mentioned.

Murder in the cathedral

Becket returned to England on 1 December 1170. His reception was hostile
in court circles. The young king refused to receive him at Windsor. Before
leaving for England, Becket had excommunicated the bishops of London and
Salisbury and the Archbishop of York. The king had given him permission
to chastise his clergy but the timing was unfortunate. The bishops found the
king at his Christmas court in Normandy and complained bitterly; there
were rumours that Becket was riding about with armed knights taking his
revenge. The king vented his famous Plantagenet rage – Becket had not
learned a thing in his six years of exile – but whether the king uttered the
infamous words 'Will no one rid me of this turbulent priest?' will never be
known. Certainly he shouted something for which he later accepted
responsibility, and four knights of his household rode off into the night to
Canterbury.

These knights – William de Tracy, Reginald fitzUrse, Hugh de Morville and
Richard le Bret – did not have a plan; perhaps they thought to threaten
Becket, take him prisoner out of England or bully him in some way into
reversing the excommunications. Three of the knights were substantial
barons and had powerful connections in England. Three of them had also
done homage to Becket when he was chancellor. What they did was not an
isolated event but within the fringes of a royal mission.

The four knights, unarmed at this stage, found the Archbishop in his
bedchamber behind the great hall at three o'clock in the afternoon, talking to
his closest advisors. The knights were known to the monks and clerics as the
king's men and were offered dinner. But a heated debate ensued, the knights
accusing Becket of breaking the king's peace by excommunicating bishops
and royal servants. Becket replied, saying that these were papal sentences.
The knights tried to arrest Becket but failed and stormed out, hurling
threats at the archbishops, who replied in kind.

Then the knights went out into the large courtyard, took weapons from their
escort waiting with the horses, and forced their way into the cathedral,
shouting 'King's men! King's men! Where is the traitor?' Becket,
determined to preserve his dignity, ignored the advice of his clerics to hide in
the many passageways of the crypt in the dark until the knights had gone,
replying, 'Here I am. No traitor to the king, but a priest of God. What do
you want?'

Eyewitness accounts become confused at this point. It was getting dark; townspeople were coming to evensong; the knights were helmeted in chain mail, the Archbishop in dark robes. Again the knights demanded Becket's arrest, perhaps still planning to take him to the king or kill him in a less sacred, less public place. FitzUrse seized Becket, who resisted. A struggle followed. Becket was hit by the flat of a sword, and his cap dislodged. He called fitzUrse a pimp. Then one of the knights, probably fitzUrse, slashed at the Archbishop's head, cutting into the arm of the monk and biographer, Edward Grim. Once blood was seen, the knights closed in, hacking at Becket so that the top of his head was sliced off and blood and brains oozed onto the floor. The knights left as they had come, shouting 'King's men!' and terrorising the people in the church on their way out. They then ransacked the great hall, searching for anything incriminating and anything of value, which they took, before retiring to Saltwood Castle for the night.

Manuscript illustration of Becket's murder

How saintly was Becket?

Becket was not seen as a martyr at first. He had died a traitor in the eyes of many. The killers were the king's men; Becket had died resisting arrest. It was only when his body was prepared for burial that evening that the monastic cowl and shirt were discovered underneath his cloak; then the hair shirt and breeches were found underneath those, and the monks began to see Becket as one of their own. Nobody but Becket's closest circle knew about this. Had Becket been wearing underclothes of silk, there might have been no martyr.

Becket's biographers present Becket as having been ready for death. He could have fled the cathedral, or bolted the doors, or hidden in the crypt. Whether

Edward Grim's account of the murder of Thomas Becket (c.1170s) 'At the third blow he fell on his knees and elbows, offering himself a living sacrifice and saying in a low voice, "For the Name of Jesus and the protection of the Church I am ready to embrace death". But the third knight inflicted a terrible wound as he lay prostrate. By this stroke the sword was dashed against the pavement and the crown of his head, which was large, was separated from his head in such a way that the blood white with the brain no less red from the blood, dyed the floor of the cathedral …'

or not he wished to be a martyr, he recognised the fact that he was so greatly opposed to some bishops and the king that his death would be the only resolution.

John of Salisbury, the famous scholar and friend of Becket, described Becket in a letter as the innocent champion of the liberty of the Church, murdered 'before Christ's altar, among his fellow priests and troops of monks'. This letter was written immediately after the event and was widely circulated. But it was the cult of Becket's blood as a healing agent that put Becket on the path to canonisation. Only six days after the murder, a poor woman named Britheva recovered her sight when the rags dipped in Becket's blood were applied to her eyes. The next day, a London priest, William, arrived with paralysis of the tongue; he drank water tinctured with blood and recovered after his return to London. By Easter, three more cures had been effected. On Easter day a flood of miracles occurred, and rumours spread that miracles were being performed by St Thomas all across the south of England. Thousands flocked to Canterbury. The cult of Becket became one of the most successful of all time. By May, ten people were being cured every day. The popular pressure was such that the Pope was petitioned to canonise Becket, which he did in 1173.

After Becket's murder: winners and losers

Despite the miraculous events after Becket's death, Henry II was not excommunicated and the killers were not tried or punished. Becket was not a hero of the Church in official eyes. His time as archbishop had been a total disaster. He had been absent for eight years. The king had pillaged the revenues of the Church and ridden roughshod over the bishops. Becket had used the issue of investiture and clerical immunity to justify his own stand against the king. In the words of the historian W.L. Warren, 'it is difficult to see in his letters any evidence that he progressed beyond a narrow clericalism, dogmatic and basically unspiritual, despite its trappings of pious sentiment'. Reconciliation with Henry II would have been impossible: their once warm friendship had turned to implacable hatred and destruction.

If he had failed in life, then Becket won much in his death. The outrage was great. Henry II was under pressure and in 1172 he conceded free elections to the bishoprics. He abandoned the key clause in the Constitutions of Clarendon regarding clerical trial in royal courts; he promised that murderers of clerics would be dealt with severely and that he would not keep bishoprics and abbeys vacant for more than a year without good cause. Bolognese lawyers changed their ideas, asserting blanket immunity of clerical criminals.

In 1174, at the height of the great rebellion throughout his English and continental lands, Henry II famously did penance at the shrine of St Thomas. He walked the last mile barefoot, prostrated himself before the tomb and publicly confessed his sins, admitting to being the unwitting cause of the martyrdom. He was then whipped by the monks and the bishops and slept on the ground by the tomb without food. In doing so, he got his own little miracle from his old friend and deadly enemy: William, king of the Scots, was captured at Alnwick and the tide of the rebellion turned in Henry's favour.

DID THE PAPACY INCREASE ITS INFLUENCE OVER THE ENGLISH CHURCH?

From the late eleventh century to the early thirteenth century, papal involvement with England became more regular and more important. Appeals, councils, threats of excommunication and interdicts all entwined Anglo-Papal relations. William the Conqueror had refused to perform fealty to Gregory VII in 1080, but his descendant John made England a papal fief in 1213. The growth of monasticism, the sophistication of ecclesiastical organisation and the clarification of canon law lay at the heart of this transformation. The papal court was the ultimate court of appeal. Popes Alexander III and Innocent III became legal experts. Bishops and abbots from England attended the great papal councils. There was a constant flow of appeals from England to Rome, reciprocated by the papal legates travelling to England with full authority delegated from the Pope.

What was the position of the papacy during the Becket crisis?

The pope throughout the Becket crisis was Alexander III, an Italian canon lawyer and theologian. He maintained an evasive middle ground between Henry II and Becket. Becket was a liability to the papacy but the Pope was not going to give into Henry's demands on absolute royal obedience. The Pope sent a Cistercian abbot, Philip of Aumône, to persuade Becket to attend the Clarendon Assizes. After Becket refused to put his seal to the Constitution, the king persuaded him to write to the Pope to confirm the customs. Characteristically, the Pope did not confirm or condemn them, leaving Becket to deal with it alone.

During Becket's exile, Henry tried to undermine Alexander III by supporting an anti-pope, Paschal, and Alexander's situation was often precarious due to the threats of the German Emperor, Frederick. But Alexander was a master of diplomacy and never openly committed to either Henry or Becket.

Pope Innocent III and King John

If Alexander III maintained the middle ground between Becket and Henry II, the pope who dominated John's reign did anything but. Innocent III was elected in 1198 and was one of the champions of the papal curia who made the ideal of papal jurisdiction over Christendom a political reality. Innocent was committed to the support of John's nephew, Otto of Brunswick, and the first years of John's reign were favoured with peaceful relations with the papacy. When Philip of France engulfed Normandy in 1204, John asked Pope Innocent to act as peacemaker, but Philip reminded Innocent that John was his vassal who had refused a summons to the royal court of France.

Why and how was Stephen Langton appointed?

Relations between John and Innocent III plunged to the depths in the years 1205–13. Once again the issue was the election of a new archbishop of Canterbury. Hubert Walter had served Richard and John faithfully, and died in 1205. The monks at Canterbury claimed their right to free election, as did the bishops of the province, but John suggested that the monks and bishops should appeal to Rome. They did, but the monks secretly elected Reginald, their sub-prior. When John pressed the monks they denied this, electing instead John de Gray, Bishop of Norwich, a man of the king's court. Innocent III, however, declared this invalid in 1206 because it had taken place whilst the first election was under appeal. Innocent then quashed the first election and suggested a third candidate: Stephen Langton, an Englishman who had spent much time at the papal court. Innocent pressurised the Canterbury representatives in Rome and they accepted. Innocent demanded John's assent and when John refused, Innocent consecrated Langton in 1207. Innocent knew that this was not his right but he wanted to prevent the election of a royal clerk from John's court.

John objected furiously. His traditional right of patronage had been denied and he did not like Langton. Langton was to become the hero of the anti-royalist, pro-baronial chroniclers writing after John's death. The Pope sent commissioners to persuade John, who raged and threatened. In March 1208, Innocent placed the kingdom under **interdict**.

How did the interdict affect John's kingship?

John wanted to retaliate but he also wanted to show a commitment to the Church. His quarrel was with the Pope, not the clergy of England. His actions against the Church were greatly exaggerated by the monastic chroniclers after his death. John did punish the clergy by arresting the illegal mistresses of priests and clerks and confiscating clerical property from those who stopped performing religious services. These measures raised money for the king and did not meet with much opposition. The barons supported the king, despite Langton's reminder to them in a letter in 1207 that their ultimate loyalty lay with the 'king of kings and lord of lords'.

How did John's excommunication affect his kingship?

Negotiations dragged on between king and pope from 1208–09. John accepted Langton's appointment but insisted that it should not be a precedent, but distrust was such that John never met Langton and the papal representatives finally pronounced John's excommunication in November

1209. This failed to make much impact. At a great council the barons agreed with John that a papal guarantee for royal rights must be part of the settlement. Not all the bishops and abbots left John's service and John was content to hold out. By 1213, the incomes of seven vacant bishoprics and seventeen abbacies were providing income for the king.

England as a papal fief and the rebellion of 1215

By 1212, however, John's political situation was worsening. If the Pope were to form an alliance with Philip of France, John's very kingship in England could be threatened. Early in 1213 John's envoys arrived in Rome to convey his acceptance of Innocent's terms, but the Pope imposed a payment of £8000 on John for the restoration of Church property and insisted on the return of exiles. John's fear of papal support for Philip's plans of invasion – which some believed to be true – was such that he gave in.

Indeed, John did more than just give in. He surrendered his crowns of England and Ireland to the Pope and made himself a vassal of Innocent III. His kingdoms were to be held as fiefs from the Pope by himself and his heirs. He would pay an annual payment of 1000 marks (£666).

It was a stroke of diplomatic genius. The Pope was now John's ally, John his devoted son. John was to have papal support throughout his struggle with the barons in 1215 and Philip never gained papal recognition of his invasion of England. Innocent regarded John as the injured party and even supported him against Langton when it came to John's choice over bishops and abbots. John got his way in all six elections between 1213 and 1216, royal clerks taking three of them. In 1214 he offered a charter for free elections, later confirmed in Magna Carta.

Innocent III may have got his way over Langton, but John gained more; he had taken revenue from the Church for years, prevented a French-papal alliance against him and had won a great ally in his struggle with the barons.

CONCLUSION: THE KINGDOM OF THE CHURCH

By 1228 the papacy had developed as a powerful institution, which had exerted its rights over the English Crown on many occasions during the twelfth century with varying degrees of success. The personnel occupying ecclesiastical offices in England and in Rome were increasingly educated and assertive. Kingship and government had developed into a more rational blend of the charismatic and bureaucratic over which the papacy and the Church in England exercised rights. The wealth of the Church had hugely increased. Kings were now in debt to the Jews; they needed the Church to help them govern the country and they ignored the Pope at their peril.

> **KEY EVIDENCE**
>
> **John's submission to Innocent III** 'We offer and freely yield to God, and His holy apostles Peter and Paul, and to the Holy Roman Church our mother, and to the lord pope Innocent and his catholic successors, the whole kingdom of England and the whole kingdom of Ireland …'

> **KEY EVIDENCE**
>
> **From the Barnwell Chronicle (early 13th century)** 'From the moment he put himself under apostolic protection and made his kingdom part of St Peter's patrimony, there was no prince in the Roman world who would dare attack him or invade his lands…'

A2 ASSESSMENT SECTION

SOURCE-BASED QUESTIONS IN THE STYLE OF AQA (THE ANARCHY OF KING STEPHEN'S REIGN)

Source A:
From *The Chronicle of Henry of Huntingdon* (1153).

For without delay came Stephen, younger brother of Theobald, count of Blois, a man of great resolution and audacity, who, although he had sworn an oath of fealty for the realm of England to the daughter of King Henry, trusting in his strength, shamelessly tempted God and seized the crown of the kingdom.

Source B:
From *Stephen and Matilda*, by J. Bradbury (1998).

We cannot doubt that at times and in some places the situation was truly awful. But we can receive an exaggerated picture if we do not approach our evidence with a certain number of questions. One would expect damage from the nature of twelfth-century war, but how widespread was the war and the damage? It so happens that nearly all the major writers who provide us with our information were based in areas at the centre of the troubles: Peterborough, Malmesbury, the west country, Worcester, the Scottish border. Inevitably they described the damage which they knew about, perhaps even were inspired to write because they were in the middle of such dramatic events.

Source C:
From *The Reign of Stephen*, by K. Stringer (1993).

In their panic at the gradual erosion of centralised royal government in England, and hence of the 'natural' order, contemporary chroniclers convinced themselves that chaos prevailed. Their exaggerated fears played into the hands of Angevin propagandists and that in turn helped to create a flourishing historiographical tradition based on the notion that violence and disorder were more widespread than was actually the case.

(a) How valid is Bradbury's view that the war was not widespread because the chroniclers inevitably 'described the damage which they knew about'? *(10)*

How to answer this question
- Summarise the content and the interpretation it contains.
- Demonstrate understanding of the interpretation and relate this to your own knowledge.
- Understand and evaluate the interpretation with reference to your own knowledge to reach a sustained and supported judgement on its validity.

(b) With reference to the origins and content of Source A, how valuable to the historian is this source as evidence that the civil wars under Stephen were a judgement of God brought upon him by his seizure of the throne? *(10)*

How to answer this question

- Demonstrate reasoned understanding of the limitations of the source in relation to its reliability and utility (usefulness).
- Understand the limitations of the source and draw conclusions about its reliability and utility.
- Evaluate the reliability and utility of the source in relation to the issue in the question to reach a sustained judgement.

(c) Using your own knowledge and the sources, assess the validity of the view that 'the anarchy of King Stephen's reign was not genuine, but rather abnormal pressures created momentous changes in English government'. *(20)*

How to answer this question

- Make a plan for this extended response.
- Include references to Stephen's inherited situation, which was the overmighty control of Henry I, to which the barons reacted after 1135, and his disputed succession.
- Include references to the various reasons for the breakdown of royal authority, such as Stephen's mistakes, the ambitions of the Church and barons.
- The best answer will query the use of the word 'anarchy' and assess if the pressures were abnormal and what the changes in English government were, and will decide to what extent the view is valid.

SOURCE-BASED QUESTIONS IN THE STYLE OF OCR (HISTORICAL INVESTIGATIONS: THE REIGN OF KING JOHN)

Source A:
From Magna Carta.

And we have fully remitted and pardoned to everyone all the ill-will, anger and rancour that have arisen between us and our men, clergy and laity, from the time of the quarrel.

(Clause 61.)

Source B:
From F. Barlow, *The Feudal Kingdom of England 1042–1216* (first published 1955, 5th edition 1999).

John, like his great-grandfather Henry I, was a youngest son, pampered, and then twisted and hardened by the failure of too many premature ambitions; and, although his vices seem ordinary enough – the conventional weaknesses of the age – and only moderately pursued, it is possible that his coarse sense of humour could aggravate his offence and that his intelligent, even scholarly, outlook could make his behaviour revolting.

Source C:
From W.L. Warren, *King John*, (first published 1961, new edition 1997).

From the moment he began to rule, rivals and traitors conspired to cheat him of his inheritance. His reaction was a display of ruthless determination: anyone who impeded him ruling as his father had done was his enemy, be he baron, king of France, or pope; but as he wrestled with one, more foes sprang upon his back. Though he flinched sometimes in moments of danger, he never gave up. It could have been an epic struggle, but the story is marred by flaws in the character of the protagonist.

Source D:
From R.V. Turner, 'John and Justice', in S.D. Church (ed.), *King John: new interpretations* (2003)

The monarch exercised close supervisory jurisdiction over the common pleas. The justices were careful to consult him about cases that touched his interest in some way, and he sent them instructions about individual cases, often in response to a fine or oblation offered by one of the parties.

---

1 Assess the different views of King John expressed in Sources B and C. *(15)*

How to answer this question

- This requires an explanation and evaluation of two different views of King John. The evidence about King John points in many directions.
- His character was shaped by his experiences as a boy and a young man and his flaws, which, as Barlow emphasises, were not necessarily a problem, were, in John's case.
- Warren, however, points out that wider circumstances led to John's problems, which he reacted to with vigour.
- Both sources point to failings in John's character exacerbating his problems and ending ultimately in his downfall.

---

2 How far do Sources A–D confirm the historical interpretation of John's reign as 'marred by the flaws in the character of the protagonist'? *(30)*

How to answer this question

- You should evaluate the sources in the context of historical interpretations of King John.
- You should make an overall assessment of John, based on the four sources.
- Did his flaws of character mar his reign? What kind of evidence suggests this?
- You should provide a context to improve on the adequacy of the sources and present a more complete and balanced picture.

- You should be able to deal effectively with the sources as part of the wider historical interpretation of the king.

3 To what extent was the loss of Normandy inevitable in 1204? *(45)*

How to answer this question
- This is an assessment of an issue which has given rise to a historical debate. The main line of debate is whether the loss of Normandy in 1204 was a result of John's failings in his character (not managing the barons, murdering his nephew, poor diplomacy with Philip of France) or whether it was inevitable in the light of financial difficulties, the growing power of the Capetian monarchy and his succession difficulties which his father and brother had not had to face.
- You should also refer to other contemporary issues and activities of John.
- You should be aware of arguments for and against the proposition ('To what extent...?') and present a variety of points.
- Avoid writing an answer that is narrative based.

4 'The charter of 1215 was a response to complaints against John's authoritarian, arbitrary and capricious government.' Discuss this verdict on Magna Carta. *(45)*

How to answer this question
- This is an evaluation of a historical judgement of Magna Carta. You should consider carefully the background of Magna Carta. There was deep distrust between the king and the barons, which predated 1204, to John's succession and murder of his nephew, Arthur.
- The barons themselves were divided and you should question whether John's government was indeed 'authoritarian and arbitrary'. The Charter was in many ways very moderate and in reality accepted much of John's government.
- You should look at John's failings of character (his treatment of the barons and ruthless exploitation of his rights) that gave rise to rebellion.
- You should examine the wider context of changes in government and kingship. How had the loss of Normandy affected John's government? What financial problems did John face that his father and brother had not had to deal with? How far were the barons pushed in John's attempts to regain his continental possessions?
- You should look at the administrative reforms of the Angevin government and assess how far it was an 'Angevin despotism'.
- You should examine the programme of baronial reform that had developed before 1215 and resulted in a radical departure from previous rebellions.

Types of essay questions asked in the A2 specifications
The majority of questions fall into three categories:

The first category consists of questions that require a reason-based approach. It is most useful to include a comparison of points and you should prioritise both positively and negatively.

Questions of this sort begin with:
- Why?
- How?
- Explain ...
- What are the reasons ...?

The second category consists of questions that require the answer 'up to a point ... however'. This means that you should agree with part of the question but demonstrate that there is an argument here in that different aspects of the topic have to be considered in order to reach a balanced judgement.

Questions of this sort begin with:
- How far do you agree...?
- To what extent...?
- Assess the validity of this view...

The exception to the above categories is a third category which requires a reason-based answer followed by a balanced assessment with a judgement.

Questions of this sort begin with:
- Why and to what extent...?
- Why and with what success...?

Plan
Recognise which category of question you are being asked. Either prioritise your reasons for the first category, or decide your line of argument 'up to a point'. If the last category, then plan both reasons and the balanced judgement.

How to write an essay
To be awarded top marks in an essay you will be expected to do the following:

- Analyse throughout the essay. Avoid narrative ('telling the story'). Analysis depends upon an argument in response to the question. Plan a line of argument before you start writing. Begin each paragraph with a statement which you will back up with evidence (for example, 'one should argue that ...').
- Make a clear attempt to reach a judgement by arguing throughout. Ensure that you address the question critically and conclude clearly.

Essay questions in the style of AQA and OCR

1) 'A personality clash lay at the centre of the dispute.'

Assess the validity of this view with regard to the situation between Henry II and Becket.

How to answer this question

This question demands an 'up to a point ... however' style of answer. You might wish to include the following:

- How much Becket changed after becoming Chancellor.
- Was his piety genuine or was he on a personal mission?
- The political ambitions of the king over the Church.
- The issues of the Investiture Contest.
- The support Becket had from the English bishops.

2) Why did government occasionally break down during the period 1066–1216?

How to answer this question

This question demands a reason-based approach. You should prioritise a range of points, perhaps including the following:

- The significance of disputed successions in 1087, 1100, 1135 and 1199.
- The weaknesses of certain monarchs, particularly Stephen and John.
- The impact of strong or even tyrannical kings, and baronial reactions to them, particularly in 1088 and 1139–47.
- The rise of administrative kingship, a growing bureaucracy and the changing relations between the monarchs, especially in relation to Henry II and John.

BIBLIOGRAPHY

F. Barlow, *The Feudal Kingdom of England 1042–1216*, 5th edn. (Longman 1999)

F. Barlow, *Edward the Confessor* (Methuen 1989)

F. Barlow, *Thomas Becket* (University of California 1986)

R. Bartlett, *England under the Norman and Angevin Kings, 1075–1225* (OUP 2000)

D. Bates, *William the Conqueror* (Tempus 2001)

J. Bradbury, *The Battle of Hastings* (Sutton 1998)

R.A. Brown, *The Norman Conquest of England* (Boydell 1995)

J. Burton, *Monastic and Religious Orders in Britain 1000–1300* (CUP 1994)

D.Carpenter, *The Minority of Henry III* (Methuen 1990)

D.Carpenter, *The Struggle for Mastery: Britain 1066-1284* (Penguin 2003)

M. Chibnall, *Anglo-Norman England* (Blackwell 1987)

M. Chibnall, *The Empress Matilda* (Blackwell 1997)

S.D. Church (ed.), *King John: New Interpretations* (Boydell 2003)

P. Coss, *The Knight in Medieval England, 1000–1400* (Alan Sutton 1993)

D. Crouch, *William Marshal: Knighthood, War and Chivalry, 1147–1219*, 2nd edn. (Longman 2002)

D. Crouch, *King Stephen* (Longman 2000)

R.H.C. Davies, *King Stephen*, 3rd edn. (Longman 1990)

D.C. Douglas, *William the Conqueror* (Methuen 1964)

D.C. Douglas (ed.), *English Historical Documents: 1042–1189* (Eyre & Spottiswoode 1953)

B. Golding, *Conquest and Colonisation: The Normans in Britain 1066–1100* (Macmillan 1994)

J.A. Green, *The Aristocracy of Norman England* (CUP 1997)

J. Gillingham, *Richard the Lionheart* (Yale 1999)

B. Harvey, *The Twelfth and Thirteenth Centuries* (OUP 2001)

C.W. Hollister, *Henry I* (Yale 2001)

J.C. Holt, *Magna Carta*, 2nd edn. (CUP 1992)

J.C. Holt, *The Northerners* (OUP 1992)

J. Hudson, *Land, Law, and Lordship in Anglo-Norman England* (OUP 1994)

J. Hudson, *The Formation of the English Common Law* (Longman 1999)

H. Jewell, *Women in Medieval England* (MUP 1996)

M.H. Keen, *Chivalry* (Yale 1984)

E. King (ed.), *The Anarchy of King Stephen's Reign* (OUP 2001)

F.W. Maitland, *Domesday Book and Beyond* (CUP 1897)

A.L.Poole, *From Domesday Book to Magna Carta, 1087–1216*, 2nd edn. (OUP 1987)

J.H. Round, *Feudal England* (Swan Sonnenschein 1909)

J.E. Sayers, *Innocent III* (Longman 1993)

M. Strickland (ed.), *Anglo-Norman Warfare* (Boydell 1992)

M. Strickland (ed.), *Armies, Chivalry and Warfare in Medieval Britain and France* (Boydell 1998)

F.M. Stenton, *Anglo-Saxon England*, 3rd edn. (OUP 1987)

F.M. Stenton., *The First Century of English Feudalism*, 2nd edn. (OUP 1961)

K.J. Stringer, *The Reign of Stephen* (Routledge 1993)

R.V. Turner, *King John* (Longman 1994)

I.W. Walker, *Harold: The Last Anglo-Saxon King* (Sutton 1997)

W.L. Warren, *Henry II* (Methuen 1991)

W.L. Warren, *King John* (Yale University Press 1997)

D. Wilkinson and D. Cantrell, *The Normans in Britain* (Macmillan 1987)

B. Yorke, *Kings and Kingdoms of Early Anglo-Saxon England* (Seaby 1990)

INDEX

To help you get the grades you deserve at AS and A-level History you'll need up-to-date books that cover exactly the right topics and help you at exam time.

So that's precisely what we've written.

The Heinemann Advanced History Series

15th - 18th Century

Spain 1474-1700
0 435 32733 X

The English Reformation: Crown Power and Religous Change, 1485-1558
0 435 32712 7

The European Reformation: 1500-1610
0 435 32710 0

The Reign of Elizabeth
0 435 32735 6

The Coming of the Civil War: 1603-49
0 435 32713 5

England in Crisis: 1640-60
0 435 32714 3

France in Revolution: 1776-1830
0 435 32732 1

The Wars of the Roses and Henry VII 1450-1509
0 435 32742 9

Oliver Cromwell
0 435 32756 9

France 1500-1715
0 435 32751 8

Medieval England 1042-1228
0 435 32760 7

19th - 20th Century: British

Poverty & Public Health: 1815-1948
0 435 32715 1

The Extension of the Franchise: 1832-1931
0 435 32717 8

Liberalism and Conservatism 1846-1905
0 435 32737 2

European Diplomacy 1870-1939
0 435 32734 8

British Imperial and Foreign Policy 1846-1980
0 435 32753 4

Britain 1890-1939
0 435 32757 7

Britain 1929-1998
0 435 32738 0

19th - 20th Century: European

Russia 1848-1917
0 435 32718 6

Lenin and the Russian Revolution
0 435 32719 4

Stalinist Russia
0 435 32720 8

Germany 1848-1914
0 435 32711 9

Germany 1919-45
0 435 32721 6

Mussolini and Italy
0 435 32725 9

The Modernisation of Russia 1856-1985
0 435 32741 0

Italian Unification 1820-71
0 435 32754 2

European Diplomacy 1890-1939
0 435 32734 8

Hitler and the Nazi State
0 435 32709 7

20th Century: American and World

Civil Rights in the USA 1863-1980
0 435 32722 4

The USA 1917-45
0 435 32723 2

The Cold War - Conflict in Europe and Asia
0 435 32736 4

Vietnam, Korea and US Foreign Policy 1945-1975
0 435 32708 9

Inspiring generations

01865 888080   *01865 314029*   *orders@heinemann.co.uk*   *www.heinemann.co.uk*
tel   fax   email   web

J652